Ocean Passages

by Mike Gemus

This book is dedicated to Neptune, the god of the sea, for allowing me to cross his ocean in exceptional style.

And to Rick Renwick (1947-2000), who first took me out in Rebel Rouser and showed me the possibilities when wind meets sail.

Mike Gemus

2

Ocean Passages
Table of Contents

The Voyage of *C'est si Bon*   Page 5

The Voyage of the *Skyelark of London*   Page 53

The Voyage of *That Darn Cat*   Page 81

The First Voyage of *Allegretta*   Page 122

The Voyage of *Tender II*   Page 170

The Voyage of *Rhapsody in Blue*   Page 201

The Second Voyage of *Allegretta*   Page 265

Note: The stories in this book are true, and the author
has made every effort to ensure the accuracy of all that
is written. Some of the names of the boats and people
mentioned were changed in order that those involved
would not be offended. – Mike Gemus

Chapter 1. The Voyage of *C'est si Bon*

Have you ever had a dream? I mean, have you ever had a passion so powerful and persistent that it made perfect sense to abandon all of life's other responsibilities? We're talking about doing something really extraordinary here—an epic adventure, one that if completed would alter forever some of your most basic attitudes. You know, like sailing around the world. Wouldn't that be cool? To buy a big sailboat and sail off somewhere, light years away from the stresses of life. To quit work and sail the world's oceans, living a life of leisure with no deadlines and no boss. Oh yeah! That would really be something...

I call it the "Sailor's Dream." It's a dream about the serene sunsets to be enjoyed at the end of a good day's sail, a glass of chilled chardonnay in hand, and a shapely bikini-clad first-mate for company. A forecast of pleasant weather always accompanies this dream. No one ever gets seasick. The boat is always on course to some faraway exotic port, and somehow it all gets paid for. It's a great dream, that's for sure, and it does come true—at least in part—at least at times.

But it can be dangerously unrealistic, that Sailor's Dream. It's a fantasy that can cause a man or woman to prioritize a boat above home and family. Without the Sailor's Dream boat brokers would never survive. Hell, the entire boating industry depends on the millions of wayward sailors, each meandering along with that deer-in-the-headlights disorientation brought about by the Sailor's Dream. It's a common affliction and has bitten many an unsuspecting host. I can recall the very day it got me:

It was back in the seventies, and my good friend Rick Renwick offered to take me and a couple of buddies out for a sail on his 25-foot sailboat, the *Rebel Rouser*. Rick kept his boat at the LaSalle Mariner's Yacht Club on the Canadian side of the Detroit River, about ten miles from where it empties into Lake Erie. LaSalle is known as an area of quiet marshes, but the damming effect of those innocent marshes forms a series of narrow river channels with fast currents. Several skinny islands parallel the channels and winds snake their way around the islands, often creating challenging sailing conditions.

The two buddies that came with us that day were Nino Buhagiar and Joe Xerri, now a couple of my oldest and dearest friends. Back then we were a trio of eager and cocky twenty-year-olds, ready to try anything and unconcerned about consequences. None of us had ever sailed before, but we all climbed aboard *Rebel Rouser*, pushing the boat away from the dock without a word of instruction. It never occurred to any of us to ask what might happen next.

Rick started the boat's small outboard engine and we putt-putt-putted out of the harbor and into the channel that runs by the yacht club. Nino, Joe and I—"the crew"—crawled forward to the mast and hoisted the boat's sails. Pleased with our accomplishment, we returned to our seats in the cramped cockpit, each of us having to rearrange ourselves numerous times so that we all could sit down. Eventually the engine was turned off and all was quiet. In the lee of the narrow man-made Grass Island there wasn't a breath of wind. We drifted along with the current, accompanied by several patches of duck-weed and a couple of seagulls. I wondered if we should run the engine again.

As we passed the end of the island, we all felt an obvious cooling of the humid conditions surrounding us. The sails flapped a time or two then pulled to one side as they filled with a movement of air still unperceived by the novice crew. The boat heeled over slightly and began to move through the water. I started to hear a strange gurgling sound.

"What's that?" I asked.

Rick laughed at my innocence. "That's the bow wave," he said.

We were moving—"making way," it's called—not very fast to be sure, but propelled by the wind alone. A moment later I felt a telling chill on my neck and little wavelets formed on the water. As a stronger breeze materialized, the boat banked more sharply and accelerated to a surprising speed. The sound of the bow wave increased, soon becoming a soft roar that I thought I could feel as much as hear. I'm sure I had a grin from ear-to-ear as the thrill overcame me. I was witnessing for the first time how a boat could be powered by the wind. I let out a scream, overwhelmed by the excitement of it all. I still recall that very moment: It was the moment I was hooked.

The joyfulness was short-lived. Scooting right along, we soon past the larger Fighting Island, fully exposing us to a powerful southwest wind that funneled up the river's channel. *Rebel Rouser* heeled over alarmingly and took off like a spooked horse. A wave broke over the bow, followed by another soon after. I was more than a bit concerned and began to plan how I might swim to shore if the boat were to roll right over and capsize.

7

"Ready about," Rick yelled out. "Helm's a lee," he said, turning the boat into wind and causing the sails to flap wildly. "Joe, let go [of] that line," Rick commanded, pointing to a rope—a "line" on a boat—that held the sail in. Joe "let go" the line and Nino and I pulled in another on the other side. With the heading of the boat changed and the wind coming from the left side rather than the right, the heel of the boat changed as well. Rick quietly steered his beloved *Rebel Rouser* while his crew of three tripped and fell over one another completing the maneuver called a "tack." The boat sped off across the channel—perpendicular to its previous course—again at full speed, and again with waves breaking over the bow. A minute or so later the "ready about" command was given again and the tacking maneuver was repeated, reversing what we had accomplished the first time. It was a lot of work for us crew, but I started to see what we were accomplishing: Within no time we were a mile or more upwind of where we had started. Also, I was relieved to see we weren't in the danger of capsizing as I had first perceived.

We tacked several times in quick succession as we worked our way upwind through the narrow channel, constantly altering course to avoid the multitude of buoys, shoals, and other boats that always seemed to be in our way. We were charging along dangerously fast, and with the sails in the way we couldn't very well see where we were going. Waves often splashed over the bow and we were all soaked. The handling of wet lines burned blisters into my hands and somehow I scraped a couple of knuckles, getting blood all over the cockpit. Also, during one of the tacks the boom caught Nino across the brow, and a bright red goose-egg had formed which could have used some first-aid. As a three-man team the crew was becoming better coordinated, but we still tripped and fell over each other every time we tacked.

Rick seemed unfazed. He ignored the mosh-pit world in which his crew existed and simply held the tiller in his

8

hand, maintaining a look-out ahead and calling out various commands to initiate one tack after another.

After an hour or so, with the crew thoroughly wet and exhausted, Rick turned the boat around to sail downwind and back to the club. It was as if we had passed into a whole other world. The boat was level and peaceful as it glided along at a manageable speed. The wind, which a second prior seemed so overpowering, died in an instant. No water came over the bow, and no tacking was required as we proceeded straight up the middle of the channel. We enjoyed a leisurely return, though it seemed to take a long time. Eventually we reached the harbor, the entire sail lasting two or three hours.

It had been my first sail ever, and in spite of the chaos and punishment my friends and I had endured, I found the experience mesmerizing. I was awestruck after witnessing so close and personal what the power of the wind and a sail could do together. Astounded by what I had seen, I felt a great passion being born within me that day, a passion that would develop and flourish into a dream. It was that dream I spoke of earlier, the one of serene sunsets and girls in bikinis. It's about quitting work and life's other obligations and taking off. It became *my* passion that day, *my* obsession, *my* Sailor's Dream.

I sailed and raced with Rick on *Rebel Rouser* for two or three sailing seasons, studying with complete abandon all I could find on sail trim, racing tactics, and cruising techniques. I sailed anytime I could, not just on Rick's *Rebel Rouser*, but also on any boat that could use an enthusiastic hand on board. I couldn't get enough. I fantasized about quitting work and heading for the ocean. I started thinking of sailing around the world. It was delusional, unrealistic thinking for sure, but I was having a ball, feeling an excitement in life like never before. Welcome to the "Sailor's Dream."

In 1981 I bought my first boat. I had married the year before, and since I maintained a well-paying job at Ford

Motor Company, and since I had access to two incomes, it didn't seem unwise to buy a considerable boat fully on credit. I, I mean *we,* didn't have two nickels to our name, but on a "land contract" we bought a nine-year-old 30-foot Pearson sailboat which we named the *C'est si Bon.* We were so proud. We made double payments and the loan was paid in less than two years. The marriage persevered a bit longer, but it too was gone after a couple more. *C'est si Bon* became my true love and passion, always treating me with fairness and grace, and remaining with me a good many years.

I was still very new to sailing when I first got the boat. I had been racing a few years by then—"learning the ropes"—but essentials such as navigation, sailing in foul weather, and watch-keeping were all very new to me. I knew nothing about sailboat maintenance, and even launching the boat for the first time was a major challenge. Once I had the boat in the water, the real learning began: Before then I had never sailed at night. I had never sailed alone. I had never sailed outside of the sight of land. Heck, I had rarely steered a boat.

C'est si Bon was built in 1972 by Pearson Yachts out of Portsmouth, Rhode Island. Built as a racer, she was a rather narrow boat with a water slicing shark's fin keel and a spade rudder. The boat had a total of nine sails—only two to be used at any given time—and these would be changed to match the wind conditions and gain optimum advantage on the race course. At the time, Pearson-30's were formidable racers, enjoying a fine competitive reputation. *C'est si Bon* was up there with the fastest of the fleet.

Regarding "creature comforts," *C'est si Bon* was a bit lacking. She had no roller furling, a common apparatus on boats now-a-days, and one that really cuts down on the work of stowing sails. There was also no auto-pilot—an electrical device that steers the boat automatically—and believe me, being forced to manually steer a boat without ever being able to step away from the helm is a major

10

inconvenience. There was no LORAN—an electrical navigation device that predated GPS—so I had to navigate "by guess and by golly." The boat had a fancy no-drag propeller, which was great for racing but an unnecessary complication for cruising. There was an engine, of course, but it was a poorly maintained, sea-water cooled, "flat top" Atomic-4 that failed repeatedly and had me sailing into harbor three or four times in my first year. The boat had entirely inadequate ground tackle (anchoring gear) and no canvas for sun protection. The interior décor, with its brown plaid upholstery and fake wood, was especially depressing. *C'est si Bon* was a race-boat, not a live-aboard. She was well-appointed for one but not the other.

Over the years I was able to make several improvements to *C'est si Bon*: I had a boat carpenter replace the entire interior in gorgeous teakwood, doing wonders to make the boat more charming and livable. I added a kerosene oven, a LORAN, and a Profurl roller furling system. I threw away almost all of the sails, saving only the spinnaker, and I bought a new genoa (that's the sail up front) and a mainsail, both very much designed for cruising instead of racing. I bought a serious 35-pound CQR anchor with an all-chain rode (anchor line), and I installed a winch on the bow (a windlass) to crank it up. I also bought an auto-pilot, which I came to regard as the best purchase I had ever made. In time, I also found a sleek-looking performance row-boat that I used for a dinghy, painting it in the same decor as *C'est si Bon*. With a new prop, a bit of engine maintenance, and a fresh bottom job, the *C'est si Bon* had become quite the sailboat. It was perfect for the Great Lakes, and it received its share of looks and compliments.

I sailed *C'est si Bon* throughout the Great Lakes for the next eight years, living aboard for five different summers. The boat and I had each become much improved year after year, and I experienced many of those serene sunsets, the distant shores, and yes, the bikinis that are all part of the Sailor's Dream. I had become a real sailor; there

11

could be no doubt. I lived aboard each summer, house-sat the winters, and sailed the *C'est si Bon* anywhere I pleased. I was divorced and free as a bird. It was a fun time. Should I have been satisfied? Maybe so. It really wasn't so bad.

But I was young and restless and I still had that Sailor's Dream. I wasn't quite the cocky twenty-something that Rick had taken out on *Rebel Rouser*, but I was still in my early thirties and not about to be rest on my laurels. I hated my job and loved my boat. And I had that dream. I wanted to untie those dock-lines one last time. I longed for the ocean. I wanted to take off!

And this I did in May of 1989 in what can be called "The Voyage of the *C'est si Bon.*" My plan was to quit work and sail to St. Thomas, one of the US Virgin Islands. St. Thomas is a major commercial hub in the Caribbean, and since it's an American territory, I could legally live and work there. It seemed like a good choice. Why did I go in May of 1989? Because that's when I had the money: It was the very first moment in time when such an undertaking was financially possible for me to do.

What an adventure and life changing experience the voyage was to be! Not only was I quitting a secure and lucrative job and leaving my friends, family, and entire life behind, I was embarking on a risky sailing venture that was far beyond my own experience or that of anyone I knew. It was to be a very long trip and I would be far out at sea. And even if I were able to make it to St. Thomas, which was in no way assured, that would only bring me to the beginning of a new life in a developing island territory. This was huge!

C'est si Bon was a great boat, but she was *not* set up as an ocean cruiser. A few essentials, such as a life-raft and an emergency Mayday locator beacon (EPIRB), I simply could not afford. I would also have to do without any overhead canvas, a real necessity in the tropical sun. Of major consequence, the tank for drinking water on *C'est si Bon* held only 20 gallons (100 would be preferred) and there was no way to change the tank. Even the size of the boat—30 feet length overall—made it too small of a vessel for an ocean voyage.

On *C'est si Bon* I would have to go *in spite* of these deficiencies. Many other would-be ocean sailors have delayed their cruises *ad infinitum*, endeavoring to make their vessels totally seaworthy. Some finally went in their retirement with boats that probably still lacked one or two essentials. In my mind I didn't have even *that* luxury: I could go with a boat that was critically lacking in several areas or I could not go at all. I chose to go.

It is important to remember that the voyage occurred in 1989. It was a time before laptops or cell phones. Even the internet wasn't available to the public. GPS, which was to become the mainstay of marine navigation, was a pioneering technology back then and too expensive for me to afford. LORAN couldn't be used either: LORAN uses radio towers and can only be used near land.

On *C'est si Bon*, I would be depending on an antiquated method called Celestial Navigation. The sole objective of Celestial Navigation is to re-establish your position (latitude and longitude) when you're far out at sea. You do this by measuring the angle between the sun and the horizon at a known time. Knowing the precise time identifies the exact position of the sun over the Earth, and knowing the angle (measured with a "sextant") identifies how far you are from the sun's position. Various tables simplify the method, but the tables used are pretty complicated, as is the math that's involved, and even the determination of correct time becomes surprisingly difficult. It's not an easy method of navigation, even for experts. Fortunately, Ron Stubing, a good friend of mine, was a course instructor of the method and he generously took the time to teach it to me.

One of the most critical steps in the preparation for the voyage was to acquire a crew member. Out at sea a boat travels 24-7 and there are no places to stop. I would have to sleep, and if I didn't want to get run down by another boat, I would need at least one other person as crew to help me.

I needed somebody whom I could trust to sail the boat by himself—day or night—and I needed somebody who could take the five or six weeks of the voyage off from his own work and family obligations. I knew from the start it would be difficult to find somebody adequate, but luckily a fellow I worked with mentioned he had a friend who might be suitable. In February—two months before the voyage— he came to my home and introduced me to Ian Glass, an experienced sailor about my age who was "between things" in life and interested in the job.

Ian and I were similar in appearance, though he was a bit taller and heavier. We both had beards, but Ian's was bushier and he wore his hair longer than mine as well. We were both muscular by nature; Ian's bigger size made his appearance more formidable. We both liked beer. Oh yeah! We both liked beer.

By trade, Ian was an Industrial Engineer, and for several years he had worked for his father's company, designing the steel framework of tall buildings. He had owned a home and was married, but his marriage had recently dissolved and he had basically given up on life— quitting his job, taking very little in the divorce settlement, and drinking more than one would normally recommend. "Between things" he called it.

Over a beer or two Ian related his story to me and I began to realize the parallelism of our two lives. Both of us were US-born Canadian residents and each of us had grown up in a Catholic family. (Interestingly, both of us had lost our way with God and each considered himself an atheist at the time.) We were also both university educated and both successful in our early adult careers. Both of us had been married; both had been sued for divorce. Both of us were quitting our very good jobs: Ian a couple of months prior, me a couple of months hence. Parallel lives, indeed. And for both of us, virtually everything in the lives we once knew

14

was ending. We both stood at a precipice—Ian at his, me at mine—looking to start a new life. Neither of us had any idea of what that new life might be.

Ian didn't have as much sailing experience as I did, but he had previously owned a sailboat and he had leased and operated a boat in Belize on his honeymoon. He had the time available—"all the time in the world," he said—and he agreed to share food expenses. We only spoke for a couple of hours that day in February, but in that time we developed a confidence and trust in each other. I agreed to take him on; he agreed to come. We spoke two or three times after that, but I didn't actually see Ian again until he showed up the day before the voyage began. Some friends of mine have mentioned that it was risky taking somebody I hardly knew, but I really didn't have much of a choice. As it turned out, Ian was a good, honest person and a very capable sailor. I couldn't have done better.

Other preparations for the voyage went along without much incident. I put on a new coat of bottom paint that claimed to be specially made for the North Atlantic. (I have no idea what that could mean.) I cleaned the boat "stem to stern" and caulked and greased everything possible. I took the sails to the sail-maker, changed the engine oil, replaced the batteries, and even bought a new flag. I launched the boat as soon as the winter-ice was out of the harbor. *C'est si Bon* was ready to go. She'd been ready for years.

A few lifestyle things had to be put in order, but these, too, went easily. Being a long-time live-aboard and winter house-sitter, I had no home furnishings to get rid of and I simply moved aboard *C'est si Bon* at the end of April as I did every year. I sold my car to my brother and gave my notice at work. I counted down the days and I was very glad when April 30, my last day at Ford, came to pass.

I should mention "the fishing rod." I wasn't much of a fisherman at the time—still not, really—and neither was my father, but my dad had an old, low-quality fishing rod and reel and he thought he'd give it to me as a gift for the voyage. It was a shameful bit of gear, this fishing rod, and to be honest, I didn't have any interest in using it. Still, it was a gift from my dad and I figured I needed to accept it. I thanked him adequately and tied the rod and reel to a stanchion near the boat's stern, not giving it much thought at all afterwards.

May 2 was the long-planned day to leave, and about 20 of us—my parents, some friends, a girlfriend, even an old girlfriend—all met for breakfast and a bit of farewell celebration. Afterwards, we all headed over to Westport Marina in LaSalle where *C'est si Bon* awaited. A newspaper article about me had appeared in the *Windsor Star* a week or two before, and looking for a story, the crews of two TV news channels had shown up to film the event. I was interviewed by a very cute news-caster, and into the camera I shyly spoke of becoming a vagabond. (I felt like such a fool.) Ian, who had arrived the previous day, was next. He was asked about his fears, and he spoke eloquently about the reality of fear associated with offshore sailing and the importance of overcoming it. Even my mother was interviewed, and with a straight face she insisted that, yes, her eldest son was doing the right thing, venturing off into the big ocean on his little sailboat. We all appeared on the news that night. We were quite the celebrities. At one point in the interview I was asked how long I expected it to take to get to St. Thomas. I didn't really know. "About five weeks," I said.

So, with publicity responsibilities covered, we hugged and we kissed and we said our good-byes. Ian and I hopped aboard and got ready to go while everybody watched and the film crews filmed. I started the engine, and the hands of a dozen of my family and friends helped guide the boat away from the dock. We motored out of the harbor and into the river's channel, the same channel that my friends and I had putt-putt-putted to on *Rebel Rouser* several years prior. I put the sails up, which by then I had done at

16

least a thousand times. A west wind pushed us along. The voyage had begun.

We sailed by Grass and Fighting Island and past Turkey Creek and the Canard River—all features along the Detroit River I had come to know so well. It was fun to show Ian my old playground. The wind became a bit fluky and we needed a little engine power, but the current was with us and we moved right along.

It was about this time that Ian started eyeing the lousy, old fishing rod my father had given me.

"What's that?" Ian asked.

"Oh, my dad gave it to me," I said. "It's a real piece of shit, but I guess it's a family heirloom now."

"Does it work?"

"I don't know. I wouldn't think so. I think it's been in the shed out back for years. I don't know where the hell it came from. I've never seen my dad fish."

"Do you fish?"

"Me? Hell no!"

Ian untied the rod from the stanchion and started looking it over. He took the cover off the reel, blew away a couple of dead spiders, and checked to see if it had any fishing line on it. He shook the rod to test its flex and made an expression that indicated his approval. There happened to be an old lure attached to the line and he began casting the rig to see if it functioned. He didn't catch any fish, but I was starting to think this wasn't such a bad idea.

As we were passing the town of Amherstburg my good friend Mike Paraschak magically showed up in his own sailboat. He came alongside us and we motored in tandem, yelling friendly words to one another. It was great to see him. At one point I tried to call him on the VHF radio, and that's when I noticed that a crystal in the radio had blown and I could no longer transmit on Channel 16, the main marine hailing station. For eight years that radio had worked fine, but now, when I needed it most, it failed. Just my luck!

17

Further along and with Mike as an escort, the very common southwest wind came up nicely, and the crews of each boat trimmed and re-trimmed their sails in an effort to out-run the other. We came to the end of the Detroit River and entered Lake Erie, heading southeast. It was a wonderful day for sailing: sunny, windy, and a bit fresh and cool. We sailed all afternoon, working our way toward the islands of western Lake Erie and the site of Put-in Bay, the home of my favorite singer Pat Dailey.

Sometime during the day I got out my brand new sextant, hoping to take a sight and compare the celestial calculated position with that of the LORAN. It was the first time I had ever used the sextant, and with the boat rocking in the waves I struggled to get an accurate reading of the angle between the sun and the horizon. (An error of just one minute of one degree equates to a whole mile of error in the final calculation of the boat's position.) I used my wristwatch to estimate the correct time. (An error of four seconds also equates to a positional error of one mile.) I took the sight and went below to work through the confusing calculations. An hour or so later, after looking up and adding in the corrections for index error, dip adjustment, solar semi-diameter and atmospheric refraction, and then working through the not-so-simple simplifying exercises of sight reduction, and finally charting all my work on plotting sheets, I eventually had a resulting "line of position." This "LOP" was seven miles off from the LORAN position—not a bad amount of error, but not that great either. Nevertheless, I had confirmed some basic elements of my offshore navigation method, and that was a very important task to complete.

We reached Pelee Island just before dusk. Mike was still with us, so we docked his boat and mine, side by side, at Scutter's Dock, located on the north end of the island. It was still very early in the boating season and the place was deserted, so we got to stay for free. Early season is like that.

18

We were all pretty hungry, and though I had provisioned *C'est si Bon* with a good amount of canned goods and other staples, we were happy to find an open grocery store near-by, one that happened to have some chicken. One of the improvements I had made to *C'est si Bon* was to install a very nice kerosene oven and stove, so within no time I was able to feed the three of us a hearty dinner of fried chicken, rice and canned corn. After dinner we talked a while over a few beers and before long it was midnight. As we called it a night, I retired to the V-berth in the boat's forward cabin, Ian to the port side quarter berth in the rear, and Mike to his own boat. It was the end of the first day of The Voyage of the *C'est si Bon*—a huge day for me. The next day my friend Mike would head west, returning to his home and family and the life he knew. Ian and I would sail east, away from our homes and families, looking to start our new lives and heading to a total unknown.

The next morning Ian started nosing around and begged a few fishing hooks and some line from a couple of locals. He used some pieces of leftover chicken for bait and again started fishing. Still didn't catch anything. I could see why I didn't bother fishing...

It took three more days for us to reach the end of Lake Erie. After leaving Pelee Island, we crossed the lake to the US side and followed the lengthy southern shore, stopping each night to sleep. One day, still 20 miles short of Erie, Pennsylvania, we encountered a light west wind, light enough to call for the engine. By this time we were running low on fuel, and I calculated that we could very well run out of gas before we reached port. Conversely, if we did *not* motor, our slow progress would surely keep us out all day and night. We kept motoring. I saw that Erie, PA had a wide open harbor. I figured we could always sail in, if necessary.

Well, we ran out of gas about midnight, in sight of the harbor but about a mile and a half away, and without even a breath of wind. So much for sailing in.

"Now what?" Ian asked as the boat drifted to a stop. We could see the unmistakable *Budweiser* lights in a window of a bar on shore. A beer would be nice right now, I thought.

"I guess we'll wait for the wind," I sighed, stating the obvious. I had been in this situation before—many times. It happens often in a race where the rules prohibit the use of an engine. Sometimes, too, the wind runs out and you just don't feel like turning on the power. Waiting for the wind is no stranger to any sailor. We waited. Ian lit a cigarette. We could almost hear the patrons in the bar enjoying *their* beers.

It had never occurred to me to try paddling a 30-foot sailboat. Why would it? I *did* have a canoe paddle aboard, however, and the idea *did* occur to me as my eyes watered—perhaps because of the cigarette smoke, or maybe because those *Budweiser* lights were so darn clear. Regardless, I got out the paddle and leaned way over the side of the boat so that I could try paddling. It worked. Not too fast, that's for sure, but we were moving.

"Good thing those TV guys aren't here now," Ian quipped.

"Shit, it's a good thing it's dark out," I said in agreement. "I can't believe we're doing this. I can't believe it's working!"

It *did* work for a while. Then the paddle handle broke, of course. So we tied the end of the paddle to a mop handle, which because it was longer, actually made paddling easier. Ian and I took turns switching between paddling and steering and before long we were making good progress. As we realized we really would make last call, we started laughing and poking fun at one another and having ourselves quite the hoot. All in good time, we entered the harbor and paddled over to a gas dock, just a stone's throw away from the bar. We made last call, and let me tell you: Those beers tasted mighty good indeed.

We reached the end of Lake Erie on May 7, entering into the city and harbor of Tonawanda, New York, which is also the beginning of the Erie Canal. There is a low bridge at the entrance to the canal area, and a sign instructs boaters to sound one long blast and one short blast on the horn to get the operator to open the bridge. *C'est si Bon* had a manual blow horn and I kept it in a little cockpit "cubby-hole." I was sure I had put it there, but when I reached for it, there it was: Gone! Somehow, we had lost our horn. Without any alternative, we resorted to a loud verbal yell of "Ooooooopeeen theeee Briiiidge." After several repetitions of this, seemingly without result, an operator appeared from around a bridge pillar, red faced and mad as hell, yelling, "All right, dammit. I'll open the bridge!" Which he did. And when he did, we passed.

We stopped at Winfield Marina at the beginning of the Erie Canal where we were able to get a chart-book for the passage and some very substantial fenders to protect the boat while navigating the locks that are a big part of the canal. Very importantly, Winfield Marina had the facilities for taking down the mast—required for getting by the seven lift-bridges in the first few miles of the canal—and we were able to complete this task and several others while at Tonawanda.

The next day, May 8, I got up and pushed open the companionway hatch to find five inches of snow on deck. In May! It was also biting cold, and I was wishing I hadn't thrown away my snowmobile boots before the start of the voyage. We cleared the snow from the deck, started up the engine, and began heading down the canal with the mast tied down to the deck. Though the Erie Canal is a huge short-cut to the Atlantic Ocean, we knew we would be motoring for the next ten days or so, and we didn't look forward to this portion of the voyage.

As we arrived at each of the lift-bridges, we would have to call upon the bridge operator—a bit difficult without a radio or horn—who would halt car traffic and lift the bridge to let us through. Once or twice we had to find or wake the operator, but in general our approach was anticipated and several times we were able to pass without even stopping. Conversely, each lock—and there were 35 of them—required quite a bit more time. For these, we would have to wait for the lock doors to open or close, for the lock chamber to fill to the new level, and for the movement of boat traffic, ourselves included, in and out of the lock. The process would take an hour or more, and travel between the locks was sometimes pretty lengthy as well. Also, the canal closed at 6:00, which made for a quick end to the travel day. On a typical day we would only make three locks or so. It was a slow process, no doubt, but I found it interesting as well, knowing we were traversing up and over the Appalachian Mountains. I don't know that I would like to do it year after year, but I enjoyed transiting the Erie Canal for the first time.

By far, the worst part about the transit was the weather. After the snow we received in Tonawanda, it remained cold and it rained virtually non-stop the entire time we were in the Erie Canal. The whole area was flooded and only the top four or five inches of the channel markers were visible above the water's surface. Getting gas—yes, my Atomic 4 engine used gas, not diesel—was a particular problem. All of the gas stations along the canal were closed because of the flooding, so we had to "dinghy-in" to a town along the way and jerry-can gasoline back to the boat. It was a back-breaking job, and it would normally take us three or four hours to re-fill the tank.

We would usually hit a bar for dinner and a couple of beers at the end of the day, and everywhere we went people were amazed at our undertaking. Our faces were red and burnt, so we stood out from the crowd. (I soon learned that you could recognize a long-distance sailor in any port by the ridiculous dark tans we all had.) Ian and I were now part of the "cruising sailors club"—new members maybe, but true cruisers, a distinction we enjoyed. We happily shared our stories and plans with anyone interested, and we enjoyed many a "good-luck beer" that was bought for us. A couple of times we were offered the use of a shower, which the boat did not have, and these were especially appreciated.

By the time *C'est si Bon* and her weathered crew reached the Hudson River, we had been traveling two weeks and we were very happy to reach Castleton Marina on the west side of the river, just south of Albany. Castleton Marina is the main place on the Hudson for re-stepping a mast, and it's a great place for finishing up repairs or ordering equipment you might need before going offshore. In Lake Erie a bird had bitten off our Windex wind-vane at the top of the mast, so I bought a new one at Castleton. I should have also bought a spare auto-pilot, but as a major error I did *not*. (Our auto-pilot was a "Tiller Master," an underpowered apparatus that's mounted in the cockpit, fully exposed to the sun and salt water spray. It was what was available in the day, but clearly not up to the task of offshore work.) Conversely, I *did* have the foresight to buy three 5-gallon water jugs. These increased our water capacity to 35 gallons—still not that much but a good improvement. We also grabbed a very welcome shower while at the marina, and took a day off for a much needed rest. New York City was still two or three days away, but the Erie Canal had taken over a week to transit, all of it cold and rainy. We welcomed the break.

At every chance he could, Ian would ask the local fishermen about their tactics: What types of fish were running? What were they using to catch them? What times were the fish biting?—all the sort of things a good fisherman would want to know. I'll tell you, you couldn't fault Ian for his tenacity. I'd see him fishing every chance he got. But you know, he still hadn't caught even a single fish. I figured when he started catching fish, maybe I would start fishing...

After just the one day off, we left Castleton Marina and headed down the Hudson River toward New York City, reaching the Coney Island area in three days. It had taken

23

us two and a half weeks to get from LaSalle to New York, and we were very glad to be finished with that long motor-boat ride that nobody could really love. We planned to sleep the night, get groceries in the morning, and then anchor out at Sandy Hook.

Sandy Hook is an anchorage and a popular staging area. It offers excellent protection from the elements, and as its name implies, it has a sandy bottom that will securely hold an anchor. Its location alone—at the very mouth of New York Harbor—makes it the ideal launch-pad for offshore voyagers.

It had always been our plan to anchor at Sandy Hook and wait for good weather. Leaving from there, we would be offshore on the big ocean for six or seven days until we reached Bermuda, and that was assuming my navigation was sound. This was the big league. The real stuff. Everything done up to this point was in preparation for what was to happen next. We needed to do this right.

The next morning, however, the weather was sunny and fair and we saw no reason to wait for any improvement. We *did* have to do some provisioning, so we walked to a grocery store and stocked up on coffee, potatoes, rice, pasta, and lots of canned goods. Since we had no refrigeration, canned goods were the standard fare on *C'est si Bon*. We must have ended up with over a hundred cans of tuna fish, corned beef, beans, potatoes, yams, stewed tomatoes, peas, corn and anything else you can imagine coming in a can. We also bought some ice and stocked up with about two days of fresh meats and produce, knowing that the ice would melt rather quickly. The icebox on *C'est si Bon* was huge, so we put most of the cans in the bottom of it, the meat on top of those, and the ice on top of it all. Seemed like a good idea. It was not. Stay tuned...

It was shortly before noon on May 18 when we were finally ready to go. We untied and stowed the dock lines and off we went—first by Manhattan, then the Statue of Liberty, then Sandy Hook, and then out into the ocean. We

24

set up watches—four hours on, four hours off—and I took the first watch at noon. It was a gorgeous sunny day, but the wind was light and fluky, and we had to tack several times just to get clear of land. We watched out for the many ships going in and out of the harbor—getting run down by a steamer was a real possibility—and even small fishing boats seemed to crowd our path. We switched watch with Ian coming on at four o'clock, and then again with me back on at eight. As the day wore on, the congestion cleared and a layer of smog obscured both the sun and the city. Darkness came and left us entirely alone. We began our first night out on the ocean, both feeling a bit nauseous, probably from nerves more than anything else. Later, during the midnight watch, I woke up to hear Ian swearing like a trucker, frustrated from the confused sea leftover from a wind that had all but died.

The wind was back the next morning, quickly gathering strength and stability. It came from the south, and though it was a bit high on the beam for our liking, it was a great improvement from the day and night before. We put *C'est si Bon* on the starboard tack (wind from the right side), a tack that was to hold all the way to Bermuda. By the third day out, our old friend the southwest wind came up nice and steady and we were able to set course directly for Bermuda. We enjoyed a few beers—yes, we drank aboard—and the warm sun perked our moods as the auto-pilot kept *C'est si Bon* on course.

As soon as conditions permitted, I got out my sextant with the goal of determining our position and finish confirming my celestial navigation. I was able to take a sun sight the second morning out and another one later that afternoon. I spent hours below, completing the awkward math routines and charting the two LOP's on my plotting sheets. The result was an estimation of our latitude and longitude—a "fix," it's called. I compared this to the reading on the LORAN—which still worked because we were only 100 miles from shore—and I was relieved to see that the

25

two methods matched. Finally I had my offshore navigation method totally confirmed, an important accomplishment and a huge relief.

I had a bit of learning to do in the category of rest, sleep, and trust. Though he proved himself completely capable, I found it difficult to "let go" and trust Ian with the boat. Several times, with Ian on watch and me supposed to be sleeping, I would get up at the slightest noise and ask Ian what was going on. He accepted my micro-managing with sufficient grace for a while, but finally he snapped and said, "Look man, you're just going to have to trust me." He was right, of course, and after a couple of days and a discussion or two, I was able to let go and give him a bit of space. After that, I slept better and I'm sure Ian found things more enjoyable as well.

The ability to fully trust Ian to handle the boat was vital. Anything could and would happen at any time, whether I was on watch or not, and it was imperative that Ian be able to handle virtually any emergency without my assistance. I needn't have worried: right from the start Ian proved himself to be every bit the sailor I was. He took almost no time at all to familiarize himself with all of the sailing controls and other systems of the boat. He even showed me some errors I was making in sail trim.

We would also have to get along for the duration of the voyage, and for a couple of divorcees, this probably wasn't one of our better skills. Normally, Ian and I got along just fine—oh, I'm sure there were one or two moments— and one thing I tried to keep in mind was that any deep down personal differences between us didn't have to be explored and resolved *ad infinitum*. (I think a small boat on the ocean is a poor place to attempt such a thing.) We *did* need to get along as a coherent team for the duration of the voyage, and this is where I tried to keep my focus.

So yes, I was able to "let go" and trust Ian, and yes, we got along just fine, but it was still a difficult time. "Four hours on and four off" is a tough watch schedule, and the electric auto-pilot malfunctioned often, which made hand-steering necessary. (Already, I regretted not buying a spare while we were at Castleton's.) Also, I was the only one to do the celestial navigation, and especially in those beginning days, doing the calculations and completing the required charting took a lot of time during my off-watch. Additionally, though the seas were moderate, "moderate" for a 30-footer on the ocean becomes "significant," and the motion was constant and extreme. We were two strong, capable sailors but it took everything we had to make it all happen.

About this time, a very large US Coast Guard ship approached us. We turned on the radio and we could hear that we were being hailed and asked to identify ourselves. Since I could not transmit on Channel 16, however, I couldn't answer. I tried other channels with no luck. He kept saying, "This is the US Coast Guard and I'm on your starboard quarter," and I was thinking, "Yeah man, I think I see you."

It was a huge ship and it was right there beside us. I could see a group of excited cadets getting ready to launch their dinghy; they probably thought this was going to be the biggest heist of the century. I kept holding up six fingers and yelling "Goooo Channel Siiiix." (Hey, it worked for the bridge operator in Tonawanda.) Finally the ship's radio operator got the message and we started talking on Channel 6. I saw the cadets in unison get the bad news and their enthusiasm died in an instant. It was hilarious! The Coast Guard confirmed who we were and where we were going and then took off, never to be seen again.

Along we went for five days, and my celestial navigation calculations were showing that we were heading straight for Bermuda. Still a day away, however, I developed a fix that showed we were significantly off course. Bermuda has a large reef area to its west, and if an ocean current were to pass over the shallow reef, the speed of the current could really intensify. This would explain our shift in position. I would have liked to take another couple of sights to get a new fix, but by this time it was dark and I would have to wait until the morning to get one new LOP, and noon before I could get a second one to develop a new fix. This is a major disadvantage of celestial navigation: To determine position, you need to take two sun sights, one several hours after the other. And for both of those sights, you need to be able to see the sun and the horizon. If it's cloudy or dark, you can't take the sight. (ps: You can also use the moon, some stars or some planets for celestial, but you still need to see the horizon when viewing them. On *C'est si Bon* I used only the sun.)

I was also unsure of my estimate of the correct time. (Recall that an error of just four seconds equates to a mile error in the determined position.) Knowing the correct time is very complicated. The song, "Does anybody really know what time it is?" had a point. Who's the authority? Me, I used the time shown on the Weather Channel, which is absurd! Don't forget: this was 1989—no internet, no satellite phones, and we didn't have a short-wave radio. What could I do? The only estimate—to the second—that I could find was on the Weather Channel. That's what I used.

So, I set my watch to the Weather Channel, as close as I could, but the two were still a bit different from each other: 10 seconds, let's say. I wrote that down. That error I would have to put in the equation every time I took a sun sight.

Oh, but we're just getting started: My watch ran a bit *faster* than the clock on the Weather Channel. How much faster? I had to monitor the TV and my watch over several months and chart the error over time. I found that my watch was gaining four seconds each month. (I got my last estimate when I called home from New York and had my mom call out the time from the TV.) Anyway, every week I would have to add one second to the 10 second correction. (Or did I need to subtract it? See how complicated it gets?)

Oh, by the way, we're dealing with Greenwich Mean Time, so right out of the gate you need to know the difference between the local time zone and GMT.

Oh, also by the way, that ocean and all its salt can alter any clock's performance, and in such a way that's not apparent. How do you know if this has happened to *your* clock? You do the whole process with three clocks, not one, and if one goes out of whack, it won't agree with the other two. Oh brother!

So yeah, the estimate of time is elusive. I thought I had a handle on it—that's why that first LOP in Lake Erie and that first fix outside of New York were so important— but here we were: five days out at sea and suddenly way off course. I split the difference and corrected our course slightly but not entirely. The next day, my sights told me that we were again coming in pretty well on target. Mind you: If our clocks were off, and they would be if the Weather Channel was inaccurate, we might never find Bermuda.

By the evening of May 24 our information said we should be getting close. We looked with anticipation where we thought Bermuda should appear. We even made a wager, offering a free drink to the one of us who saw land first. We stared at the horizon for what seemed like hours.

At 8:00 Ian went off watch and I went below to re-look over my charts and calculations. Back on deck, I gazed at where Bermuda should be. "It should be right there," I pointed. Then, right where I was pointing, I saw the little hump of an island on the horizon. I had made my first ocean landfall after six and a half days of celestial navigation. What a wonderful accomplishment in sailing and navigation! Now we just needed to get in safely.

As I mentioned, Bermuda has quite a mass of reefs on its west side. The piloting instructions clearly warn that you should always come in during daytime hours, never at night, and always from the southeast—never from the west.

The nighttime warning puzzled me: For daytime entry, the piloting instructions have you lining up fixed physical objects and coming in that way. (I recall the instruction of lining up a flagpole and Sugarloaf Hill to find an important channel into the harbor.) I had heard of such coastal navigating methods before, perhaps to be used when there are no other navigational aids available. This, however, was a major commercial port. I thought that the daytime piloting instructions were entirely inadequate. At night, and it happened to be nighttime, we could use normal navigational lights and buoys. They're clear and unambiguous. What the hell is wrong with that? It's true, we might be able to see the lights and nothing else—tidal currents could present a problem—but I still didn't see much risk in coming in at night.

I also thought the insistence on a southeast entry was unwarranted. A north entry would have been much more convenient for us—we were going to St. George's Harbour, which was on the north end of Bermuda—and there's a huge sector-light on the north end that appears red if you're in unsafe water and green if you're coming in correctly. It all seemed fine to me.

We came in from the north, not the southeast, and at night—everything contrary to the piloting instructions. The sector light directed us perfectly as did all the other lights leading into the harbor. Looking at the floating buoys, I could clearly see there was no tidal current. We found our way to the inner harbor, right where we wanted to go, and at 1:00 AM, May 25, 1989 (my 34th birthday) we dropped anchor in St. George's Harbour, Bermuda.

We were supposed to check in at Customs before doing anything else. We didn't. Also, neither Ian nor I had bathed in a week and we probably should have jumped in the water to wash off the stink. We didn't. We also hadn't had a drink in a week, and we could see those familiar red and white *Budweiser* lights in a bar window on shore. We launched the dinghy and rowed over to *Chick's Bar and Grill* for a well-deserved drink.

It was the best birthday I ever could have had: I had just made my first ocean landfall, navigating by sun and sextant, and I was in a waterfront bar in Bermuda with a nice cool drink in my hand. I could still feel the world rocking from six and a half days of non-stop motion, but the Reggae music in the air brought comfort to the apparent motion and made it seem perfectly natural. Also, a woman wearing perfume walked behind us several times and the fragrance was absolutely electrifying. It was a grand birthday indeed.

In the morning we reported to the Customs dock—Liberty Island it's called—something we were supposed to do immediately upon landing. Liberty Island was close to where we had anchored—we had rowed right in front of it on the way to the bar—so we took *C'est si Bon* over and tied her up to the dock. We knew we had ignored proper procedure; we hoped the officials would let us off easily.

After waiting only a few minutes, Ian and I saw a Customs official coming toward the boat. He carried a black satchel and stepped slowly and with purpose. He stood tall and straight but also appeared unstressed and relaxed. He exuded the dignity of a proud Ethiop. His hair appeared recently cut; he had shaved that morning; his clothes were laundered. He wore the traditional black shorts that are seen only in Bermuda. I noticed the fine cloth from which these were made and the sharp creases in them that extended from the shiny black belt to the cuffs a few inches above the officer's knees. The whiteness of his formal shirt, collared and accompanied by a thin black tie, blinded my eyes as it reflected in the sun. The tall black gartered stockings he wore were as perfect as his polished black Oxfords. All this contrasted with how Ian and I presented ourselves: bearded, sun burned, unbathed, and dressed in the same clothes we had been wearing for a week out on the sea.

The officer approached *C'est si Bon* by way of her bow, and looked her over without emotion as he passed by her length. Though his face remained neutral at best, I imagined I saw in his lack of expression a hint of appreciation, of admiration, of pride. Perhaps, I thought, he would have a soft spot in his heart for the fine sailboat in front of him, manned by two sailors who were only following their dream. It was a fantasy, of course: I knew we were dead meat for sure.

"Hello," he said. "My name is Officer Lee. Welcome to Bermuda. Do you mind if I come aboard?" Still stoic and formal, he smiled slightly and extended his hand for me to shake. I noticed again that he had a manner about him that balanced the formality of his occupation with an inner peace and comfort he possessed. I saw kindness in his face. I shook his hand, introduced both myself and Ian, and welcomed him aboard. He stepped over the life-lines and went down the companionway and into the cabin. I motioned for him to sit at the table and placed a glass of water in front of him. He thanked me for the water, but put it to one side where it would remain unsampled. He pulled some paperwork out of his satchel and spread it out on the table.

"What time did you land?" was his first question.

"One o'clock in the morning," I answered. I knew this answer identified our breach in procedure, but I tried to appear innocent.

"One o'clock?" he asked in apparent alarm. "That was ten hours ago!"

We were busted! You would know it if you were to hear the officer's words and the accusing manner in which he stated them. Also, if you were to see him raise his eyebrow in the telling manner with which he did, you would conclude we were already judged guilty and that we would be fined, deported or incarcerated. I heard and saw all of that too, but it was the manner in which Officer Lee instinctively jerked his head and looked over his shoulder toward the Customs office that alerted me that something else had caused his alarm. As we found out later, it was his own agency that had failed to see us enter on the radar they were supposed to be watching at all times. To Officer Lee, this was a great concern, great enough to interrupt his concentration and allow our indiscretion to be forgotten.

The glance over the shoulder as well as the inner turmoil lasted only a moment, and with his inner peace and stoicism restored, Officer Lee returned his eyes and attention to the matter at hand. The paperwork process, formal the whole time, took about an hour. Several forms had to be completed and several dozen questions were asked and answered. We had to give up the ship's flare gun (a possible weapon) and there was a minimal landing charge of $25. At the end of it all, Officer Lee stamped our passports and told us we were free to go. Before he left, he offered a suggestion of the best place to anchor. It was the very one we had used the night before.

We spent the next three days at Bermuda, my second time to the lovely four-island ocean paradise. We caught up on our rest, rented scooters, snorkeled the reefs, and hit the bars. We met a few new friends, mostly fellow cruising sailors, and it was both fun and educational to mix with this new crowd, a group of sailors I had wanted to join for so long.

One kind, older fellow named George had a particularly interesting story. He had been cruising on his Nicholson 35 for several years, and I quickly realized that the life he had been living was the life I sought. George told us of the years he spent gunk-holing the Bahamas and the Eastern Caribbean, the hurricanes he waited out in Trinidad, and about a Jamaican who snuck aboard one night and robbed him at knifepoint. We had him over for a lamb roast dinner one night, and he had us over to his boat a couple of times as well. He once served us crackers and a fish spread, made from a fish he had caught on the way over and "canned" in the canning jars he had aboard. He canned all sorts of things—meats, fish, fruits—and I found that other sailors did the same. How civilized!

We met another group—Todd and his wife Marsha, and Marsha's brother Jim—all of whom were sailing on another Nicholson 35, theirs out of North Carolina. This trio, as well as George, became a great set of mentors, explaining to Ian and me the realisms of cruising life. I recall one afternoon, sitting with the whole group on Todd and Marsha's boat, when one of these *realisms* was shared:

We had been out snorkeling that morning and we were relaxing in the afternoon breeze, enjoying the motion of a sailboat at anchor. Lounging in the shade of the cockpit awning, all of us on "island time," we chatted away and sipped our beers. At one point I looked out from the boat and saw dozens of small silver fish jumping out of the water, here and there, all around the boat. Ian saw them too and went totally nuts! He was up on his feet and wanting to rush back to *C'est si Bon* and get the fishing rod. Todd grabbed him by the shoulders and steadied him saying, "Relax, man. Fish don't bite when they're jumping out of the water. Try later. Perhaps at five. Fish bite best at five. AM or PM."

Now, to this day I still don't know whether or not fish bite best at five, AM or PM, but it seemed like knowledgeable advice, at least at the time. Ian, slow to lose his agitation, stared into Todd's eyes in a most serious manner, absorbing the privileged information. They appeared as if they were two well-seasoned old salts sharing the scarcely known true secrets of marine animal behavior: "Yes, they eat at five."

We went back to our beers and our stories. Life was slow. It was great. I'm sure that if I had cruised longer I would have run into at least some of these kind folks again, but such was not to be. I miss them all. I sure am glad I was at least able to enjoy their friendship for a short time though. Good folks.

(By the way, Ian didn't catch any fish at Bermuda. Not at five nor at any other time. AM or PM...)

At one point during our stay at Bermuda it became apparent that we had a problem in our icebox: It stunk like hell! In New York we had packed cans in the bottom of the icebox, packaged meat on top of that, and ice on top of it all. The ice had melted, dripping over the meat, with the meat juices then dripping over the cans and contaminating the labels. What to do??? We had ignored the problem too long, and it was escalating faster than we could eat through the canned goods. We would have to remove the labels and wash the cans but we couldn't figure out how to identify the contents of each can. But we were men, or so the song goes, and we handled the problem in a very "manly" way:

We got out a hammer and a punch and we put a "ding" on the top of all cans that contained some type of meat or protein. Likewise, if a can contained vegetables, it got two "dings." If it contained potatoes or some type of starch, it got three. We didn't know exactly what was in each can, but for any particular meal if you chose three cans—a one, two and a three "dinger"—at least you would have a balanced meal. Meals, after that, were always a surprise. Usually the result was okay—as okay as a meal entirely out of cans can be—sometimes not so okay. We survived. And the stink in the icebox was gone.

The next leg of the voyage would be an 800-mile passage straight south to St. Thomas. It would be my first attempt at this particular stretch, but the sailing strategy seemed simple enough: Wait for an east wind, and when it comes, take it. The wind should remain out of the east at least for a while, my strategy predicted, and after a few days the trade winds should appear. If we were lucky—and on *C'est si Bon* we were *always* lucky—we'd be on the port tack the entire distance.

Ian and I awoke rested on the 28th with an east wind blowing and a forecast for fair weather. It was time to go. We had already said our good-byes, so we raised anchor and motored over to Liberty Island to clear Customs. Officer Lee was again on duty, and again well-presented and displaying the same enviable dignity we saw in him three days earlier. He stamped our passports, returned to us our flare gun, and bid us farewell. After shaking his hand, we untied and stowed our dock-lines then pointed *C'est si Bon* eastward and motored out of St. George's Harbour, leaving Bermuda about 9:00 that morning.

Immediately out of the harbor, we were greeted by a choppy incoming surf that reminded us instantly of the sea's authority. I revved the engine and *C'est si Bon* powered through several breaking rollers while Ian and I hung on for our dear lives. Once clear of the surf, we put in another mile to make sure we were in deep water, then turned south, catching the wind just forward of the beam. Ian went forward and put up the main while I unfurled the genoa. *C'est si Bon* took off in a great hurry, the conditions being ideal for a gal like her. As we had experienced on the previous leg, the wind would consistently come from one side only. On this leg it was from the port side and we would sail over 700 miles to the Caribbean Sea without changing tacks even once.

Since it was just a few days short of June, and since we were now getting into more southern latitudes, the day's warmth allowed Ian and me to wear our summer garb of shorts and T-shirts. (I could hardly believe that only two weeks prior we were suffering miserably in the cold and rainy conditions of the Erie Canal.) We were blessed with a gorgeous sunny day, one that surpassed even the most promising predictions we had received from the Bermudian Coast Guard. The unblemished deep blue sky created a perfect panorama, its purity interrupted by dozens of chicken-dumpling clouds that hung in the air as if pinned in place. We set the auto-pilot—which no longer performed very well—and once again began watches, anxious to re-settle into a sea-going routine. Later in the afternoon we boiled some cabbage and mixed in some corned beef, a splendid Irish meal that Ian had suggested and one that kept us in good cheer all day. We had a few ice-cold beers aboard, and we broke these out to toast the continuation of our great adventure. Evening came soon enough, and the night that followed passed peacefully as did the next few days. I found that days on a boat offshore sometimes fly by, especially when the company is good, the conditions are even better, and there's sufficient, but not too much, cold beer.

For this leg we set up a watch schedule opposite of what we had before. (For example, I now slept from 8-12 PM whereas before I was "on watch" then.) I had thought that the change would be seamless, but I found I couldn't sleep during my newly allotted times. I asked Ian to switch back but he preferred his new schedule. (He probably slept better.) The auto-pilot was acting up more and more, and in addition to having to hand-steer while on-watch, I was spending quite a bit of my time off-watch—my sleep time—trying to fix it. Also, I was still spending a lot of time navigating and this dug into my sleep time as well. The first few days out of Bermuda were delightful indeed, but before too long I was desperately low on sleep. I even tried letting the boat sit "hove to" and just bob in the water while I tried to rest, but that didn't seem to help. Totally exhausted and beginning to see little rowboats out on the water—a common hallucination; it's really just the water sparkling—I finally fell asleep, simply because I couldn't stay awake any longer. At the time the experience seemed like total agony, but looking back I wish all of life's problems could be solved so easily.

By any analysis, this leg of the voyage should have been the very best sailing passage of my life. This leg was what the voyage was all about. This was why I had struggled and come this far. The dream! I was living the Sailor's Dream! Three or four days out of Bermuda, however, a painful anxiety developed within me, one that took away much of the pleasure one would normally expect from such beautiful days of sailing. It was a feeling of impatience, a sense of irritation, a painful longing simply to get into port. I began wishing away the voyage, the very voyage that for so long I had dreamed of doing. What a horrible state of mind!

The watches, especially the night ones, became four-hour endurance contests and everything seemed to be going wrong. The plastic gears in the auto-pilot were wearing out and I could get the damn thing working only a few hours each day. The days were becoming progressively hotter, and hand steering unprotected in the tropical sun really became a bear. Cooking and eating our "surprise" meals of 100% canned food was hard to get enthusiastic about. The wooden mast-supporting beam inside the boat developed a bend in it, threatening to break with who-knows-what results. I started to pray, something I hadn't done since I was a child. I was in a terrible state of anxiety. Though I had known it all along, I couldn't shake the thought that we were a very long way from shore and helpless if anything serious were to go wrong.

So, it was in spite of this horrible mental disposition—and it stuck around for more than a couple of days, I'll tell you—that we sailed on, working to complete what really was a passage of a lifetime. I kept my unpleasant thoughts to myself, never mentioning even a single word to Ian, and half-way between Bermuda and the Caribbean Sea a most persistent wind began to blow. The star of the show had arrived: It was the North East Trade Wind.

It's a wind born in the Sahara Desert, the world's largest high pressure area and a huge solar furnace of stagnant air, super-charged by the unrelenting equatorial sun of northern Africa. Sufficiently strong as it leaves the African coast, the wind would only gather momentum as it crossed the entire ocean before reaching *C'est si Bon.* With this "fetch" of almost two thousand miles, the trade wind would create 20-foot swells—scary but safe and majestic walls of water that would slowly raise and lower us in a repeated 30-second rhythm. Up top from the crest of one swell we could see the next one several hundred yards away, and from down in the trough between two swells we would be awestruck, hardly believing the wall of water we had just been over.

I would have been sufficiently entertained by the swells alone, but instead of being featureless mammoth waves, the surface of each swell bore a confused and chaotic system of four or five-foot seas coming from three different directions at any particular time. Resembling the "mogul hill" of a ski slope, the seas created a constant and thorough motion, rocking the boat from side to side, pitching it fore and aft, and attempting to buck Ian and me overboard. (We wore a life-harness and tethered ourselves to the boat to prevent this.) Before long our legs felt like rubber, totally spent from trying to balance against the arduous motion.

The sea was a gorgeous transparent sky-blue, and as I looked down into it, it appeared not so much like water but like solid ice with the sun's rays extending infinitely into its depths. The incessant movement of the ocean surrounded us everywhere. Thousands of white caps roared in our ears and we had to yell to be heard over the noise. Seas smashed into one another, creating vertical geysers of water, which the wind quickly took hold of and changed into horizontal spray. Day after day, I sat out on the boat's coach roof and watched the incredible cinema of the trade winds. I knew it was one of life's most special experiences. I absorbed all I could.

C'est si Bon loved the sea, reminding me of a puppy that was finally let outside to play after a day cooped up in the house. Yawing wildly from left to right, the boat would quickly be brought back on course by the forceful wind. Every hour or so—at least once every watch—a sea would hit the side of the boat, sending a huge mass of water straight up into the air, which the wind would then dump over the deck, soaking everything and everybody with warm but refreshing salty water. *C'est si Bon* sped along, jumping and splashing and having the time of her life. We raced along at maximum speed for two or three days. I was taking sights and calculating positions each day, and we were making some great 24-hour runs—two of them over 140 miles.

On June 4, just before dinner, I developed a fix that put us 70 miles north of the Sombrero Passage, a fifty-mile wide separation between islands that would lead us into the Caribbean Sea. To the right of the passage, downwind or "to leeward," was the low-lying island of Anegada with a large shallow reef we would need to avoid. The chart stated that one could hear waves breaking on the reef if you were too close. (I wondered if I was supposed to use that information or if it was put on the chart just to scare me.)

Evening progressed and the sun went down, putting us "in the dark" as far as navigation was concerned. We were expecting to go through the passage at approximately 4:00 AM—12 hours after my last position determination. At the time we hadn't seen land in almost seven days and I was still a bit unsure of my navigation. It was that time thing again: Even a minor error in time would put us up on the reef. Also, the chart identified an east-to-west current in the area, and recalling our experiences when we were approaching Bermuda, I was worried that the shallowness of the water in the passage might increase the speed of the current toward the reef.

As the night wore on the anemometer showed a steady 30-knot wind, quite a bit of punishment for a 30-footer. We put a third reef in the mainsail and left only a few feet of the genoa exposed from the furler, hoping the wind wouldn't get any stronger. *C'est si Bon* surfed down one wave after another, racing along well over hull speed but making only an eerily quiet hissing sound. I stayed up all night, watching—and listening—for the reef. I prayed. (I prayed often those days.) I waited. It was a long night.

As the morning sun was rising I saw the lights of a large ship pass a few miles to starboard of *C'est si Bon*, granting us a huge relief by verifying we were in safe water. We held course and sailed into the Caribbean Sea, not yet seeing any of the islands we believed to be on either side of us. Later in the morning, well through the Sombrero Passage, we made our long anticipated right turn and sailed downwind in an uncomfortable slog that lasted the whole day. We spotted Anegada about noon, the first sighting of land in seven days, and one that confirmed all of the celestial navigation I had done thus far. It also meant that henceforth we would simply spot and identify various land forms and make our way with a method called "coastal navigation." Although we didn't particularly enjoy the downwind slog, Ian and I took delight as we called out the numerous Caribbean islands we passed, anticipating fully the end of our long journey.

Late in the afternoon on June 5, seven days and seven hours out of Bermuda—exactly five weeks out of LaSalle—we arrived at St. Thomas. As *C'est si Bon* sailed to a position where I could look into the large natural harbor on the island's south side, I saw for the first time the panoramic vista of what would be my new home. Green volcanic mountains monopolized the landscape, and scattered throughout the hills I could see numerous residential buildings. Instead of the attractive sort of homes I had expected, however, the ones I saw seemed squalid and depressed. Most were stucco and painted a single color; an ugly faded peach color seemed to be most popular. There were no large picture windows to be seen, no cozy patios, no welcoming landscaping. I felt disappointed. The village of Charlotte Amalie lay along the waterfront, and it, too, was not as I had imagined. It looked drab and unkept. Trash littered the flowerbeds by the water. Everything looked as if it needed a coat of paint. I had expected to see a Caribbean island paradise; it appeared as if I had arrived at a south Chicago slum.

It happened to be a Friday afternoon when we reached St. Thomas, and by the time we located the Customs dock it was just minutes before 5:00 PM—quitting time, I was thinking. If we didn't clear Customs, by law we were

41

supposed to remain on the boat until it reopened, which might not be until Monday morning. Knowing the time constraint, I revved the engine to full blast and raced the boat across the harbor to the Customs dock, kicking away the tiller and yelling out to Ian to handle the boat as I jumped off of it and burst into the Customs office.

I must have made the worst possible impression as I staggered through the door like a drunkard, my equilibrium destroyed by several days of exaggerated motion at sea. I hadn't bathed since Bermuda and I'm sure I stunk like hell. My unshaven face was both burned and blistered from the sun and my hair and clothes were caked with salt. And just in case my ghastly appearance wasn't by itself sufficiently offensive, I abandoned all evidence of learned manners and immediately blurted out my desire to land as if my personal needs superseded those of all others.

The Customs clerk, demonstrating that total non-hurried "Caribbean Time" mannerism that I was soon to see quite often, slowly approached me and voiced a concern, not about my appearance, or the way I stunk, or my poor manners, but about how rude and unreasonable it was of me to report to Customs five minutes before closing time, and on a Friday at that. I pleaded my case, stating that I had little choice, but the clerk was unimpressed. She gave me a form and instructed me to fill it out and leave it with the janitor when I was done. She started to walk away and showed a real annoyance when I asked for a pen. With the pen delivered, which apparently was her last obligation in the matter, she left the premises via the same door I had entered, presumably to begin her weekend. I completed the form as I was told, gave it to the janitor, and to this day I don't know if I was ever "cleared" or not.

Finished at Customs, as much as possible anyway, we anchored *C'est si Bon* among several other boats in the eastern end in the harbor. Anxious to re-engage in society, we jumped overboard for a couple of quick salt-water baths, launched the dinghy, and rowed to shore. We began our lives as residents of St. Thomas, meandering through the central area of Charlotte Amalie, hitting a local bar or two, enjoying a few beers, and chatting with our new neighbors. Over the next several days we would meet several other "residents," telling them our story and hearing theirs. Some of the sly-types saw Ian and me as fresh opportunities: One two-year veteran to the island tried to sell me his boat and motor. Another said I needed to buy his scooter. Several people proved overly eager to befriend me, each wanting to gain free lodging on *Hotel C'est si Bon*. One day, a particularly troubled individual tried to sell me drugs. He became inflamed when I told him I didn't want any; then he tried to rob me. Welcome to St. Thomas.

Very quickly I saw the ugly world of living as an island local. It was what many people call "third world" but in fact, it was really just a two-level society with a distinct and impermeable contrast between the prosperous upper class and the impoverished lower one—the "haves" and the "have-nots." One aspect that made it particularly distasteful on St. Thomas was that the division was racially oriented: Sure, there were whites in the lower class, but I saw no blacks relaxing on yachts, dining at fine restaurants, or engaged in any of the other activities that would demonstrate some level of prosperity.

Many impoverished people, I think, would find life difficult. It is said that "money doesn't buy happiness" but I wouldn't expect agreement on that from any chronically poor person. I can easily imagine the hopelessness a man (or woman) must feel if he were poor, uneducated, lacking of marketable skills, and living within an isolated island economy. That hopelessness could quickly change to anger, I'm sure, especially if ethnic prejudice were a significant factor. It becomes difficult to predict what a person would do when placed in such a desperate situation.

One of those in the less affluent class I met was a woman named Maggie. Maggie worked at the *New York Bar*, one of the bars in the back streets of the village. The bar was frequented by locals, both black and white, but not by tourists and generally not by anybody who took pride in belonging to the more prosperous upper class. It was a fun place, filled with laughter and smiles from a few folks born on the island, but mostly by people who, like me, had come to St. Thomas chasing the Caribbean sun. Ian and I took to going to the *New York* to meet and mix with folks like us. Maggie was often there, working the bar. She was friendly and easy to talk to and she introduced Ian and me to the rest of the crowd.

I saw Maggie as myself, two years in the future. She was from upstate New York and she had come to St. Thomas chasing a dream: She wanted to move to the Caribbean and live the island life. She was tired of a boring life of "working for the man" and she wanted more. She didn't have much money, and even less of a plan, but she knew upstate New York wasn't going to do it for her anymore. She quit her job, sold her car, and packed her bags for St. Thomas. Sound familiar?

Maggie worked most days but she was broke. Her paycheck barely covered the rent, and she was fully dependent on tips for food, clothes and everything else. She told me about how back in upstate New York she always had a full refrigerator. "If you came to my home now," she told me, "all you would see in the fridge is a jug of water."

Maggie introduced me to several of the locals of Charlotte Amalie; all of them were possible variations of me in a varying number of years in the future. They were a happy group, but surely not prosperous. They would work when they could, but there never seemed to be enough work and it never paid very well. Any money saved went to buy some necessity, all too often booze. Nobody was getting ahead. Nobody thought about retirement, or investing, or even buying a home. The sad fact was that nobody could see any escape from the impoverished world in which they lived.

I actually got a job at St. Thomas. I heard about a resort on the east end of the island that needed a bartender. (I used to be a bartender, briefly, in my younger years.) I applied for the job and for some reason I was accepted. At the time the resort wasn't yet open, but apparently it was going to open soon. Anyway, I got the job.

Each day, Ian and I would go through a routine of buying food and preparing meals, of wandering around town in the mornings, and taking a nap in the hot afternoon. We finished our daily routine by hanging out at the *New York Bar* in the evening and returning to the boat half-drunk afterward. Hurricane season would be starting in a week or two and I was wondering what I would do if one ever came through. (As it was, a very destructive hurricane named *Hugo* hit St. Thomas later that year.) The bottom paint on *C'est si Bon* was entirely gone and barnacles were starting to grow. I was getting low on funds and Ian was almost completely broke. (He kept wiring money from home but apparently the money from his divorce settlement was depleted.) It wasn't difficult to see the writing on the wall: My boat was going to rot under my feet and I was going to be broke and hopeless like all my new friends at the bar, working as a bartender and drinking my life away. I decided to sail back home. I asked Ian if he would crew for me. He said yes. We left immediately. We were on St. Thomas for only ten days.

On the morning of June 15, the *C'est si Bon* sailed out of St. Thomas, bound for New York City, 1380 miles away. It was a beautiful day—all of them were—and soon we were dancing away in the glorious sea of the trade winds just like before, simply going a different direction.

You may recall I mentioned that when sailing south you just wait for an east wind and sail with that until you reach the trades which always come from the east. It's pretty easy. Going north, however, you start in the trades and then you gradually come out of them and take whatever is there for you. What you normally get is some very light or

45

non-existent air. In fact, it's so non-existent that the area is called the "Horse Latitudes," supposedly because the crews on traditional ships had to jettison their cargo of livestock to conserve water while they waited for the wind. I don't know if any of that is true, but I do know that when you get out of the trade winds at about 25 degrees north or so, you're bound to have trouble finding wind. It's also the area known as the Bermuda Triangle, but I wouldn't get too excited about that.

For the first two or three days, things were fine. We had stocked up on food and water, and some of the errors we had made on the way down we knew not to repeat on the way back. The trade winds were again giving us some remarkable daily passages, and I didn't yet know how severe the problem of the Horse Latitudes could be. Of course, the auto-pilot continued to give us trouble. I had tried to buy a new one before we left St. Thomas, but I couldn't find one anywhere. (Apparently, everybody knew that you should never use an exposed electric auto-pilot on the salty ocean.) We were still getting some utility out of the old one, however, and I was hoping it would hold.

About three days out, I heard the pump for our drinking water cycle one time. I wasn't alarmed: If the pump cycles without someone using water, it means there is some sort of a pressure leak in the water system. One pump stroke, I thought, was no reason to worry.

The next day I noticed there was quite a bit of water in the bilge—not all that unusual on *C'est si Bon*—so I pumped the bilge empty with the manual pump. Just then I heard the water pump cycle again. (Not good.) Upon investigation, I noticed that the spigot on the water tank had broken and all of the water had spilled out of the tank and into the bilge. (That's what I had pumped overboard.) Thank God I had bought those three 5-gallon water jugs back at Castleton. Without those (and without a radio to call for help, don't forget), we would have been in big trouble. With the water jugs we still didn't have much water, but we

46

did have 15 gallons. Mind you, we still had about 10 days of sailing left, assuming the wind held.

The auto-pilot continued to give us trouble and it was mal-functioning more and more often. I was an expert at fixing it for any mechanical problems, but a day or two after the water tank disaster, the auto-pilot stopped running for no apparent reason. I tinkered with it a bit and found that if you turned it off and let it set a while, it would work again, but only for a minute or two. It was clear to me that we had a burnt out transistor, something I couldn't fix. I opened up the auto-pilot case, cleaned and fixed what I could, then closed it up to see if it was going to work.

If it worked, great: we could sit back and *C'est si Bon* would steer herself, hopefully all the way to New York. If it didn't work, Ian and I would have to steer the boat 24 hours-a-day—in that hot tropical sun—with very limited water—for the next nine days or longer.

So, before I turned on the auto-pilot, I looked up into the sky and asked God if He would make the auto-pilot work. I reasoned with Him that I was a good, moral person. I'm sure I made a whole lot of promises. All I needed Him to do was to make the auto-pilot work. *I'm going to turn it on*, I prayed. *I know it will run for a minute or so. Please God*, I begged, *make it run a good long time after that.*

I turned it on. It ran for a minute. Then it stopped. It never did re-start. I haven't been to church since.

We got pretty good at hand-steering, Ian and I. By this time we had both become marathon readers and each of us could read a book, steer the boat, and watch the compass—all at the same time. The trade winds hung on for a few more days and then they gradually abated. It was great for a while: the seas diminished, the wind pushed us along at a respectable five knots, and we stopped getting the regular soaking of waves coming on deck. Eventually the wind all but stopped and we thought it was quite a novelty, being six or seven hundred miles offshore and becalmed. We sailed even in very light breezes, not knowing when the good wind would return. Sure was hot. There wasn't a cloud in the sky and we had to stay at the helm 24 – 7.

By and by, the wind stopped completely and the ocean went flat except for a pesky roll that never abated completely. In the still air we would have to take down the sails so that they wouldn't get damaged by the constant flogging. We watched the sea for telltale "cat's paws," and at every breath of wind we'd again put up the sails, hoping to make a mile or two. I'm sure we took them down and put them back up dozens of times, but at one point we had not put up the sails for three days as we waited for wind. During that time we didn't move an inch, of course, but we still continued to use up our water supply. The use of one gallon of drinking water per man per day is considered a minimum, but because we had so little, we were allowing ourselves less than half of that. We were thirsty all of the time.

I was on watch during one of these periods with no wind and the sails down, sitting in the cockpit and waiting for the wind. Ian was down below, off-watch and asleep. I looked down into the water and saw a fish swimming around and around the boat. It was a pretty fish. Colorful. Peaceful. I probably watched him for a half an hour before it occurred to me that I should try to catch the son-of-a-bitch.

So, I reached for the fishing rod. I don't think Ian had used it since Bermuda and I hadn't touched it even once since I tied it up to the backstay way back in late April. By chance, it once again had the original lure attached to the end of the line.

I cast the lure out into the water and the fish went at it like a bullet, stopping inches from the lure, staring at it intensely. I wiggled the line a bit, trying to make the lure look like a little fish. The big fish approached the lure, seeming to sniff at it and trying to figure out if it was edible or not. Eventually the fish figured out that the lure, indeed, was *not* edible, and returned to swimming around and

48

around the boat. I cast the lure out again and again but the fish didn't give it any more attention what-so-ever.

Way back in New York we had bought two cans of ham and upon opening one of them, we discovered they contained the worst ham you could ever imagine. We still had the second can; we were keeping it "for emergencies." I figured it was time to invest that can of ham. I opened the can and picked off a little piece of ham and threw it in the water near the fish. He swam over to the ham and sniffed at it, much as he had done with the lure. He prodded it with his snout several times, taking his good-old time figuring out what the strange piece of meat was all about. By and by, all in good time, he ate it. And so, I got out a second piece of ham and threw it toward the fish. This too, he ate, and a little bit faster than the first one. I offered some ham over and over and soon I had that fish eating like no tomorrow. I woke up Ian. "Get a hook," I told him.

Ian got up and got a piece of fishing line with a half-inch hook on it—a small hook for a pretty big fish, I thought. He put a bit of ham on the hook and I warned him, "Whatever you do, don't put that hook into the water until I get the net."

Well, I got about half way to the net, which was no more than a single step away, when I heard Ian's frantic yell, "Get the net!"

I looked over and I saw that Ian had the fish on the hook, half out of the water and flopping wildly, you know, as any fish out of the water will do. I reached the net over the gunwale and the fish fell off of the hook and right into the net. We finally had our fish: a two-foot mahi-mahi. Ian cut it up—"cleaning it" it's called—and I cooked it up for our dinner that evening.

And that, friends, is the end of the fish story: a great fish story, for sure, but even a great fish story would not solve the problem we were having on *C'est si Bon*. We hadn't had very much wind for quite some time, and we were desperately short of water. I recall looking Ian in the eye when we broke into our last 5-gallon jug of water. It was not a happy time.

We *did* have a bit of gas in the tank. *C'est si Bon* had a 20-gallon fuel tank, which equated to a range of about 100 miles. We started with a full tank, but each day we had to run the engine to charge the boat's batteries. By this time we had only a bit over half a tank. Being mid-June, it was getting pretty close to hurricane season, and generally there were four or five small squalls surrounding us. We took to motoring toward a squall if there was one near-by and grabbing a bit of wind that way. That took quite a bit of precious gas, however, and it didn't provide us with much sailing. We still had a long way to go; we were desperate but we had to be smart about things.

I didn't have any charts of the US eastern coast but I did have a "catalog map," which was simply a very low-detailed picture of the coast with some boxes drawn on it, indicating which charts could be purchased. From the picture, though, I could see that we were a lot closer to North Carolina than we were to New York, and since our water situation was clearly desperate, we elected to sail—without a chart—to a place in North Carolina called Morehead City. We altered course and headed for the coast. Progress was slow, but time and time again we would get a bit of wind. By the time we came to and crossed the Gulf Stream we seemed to be doing okay.

One day when we had been out eleven days, no doubt getting close to the coast but still out of the sight of land, the alarm on the depth sounder went off. There was only ocean around us but we were in water only eight feet deep and about to go aground! It was some sort of a reef, we guessed, but we had no choice other than to continue on course. Thankfully, after a while the water started becoming deeper.

A day or so later we came upon a red channel marker. Still, we hadn't seen land for close to two weeks, but here was a marker, warning us of danger and telling us that we needed to go on one side rather than the other. We

50

recalled the mariner's phrase of "red-right-returning" and interpreted that as best as we could. Apparently we did okay.

Finally, 13 days after leaving St. Thomas, we started to see boats and we noticed that most of them were heading toward the same area, probably to some sort of channel leading to some sort of port. We followed these boats, utilized our own good common sense, and eventually found the port of Morehead City. Then, up what appeared to be the Inter-coastal Waterway (ICW), we came to a waterfront town, the name of which we did not know. We saw a gas dock and tied up. A sign said, "Welcome to Beaufort, North Carolina." Total time from St. Thomas was 13 days, 8 hours.

C'est si Bon and her crew were still a long way from home but I guess the story of The Voyage of the *C'est si Bon* ends here. Beaufort, North Carolina was a wonderful town and after a few days Ian decided that he would make it his home, at least for a while. I bought him a steak dinner as a gesture of gratitude, left him and the *C'est si Bon* at anchor, and took a bus home so that I could get things in order for my re-entry into the civilized world. I came back after a couple of weeks to find that Ian had secured a job on a shrimp boat and he was heading out for the first time that night at midnight. He was broke, so I bought him some cigarettes and gave him a bit of money. His last pair of sneakers had rotted away and he walked in his bare feet. *He didn't even have a pair of shoes to his name.* We hit a bar that evening, had ourselves a couple of beers, and shared some stories with a crowd that wanted to hear about our adventure. Still barefoot, Ian headed off to work at midnight. I never saw him again. I heard he eventually took a job on a fishing boat bound for Nova Scotia. I hope he is well.

The next day I took up the anchor and started heading up the ICW alone, finding my way to Elizabeth City a week later. It was there that a boat transporting company offered to truck *C'est si Bon* home, saving me a very long motorboat ride and quite a bit of money. The voyage was over. I gladly accepted.

Chapter 2. The Voyage of the *Skyelark of London*

Life changed in unimaginable ways following the voyage on *C'est si Bon*. Coming back, I was broke and without a job. I had no car or home. The boat looked like hell. I was drinking too much. I had even acquired a cigarette habit.

I set about networking for a job, and in a major stroke of luck Ford hired me once again, this time in the US at the company's flagship Romeo Engine Plant. Being out of a job for six months had created in me a totally revised work-attitude: Whereas I loathed my work before, I loved my new job and attacked all work assignments with total gusto. And where I previously had no chance of advancement, in my new career I became quite the "golden boy" and received three promotions within three years. The job paid well—better than before—and before long I had a pretty good chunk of change put away.

Luck played a major part in this good fortune, no doubt, and so did the help I received from of a couple of high-level managers. But it was my new attitude—one of enthusiasm, of persistency, of attention to detail—that first and foremost paved my path to success. That change of attitude came from the voyage: from quitting work, going sailing, and starting life anew.

I also acquired a whole new outlook regarding health and fitness. I took a company provided smoking cessation class—good riddance to *that* habit—and I cut back on the beer, eventually cutting out alcohol altogether. I began lifting weights at the company fitness center, and that grew into a habit of daily gym work-outs that I maintained for years and years. I also took up the hobby of bicycle riding, and in no small way. At first I pedaled on my own along the rural roads in the Romeo area; later I joined a couple of bicycle clubs and toured all around the state of Michigan. Over the years my passion grew, and I was able to take several exciting cycling vacations in foreign places like Mexico, Italy and Thailand. My "big ride" was an 83-day crossing of the United States.

Regarding boating, after the voyage I quickly put *C'est si Bon* back in ship-shape condition and sold it that winter. Still succumbing to the Sailor's Dream, however, I bought a bigger boat—a Morgan-38 called the *Wavelength*—which I kept on Lake Huron for seven years. I had a lot of fun with *Wavelength*, but it wasn't like my beloved *C'est si Bon* and I didn't feel the passion as I did before. Also, being a big and thus costly boat, it taught me the painful financial consequences of the Sailor's Dream. I eventually sold it in 1997 and went "boatless" after that.

That's not to say I ever lost that damn fantasy I had with sailboats. I would feel it every time I saw one, especially if the boat appeared to be suitable for the ocean. I would stare in awe at the powerful winches that surrounded the cockpit, the salt-water oxidation on the boat's stainless steel, and the well-coiled lines hanging at the mast. I would see two boats docked alongside each other and I would judge that *this* boat would do well in a storm but *that* one would not. I would continue with my dream, the one of the beautiful sea and of its distant shores.

With the downturn of the automotive industry in 2007, I was offered an attractive early retirement just short of my 52nd birthday. By then I had worked my way to a staff position, which really wasn't too bad at all. It was good work, and I'm very grateful, but it had its stresses. Life was going by: My dad had died a couple of years earlier and my mother had terminal cancer and wasn't expected to last long. I accepted the retirement offer. I now sometimes joke that the work-nightmares are finally starting to diminish, but that's really only "half joking."

Over the years, my thoughts would often return to the voyage I made on the *C'est si Bon.* It changed my life, I would recognize, my whole attitude of life. I would remember the Ocean Passages I completed. I could recall the wonderful clear blue color of the sea that *"appeared not so much like water but like solid ice with the sun's rays extending infinitely into its depths."* I remembered the swells, the fish I caught, the ports I visited, the people, the good times, and the hard times. Indeed, it was an "experience of a lifetime" and I often thought and said, "If I died today, at least I did that!" As difficult as the voyage proved to be, by cutting all my previous ties and completing such a fantastic endeavor, I experienced in life an exuberance that few people will ever know.

At times I would dream anew: *Maybe it would be nice to return to the ocean. Perhaps I could sail another Ocean Passage. Or two! Maybe I could do two.* It occurred to me that if I did sail again, I would like to *cross* the ocean. Indeed, I thought that if I did do another ocean voyage, I would like to *sail across an ocean on some big-ass sailboat, one I could never afford.*

It was with the ambition of sailing across an ocean, any ocean really, on some well-founded, fairly large and capable ocean-sailing yacht, that I joined Offshore Passage Opportunities in early 2011, more than twenty years after the voyage on *C'est si Bon.* Offshore Passages (OPO) was a company that hooked up experienced sailors with boat owners seeking crew to help with an offshore ocean passage. Hank Schmitt, a very experienced sailor from Huntington, New York, owned and ran OPO. For an annual fee of $125, I would receive several e-mails from him, one for each of several dozen voyages requiring crew. Each e-mail would describe the boat, the captain and crew, the passage route and timing, and importantly, the cost obligations. The process was as follows: I would read the e-mail and reply to the captain if I was interested; the captain would collect e-mails from those interested and select the crew he wanted.

It was through OPO that I heard about *Skyelark of London*, or simply *"Skyelark,"* a charter-boat owned and captained by British husband and wife team, Dan and Emily Bower. The OPO e-mail I received described the two: Dan was only 29 years old but he had extensive sailing experience, including 14 Atlantic crossings. Emily was slightly older and had even more experience, including a passage to Antarctica and a rounding of Cape Horn at the age of 22. Together, they chartered *Skyelark of London*— winters in the Caribbean, summers in England—and offered passages between the two locations at the change of seasons. (They also "delivered" several yachts across the ocean, not sailing on them but hiring captain and crew and organizing the trans-ocean passages.)

At the time (2011), the annual passage to Europe for *Skyelark of London* began in early May at the Caribbean island of Antigua and ended a month later at Southampton, UK, with a stop at the Portuguese mid-Atlantic Azores Islands. Dan captained the boat and he was assisted by one professional sailor (the "first-mate") and three paying

56

"crew." (Because she had the capability, Emily captained on another boat that she and Dan were moving to Europe as part of their boat delivery business.)   The privilege of working as crew would cost $4000, which included all boat-related expenses and on-board meals. (Airfare to and from the boat and meals while in port were not included.) At a minimum, it seemed to me to be a wonderful and affordable five-week sailing vacation. Considering the substantial boat involved and the experience to be had—sailing across the ocean on a big-ass sailboat I could never afford—it appeared to me to be nothing less than another "experience of a lifetime." I applied for the position, provided a credit card number, and waited for May.

Well, not quite May: For me, the trip actually began a few days early when my girlfriend Lisa and I flew to Puerto Rico for a mini-vacation before the voyage. We found a comfy hotel in Condado near San Juan and had a fun time hiking El Yunque Rain Forest, driving along the Ruta Panorámica and experiencing as many beaches and restaurants as time would allow. Finished and satiated, tanned a shade or two darker and perhaps a pound or two heavier, Lisa returned home on May 2.   Itching for adventure and longing for the sea, I hopped on a Cessna propeller jumper that would take me to Antigua.

Arriving on the island, I took a taxi to Nelson's Boatyard in English Harbour and found the *Skyelark of London*, moored stern-in "Mediterranean style" with several other 50-foot-plus boats on either side. Here I met *Skyelark* owners Dan and Emily Bower and also two crew members: Mark (49), a professional sailor and the boat's first-mate; and Chris (44), another paying customer like me. All mentioned thus far were "Brits"—people from Great Britain. Eventually I would also meet two other paying customers: Tina (58), a speech therapist from California and the only woman on board; and Lenny (31), an unemployed aircraft mechanic Irishman, currently living in Switzerland with his English girlfriend. In the next couple of days I also met several other professional and non-professional sailors from three other sailboats that were to sail in tandem with *Skyelark*, these boats being *Great Escape* (the boat Emily would captain), *Northern Child* and *Snow Wolf.*

Skyelark of London was a 51-foot American designed, Taiwanese built, no-nonsense ocean-going sailboat. It was a big boat—far bigger than any other boat I had sailed—and heavy enough that I couldn't push it away from a dock manually. Built in 1987 and hence 24 years old, *Skyelark's* well-maintained dark blue hull, her polished white fiberglass coaching, and her teak decks defied her age. She had a rather shallow keel that ran half the length of the boat and the skeg-supported rudder, two elements that provided *Skyelark* with a trustworthy under-water structure, one designed to take any punishment the ocean would offer. Above, the single-masted sloop rig, simple enough to be handled by only a couple of sailors, had the robustness to withstand the severest of conditions—perhaps even a roll-over. *Skyelark* had only four sails: the normally used mainsail and genoa, a storm jib, and a rarely-used spinnaker. All of these sails, except perhaps the spinnaker, were cruising sails: three times as thick and heavy as the racing sails normally found on boats. As with the boat's structure, the sail inventory was engineered to be strong enough to endure the relentless elements found offshore and simple enough to be handled short-handedly.

Down below, *Skyelark's* interior was also designed for extended ocean sailing. I counted eight ocean-going berths (beds) with two semi-private cabins forward, a pair of pipe berths amidships, and a spacious captain's cabin aft. The galley just forward of the companionway had a propane oven and stove, and I could see that the huge vertical loading refrigerator and the matching freezer beside it made pointless any discussion of an ice-box like the one I had on *C'est si Bon.* I noticed an abundance of storage lockers throughout the boat—very necessary to store the food, clothing, foul weather gear and everything else for eight sailors (we would have five on board) for a month or more. Even the head (toilet) was designed for the sea: forward, centered, and facing aft so that it could be used on either tack.

I was a day early getting to *Skyelark*, and since we ended up leaving a day late, I had four days to hang around and get to know everybody and acclimate myself to "Caribbean time." During this period a couple of noteworthy things occurred: One was that Chris, one of the paying customers, abruptly withdrew from the trip. He claimed that he missed his wife, but I imagine there was more to it—maybe fear, maybe seasickness. (Yes, it can happen even at a dock.) Who knows? I hope it wasn't simply lack of courage. That would be tough to live with. Mind you, canceling an ocean crossing at the last minute simply because you missed your wife would be tough to live with as well. Anyway, Chris left.

The other occurrence of note was a conversation I had with a sailor named John Blair, owner of a wonderful boat, a Hans Christian 44. John was about to embark single-handedly for England and he was quite distraught because his girlfriend had just dropped him for another man, something John now understood was her recurring habit in other relationships. I couldn't help thinking that this wonderful voyage John was about to begin, his first solo crossing of the Atlantic, could easily become a time of lonely agony if he didn't mentally "let go" of the woman he now missed. Another friend of his came by, and the two of us tried to give John reassuring advice, something to pull him out of the anguish he was feeling. I think we might have failed: Well into the voyage we heard John on the radio, rambling on for at least a half an hour to an imaginary listener, seemingly with no real purpose. It was heart wrenching. I think we all have had our hearts broken at one time or another and I know it hurts like hell. Out in the middle of the ocean, alone and lonely, the pain could be extreme. (There are numerous accounts of people killing

59

themselves out at sea because of unrelenting mental anguish.) I just hope John was okay. It must have been some gal.

On Tuesday, my second day on Antigua, Dan, Mark and I went to a market in St. John, the capital of Antigua, to order many of the fruits and vegetables we would be taking on the voyage. Dan knew all of the vendors at the market, most of whom were women, and as he pranced from one stall to another he would charm each one in turn. I noticed he employed a standard routine, starting with a quick hello and a minor touch such as the grab of a forearm, followed with a deliberate smile and eye contact, and finished with a phrase or two of idle chit-chat. Dan understood the Caribbean way: Business is always preceded by a few pleasantries. He must have gone to two dozen stalls that day; he moved quickly and accomplished much, but he never skipped that important first step. Dan was an expert at charming people, especially the women. He knew it; they loved it.

The next day Dan gave the crew a thorough lecture on the procedures we should follow while underway and the workings of the boat's safety equipment. We learned how to use the stove so that settling propane fumes wouldn't blow up the boat. He explained that using a hand pump conserved water over the use of an electric one. He showed everyone how to use the toilet so that we didn't have to live in a boat that smelled like pee. (He tactfully suggested that, "whilst at sea, real men sit to pee.") He also showed us how to safely handle a line around a winch, how to use our life-harness tethers, and what to do if someone were to fall overboard. The lecture went on for over two hours, and though I forgot plenty, I don't think Dan missed anything. He obviously had given this lecture many times. I was glad to be a beneficiary of his extensive experience.

As Dan continued with his identification and instruction on the safety equipment aboard *Skyelark of London*, I began to realize the insufficiencies in similar systems I had on *C'est si Bon*. *C'est si Bon* was a great boat (I've said that), though perhaps not a proper ocean-going yacht. (I've said that too) Over the years I have come to understand how lucky Ian and I were just to survive our voyage. A comparison of the safety systems on the two boats—one a proper ocean-going boat, one not—might make this clear:

1. Water. *Skyelark* had four water tanks with a total capacity of 150 gallons; we also carried 50 gallons in 1.5L plastic bottles. The boat also had a water maker that could desalinate saltwater into fresh drinking water at the rate of 12 gallons per hour. On *C'est si Bon* we had one tank of 20 gallons, and as an after-thought I bought three 5-gallon jugs, increasing the total capacity to 35 gallons. (Back then (1989), water in the ubiquitous plastic bottles we have today was unavailable.) Also, a water maker was clearly out of the question.

2. Fuel. *Skyelark's* engine used diesel fuel, much safer than the gasoline used on *C'est si Bon*. *Skyelark* had two tanks with a total capacity of 90 gallons and we carried 60 more in 5-gallon jugs. *C'est si Bon* had one 20-gallon tank and because gasoline is so explosive, we could not carry any additional fuel. (*Skyelark* could travel 600 miles on the fuel she carried; *C'est si Bon's* range on fuel was only 100 miles.)

3. Navigation. *Skyelark* had several GPS navigation devices aboard, plus two chart plotters which instantly provided complete navigational information. Also aboard was a complete set of paper charts. We even had a sextant and at least two people on board knew how to use it. *C'est si Bon* didn't have GPS and we relied on celestial navigation—and only I knew how to do it.

4. Electricity. Electricity runs the running lights and navigation systems, the refrigeration, and even turns the engine starter motor. On *C'est si Bon*, we had two batteries and they could only be recharged by running the engine using our scarce fuel. *Skyelark* had six batteries. These could be recharged with the engine or with the more fuel efficient generator or even with the "energy free" wind generator. *Skyelark* also had an "inverter" which could produce "household" 110V or even 220V AC electricity.

5. EPIRB. (Emergency Position-Indicating Radio Beacon) These are radio devices that automatically inform rescue personnel (e.g.: Coast Guard) the identification and location of a boat in distress (sinking or otherwise). *Skyelark* had two or three aboard; *C'est si Bon* didn't have any. (EPIRBs might not have been available in 1989.)

6. Life-raft. *Skyelark* had two automatically inflating life-rafts, each with a grab bag (with water, food, fishing equipment, blankets and EPIRBs). *C'est si Bon* had no life-raft.

7. Satellite telephone. *Skyelark* had a satellite telephone; *C'est si Bon* did not. In addition to chatting with your mom, satellite telephones can be used to arrange an emergency rescue or acquire medical advice. All internet applications are also available via satellite telephones. They're expensive, but they sure do improve safety. *Skyelark* also had a working marine radio (*C'est si Bon's* didn't work) and a side-band short-wave radio.

8. GRIBS. Weather data and forecasts for any spot on the ocean. Invaluable. *Skyelark* had GRIBS; *C'est si Bon* did not. Marry this up with meteorological advice Dan purchased from shore-

based weather experts (available via satellite phone, verbally or by e-mail) and you've really got reliable weather info. On *C'est si Bon,* we used pilot charts, which provide average conditions for a particular month. (Editor's note: Pilot charts work fine and too much weather information is still "TMI.")

9. Radar. Great for seeing other ships so that you don't get run down in the middle of the night. Also very good (at night) for seeing a squall coming in. Neither *Skyelark* nor *C'est si Bon* had radar.

10. AIS. Automatic Identification System. This tells you what ships are around you, how close they will come to you, and when that will be. *Skyelark* had AIS, *C'est si Bon* did not.

11. Life-harness. (automatically inflated, with light, whistle, crotch strap, spray hood and PLD) These tether you to the boat, so that if you fall overboard, you're still connected. The inflation, light, whistle and everything else becomes useful if you're not tethered and the people *not* overboard are trying to find you. (Editor's note: If you fall overboard untethered, you're probably a goner anyway.) *C'est si Bon* had only one life-harness aboard and it was always given to the person on watch to wear. It wasn't the inflatable type, and it didn't have any of the other items mentioned. A second harness would have been prudent. *Skyelark* had harnesses for everybody, with all the items mentioned except PLD's. A PLD (Personal Location Device) is like a mini-EPIRB and will direct rescuers (either those on the boat or the Coast Guard) to the overboard person.

12. MOB (Man-Over-Board) equipment. *C'est si Bon* had minimal gear; *Skyelark* had more. Again, if you fall overboard, you're probably a goner. Even

if you get back to the boat, getting you aboard is a major problem. And if you do manage to get aboard, those that were careful enough to not fall overboard, and who risked their lives to save your careless ass, are going to kill you anyway. Solution: Wear a harness; remain tethered; don't fall overboard.

So, yeah, *Skyelark of London* was a big-ass sailing boat, one that I could never afford, and well-equipped for long ocean crossing passages by her knowledgeable owners. As alarming as it was to realize all of the ignored safety risks on *C'est si Bon*, it was equally comforting to see them adequately addressed on *Skyelark*. On that vessel too, we had a strong and adequate auto-pilot, which would save the exhausting work of hand steering. We also had a canvass dodger to shield us from wind and spray, and even a Bimini cover to keep us out of the relentless tropical sun. And to help with cooking, dish cleaning, and other chores, we had five able sailors instead of two. The voyage on *C'est si Bon* was a grand one—I would never give back even one minute of it—but the voyage on the *Skyelark of London* promised to be just as good, if not better, and much safer as well.

With the safety presentation completed, and with the afternoon free to accomplish whatever we thought useful, we untied *Skyelark* from her Mediterranean mooring and took the boat over to the gas dock for refueling. This was the first "work" we performed on the boat, and between the filling of the boat's two 45-gallon fuel tanks, the filling and storing of the twelve 5-gallon jerry cans, and the completion of a few other jobs Dan wanted done, "getting gas" took us most of the afternoon. As a reward, on our return from the fuel dock we anchored out in the harbor so that the overheated crew could take a swim and Dan could inspect the boat's bottom. It had been quite hot and humid since I had arrived in Antigua, and it felt wonderful to jump in the water, this being the only time we were to go swimming on the entire voyage.

We were supposed to leave on May 5, but the forecast called for light winds which would threaten our fuel supply with required motoring, so the departure was delayed until May 6. May 5 then became "provisioning day," and Dan rented a car and went to the market and grocery store, returning with well over 100 bags of groceries. We spent the next several hours storing dry goods in the boat's numerous lockers and packing the perishable items into the refrigerator and freezer. Tina set up a washing operation and carefully washed and disinfected all fruits and vegetables to get rid of bugs and their eggs. After being allowed to dry in the sun, we then stored them in small hammocks that hung in the cabin. Dan's sister Deb, who had been crewing aboard *Snow Wolf* (with her boyfriend and captain Matt), cooked up five or six lasagnas which we put into the freezer for later. Countless tasks remained to be completed, not only on *Skyelark* but also on the three other boats that were departing with us. Fortunately, we had several hands to do the work and each task got accomplished in its own time.

The captain and crew of *Skyelark* and of the several boats in our vicinity all met at a near-by bar for some libation and celebration the night before we left. We all shared the imminent plan of sailing across the ocean, and in our short time on Antigua we had all become good friends. Many a beer mug was lifted to wish each other fare-well and *bon voyage*; I'm sure many bar patrons were over-served. Boating and drinking often go together, and in the past I would have been there with the best of them. As I mentioned briefly, however, I had decided to give up all alcohol several years prior. During that night of celebration at Antigua, as well as in all other occasions as yet unmentioned, I drank something non-alcoholic. The party that night went quite late, I'm sure. I socialized a bit, but I was early getting back aboard *Skyelark*, and fast asleep in my bunk when the others retired.

With five of us on board (Dan, Mark, Len, Tina and me), we left Nelson's Boatyard and Antigua at 3:30 PM, Friday May 6. Accompanying us were *Northern Child*, a wonderful 51-foot Swan sailboat sailed by a highly skilled crew, and *Great Escape*, a Jeanneau-51 captained by Dan's wife Emily. (*Snow Wolf* was delayed because of a refrigeration problem.)

Our destination, the Azores Islands, was northeast of Antigua—straight upwind into the northeast trade winds. (Of course!) We headed east to round the island, then tacked and headed north on the starboard tack, which would hold for much of the first leg. (I didn't know it, but standard world cruising routes by nature usually put sailboats on the starboard tack, and because of this the interiors of many boats are set up assuming that the boat will be leaning to the left rather than to the right.)

The Azores Islands, some 2180 miles away, lie in a huge high-pressure area called the Azores High, which the winds of the North Atlantic circle in a clock-wise direction. We planned to sail north through the belt of trade winds and continue through the Horse Latitudes, the area of light winds that gave Ian and me so much trouble on *C'est si Bon*. Once past the Horse Latitudes, we would be looking for westerly winds that should start about latitude 40. These, we figured, would take us east over to the Azores Islands in comfortable fashion. That was the theory anyway. We had GRIBS, which showed us the current and forecasted winds of the whole North Atlantic, and also the weather advisory service Dan had purchased. Still, it's all a crap shoot once you're out in the ocean.

As it happened, *Northern Child* sprinted off ahead of us right from the start and continued on a northerly course well after we eventually turned east. They experienced very heavy winds and wild conditions much of the way, and I heard that some members of the (very experienced) crew were thinking of abandoning at the Azores. Also, having arrived at the Azores several days before we did, they also

66

left several days earlier—right into the teeth of a gale force northeasterly that again gave them a severe pounding.

On *Skyelark* (and *Great Escape*), upon hearing advice from our shore-based weather experts, we turned right and headed east quite a bit earlier than one would normally expect. This put us into the Azores High earlier than desired, making for a peaceful, if a bit slow, passage. Me, I had all the time in the world. And ya' know, we could all use a little peace. I was glad we did what we did.

As peaceful as it would be a bit later, it wasn't comfortable the first couple of days out. We were sailing in the trade winds, which blew at a steady 20 knots and created what Dan called a "moderate sea" with waves of six feet. We were also sailing "best course to windward," or into the wind as much as a sailboat can go. Sailing upwind on the 51-foot *Skyelark* was not much different from how it was on Rick Renwick's *Rebel Rouser* so many years ago. We crashed into the seas with the boat leaning over 20 degrees as one wave after another came over the bow and soaked us in the cockpit. The normal activities of cooking, dressing, using the bathroom—even sleeping—all became contests with gravity and momentum.

Tina became seasick during this time and remained so for three days, even though she had medications that were supposed to prevent it. I felt some nausea as well, but elected to apply one of the *Transderm-V* motion sickness patches (which contain the drug Scopolamine) I had brought. I had never before used the patches, but I had seen them dispensed and I knew that they worked well. Within a short time I felt fine and the butterflies never came back. Len also became seasick, though I didn't know it until about two days out. When I did find out, I applied a patch behind his ear and in 20 minutes he felt okay as well. I offered a patch to Tina but she declined and I think that was unfortunate: Tina really suffered those early days.

At 6:00 the first night out we began watch rotations, a system designed to operate the boat with rested and refreshed crew day and night on a continuing basis. Two watch teams were created: Mark and Len were one team, called the Screaming Eagles; Tina and I were the other team, comically called the Pretty Petunias. The night watches, those from 6:00 PM until 6:00 AM, were three hours long each; day watches, those from 6:00 AM until 6:00 PM, were four hours each. You were "four hours on, four hours off" all day, and "three hours on, three hours off" all night. Since there were a total of seven watches, those you had on one day would be opposite from the ones you had the next. Duties while on watch included the actual sailing of the boat and also the cooking or cleaning up of the dinner meal. If you were off watch you could do as you please, but getting sleep would normally be the priority. Dan, the captain, didn't keep watches but he was always "on call" to help with complicated maneuvers such as reefing or sail changes. He would also have to cover for any crew members who were overly fatigued or sick, and on the first leg of the voyage that occurred two or three times.

It probably took a week or so before I got acclimated to the routine of watch keeping and sleeping in increments of three hours or less. For the first several days I found it extremely difficult to stay awake on watch, especially during the nighttime hours. (Some of the others didn't even try and I noticed several instances of people sleeping on watch.) To make matters worse, Dan insisted that we hand-steer the boat and the fatigue got so bad I lost all ability to focus on the compass card. We took 30-minute tricks at the wheel and as I tried to steer a straight course, the compass would appear to spin wildly, giving me no utility whatsoever. (I questioned Dan repeatedly why he wouldn't allow us to use the boat's auto-pilot. I thought maybe he'd say that hand steering saved electricity, or that it ensured the alertness of at least one person on watch. Instead, he claimed that a human helmsman could out-steer an auto-pilot, which was entirely whack! Nevertheless, he never relented and we hand-steered the boat across the entire damn ocean. Geez!)

The 3-hour sleeping periods—made shorter by the time it took to get dressed and undressed at the change of watch—were entirely too short for proper sleep. Once in bed I would fall asleep immediately but I would have the most bizarre dreams, dreaming that I was perhaps on another boat or maybe in another location on *Skyelark*. Once I dreamed I was in the engine room, a place I had never been. Often I would wake up, either on my own or after being called for the next watch, and I'd have no idea where I was until I turned on the light and spent a minute or two figuring it all out. I mentioned my experiences to Dan and he said they were common with sailors new at the watch keeping routine. "It has to do with the short sessions of sleep you get and the interruption of REM sleep," he said.

After several nights, however, I developed a sea-going rhythm, sleeping well when I should and feeling rested when on duty. The crazy dreams stopped, and though I always resented the hand-steering, in time I was able to maintain a proper course with little effort. I recall one of the last days of the voyage, a day that was particularly bouncy. Lying in bed, the boat's motion threw me from one side of my berth to the other. The noise bellowed in my ears and I could hear the boat fall first off one wave and then "bam!!" it would plow into another with a loud crash. You would think that any boat would simply fall apart with such punishment. The noise and motion, however, had long lost my attention: Although at the time I wasn't overly tired or fatigued, I simply drifted off to sleep, quickly and without ceremony. What a strange way to find peace.

Speaking of watches, I don't think I'll ever forget the "Watch from Hell," the 3:00 AM one on Thursday, May 12. Awakened from a deep sleep and still disoriented—it was still early in the voyage—I was called to watch and informed that a squall was coming in. Tina and I needed to get on deck right away and get the sails properly shortened so that the boat could take the mini-storm safely. The sliding

69

companionway hatch was closed, and it would normally take quite a bit of force to pull it open. In a bit of a rush, I pulled hard on its handle. Since it was raining, however, the slides were well lubed and the hatch pulled open easily and quickly, smashing my thumb severely between the hatch handle and its frame. The whole thumbnail immediately went black and I don't think I've ever experienced more pain than I did right then. Regardless, Tina and I—and Dan too—had to get up on deck and fight off that first squall and then two others that followed shortly afterward. At one point the boom-vang broke and then Tina accidentally jibed the boat, almost sending Dan over the lifelines. The whole time it seemed I would bang my thumb with every task, each time creating a new wave of unbelievable pain. It truly was the "watch from hell" and though it was over in just a few hours, I would have a very painful thumb for the remainder of the voyage. The thumbnail would eventually fall off, though it hung on until the very last day of the voyage, and afterward it would take over a year to grow back.

We continued on our northerly course, close-reaching across the northeast trades, and inching upwind whenever possible to gain any easterly progress available to us. Dan kept a constant watch on the GRIBS forecasts and the weather related e-mails he received. He showed us the charts on the computer and we could clearly see the early demise of the normally reliable trade wind belt. All too soon the wind speed dropped sharply, convincing us that the end had come and that we had exhausted all utility the trade winds might provide. Dan ordered a revised course and we steered northeasterly, directly toward the Azores Islands.

We were still in the tropics, and with the reduced wind the weather became unbearably hot and humid. Several weak squalls came our way, and though they kept us on our toes, they caused little harm. We spent a lot of time close hauled, banging away into the left-over seas, but the variable wind also allowed us our fair share of comfortable beam reaches and even some time sailing straight downwind. For the downwind runs we would pole the genoa out to one side with the mainsail to the other and run wing-on-wing—"goose necked" the Brits called it. With this wonderfully stable rig, we'd rise up and surf along with the waves, at times accelerating up to ten knots.

There were times, too, when we wouldn't have any wind at all, and for these periods we would use the "iron genoa." Indeed, as we came closer to the Azores High, that huge high pressure area that is normally a real dead hole without wind, we came to rely more and more upon the engine. It was during these times under power—and only during these times—that Dan relaxed his mandate on hand-steering. As I had experienced on *C'est si Bon,* use of the auto-pilot on *Skyelark of London* was a tremendous pleasure, significantly reducing the energy and attention required by those on watch. And as an improvement from my previous experience, the auto-pilot on *Skyelark* worked flawlessly.

Hours spent motoring along on a sailboat are normally long and tedious. Diesels are noisy, smelly, smoky contraptions, their dreadfulness often accompanied by the heat and humidity of a windless day. On *Skyelark,* however, we were entertained by a spectacular natural wildlife preserve, one created by the tranquil conditions of the area. It didn't come to us in the blink of an eye; we crept upon the magic of the Azores High over the course of several days. Watch by watch, the wind lost its punch. Day by day, the sea settled down more and more. In time the wind went still. Very still. And for 500 miles the ocean became a vast moon-like expanse, flat and unmoving except for a small but spooky undulation. *Skyelark of London* hummed through this sea, which, because of its lack of features, reminded me more of a desert than an ocean. Jelly fish began to appear. Soon we saw thousands of them. We saw a turtle, then ten more. Dolphins came around every few hours. Fully amused, they would play "chicken" with the boat's bow for ten minutes then boogie off to other adventures. Their intelligence and humanistic qualities were as apparent as that of a pet dog. Once I leaned over the bow and saw a dolphin turn his body and look me squarely in the eye as he swam along. We remained for some time with our eyes locked in a hypnotic connection that only two mammals could create. That one of us was from land and the other from the sea seemed to have no bearing. Other dolphins came and did the same, they too, obviously entertained. We lingered for half an hour, totally spellbound, until I looked away and reached for my camera and the connection was broken. Without their human dance partner they had no reason to stay, and when I looked back they were already gone.

Len saw the first whale. In the flat featureless sea, the steamy cloud of fresh exhaust was unmistakable. Soon we could see three or four podded together, their indiscernible black bodies identified by the more evident dorsal fins. They ambled along with scarcely the flip of a flipper, pretending to ignore the foreign fiberglass intruder they must have found obnoxious. How long they remained, we would never know; in only a few minutes we had moved on without them. That was our first sighting. We would see whales three or four other times before we reached the islands.

I would be remiss if I didn't mention "tea and biscuits"—English tea and biscuits, that is—and the related funny occurrence that took place in the light winds of the Azores High.

The Brits love their tea. Being on a boat with a bunch of them, well, we drank a lot of tea. It wasn't the fancy loose tea one might expect, but a rather low-quality bagged tea, easily prepared in most sea conditions. It was light and tasty and low in caffeine. We would drink it six or seven times every day, often accompanied with biscuits.

There were two sayings that were voiced with regularity concerning tea and biscuits:

The first one was, "Mike, what comes after 'S'?"

"T," I would answer.

"Tea, you say? Why sure, I'd love one!"

Then I'd have to make tea for everyone, it being totally rude not to do so.

The second popular saying was, "Wouldn't have any biscuits, would ya?" It struck me as a strange way to ask for something, but it was uncanny how often biscuits were requested precisely in this manner. Strange, too: the more I heard it, the more appropriate the saying became.

An English biscuit, quite unlike anything normally found in America, is a cross between a cookie and a cracker. There are hundreds of varieties, and they come in packages of 50 or so. We must have had 30 or more packages of biscuits aboard *Skyelark* in our initial provisioning. We ran out.

Having two or three biscuits with a cup of tea truly is a special pleasure, and all of us thoroughly missed them after the last were consumed, a few days before reaching the Azores Islands. By this time we were well into the Azores High, motoring along extensively and more than a bit bored. A biscuit or two would have been very much appreciated indeed.

By and by, we came upon another sailboat, apparently bound for the Azores, sailing along very slowly in the light breeze. It seemed obvious that there was a need of some fuel. Dan made contact by radio and offered to come alongside and hand over a couple of 5-gallon jugs. After the arrangements had all been made, and after all of the obligatory verbal pleasantries had been completed, Dan—displaying the most proper British etiquette imaginable—asked, "Wouldn't have any biscuits, would ya?"

A few minutes later we transferred the fuel and received three packages of biscuits—just enough to get us to the Azores if we utilized a little bit of constraint.

"Tea, you say? Why sure, I'd love one! Wouldn't have any biscuits, would ya?"

While underway, we had a bit of communication with the outside world on land. One form of the communication was the voyage blog, which one of the crew would be asked to contribute to on a rotating basis each day. I was asked to do the first blog entry, and though I was only supposed to do one every fourth day, I enjoyed it thoroughly (while the others did *not*) and I was able to do more entries than anybody else. Dan had been publishing the blog for several years and had acquired an extensive audience. Many of my friends sent responses to my blog entries and these allowed me to send return e-mails. Certainly the most special of these were the notes that Lisa and I sent to each other. (You remember Lisa, right? That girlfriend of mine?) I couldn't answer all of the e-mails that came my way (it's an expensive process), but every day I looked forward to whatever e-mails were in my queue, and those from Lisa warmed my heart like no other.

After almost 17 mostly hot but getting progressively cooler days at sea, we arrived at the Azores Islands on May 23. As he did with the whales, Lenny spotted the islands first, right at daybreak. All of us spent the day gazing at the islands, anticipating what was to come. I thought the Azores would be merely a few small island dots easily explored in a day or two, but in reality each island is of sufficient size, and in totality the Azores Islands extend across several hundred miles of sea room.

We landed at the harbor and city of Horta, the major port. The harbor was crowded and busy, with boats normally rafting off one another three and four deep. I couldn't help but be reminded of Put-in-Bay in Lake Erie near home. We rafted off an absolutely gorgeous and huge 150-foot-plus mega yacht while we re-fueled and cleared Customs; afterwards we moved to a more permanent location. We were always surrounded by a cluster of ocean going yachts from all around the Atlantic. With the varied languages spoken and the fact that everyone was an ocean sailor, many of whom were circumnavigators, it really was a special place for a sailing lover like me.

Skyelark was a "dry boat" in that no alcohol was consumed aboard while underway. Once tied up, however, several dry throats regularly required attention and this was usually rectified at a very popular bar called *Pete's Café*. *Pete's* is the place that sailors go to (locals seem to avoid it) and it was always busy. While not a large place, it had overflow tables across the street plus a banquet room a couple of doors down the street, so its capacity was respectable. There was even a boat chandlery, a gift shop, and indeed, a museum on the premises to complete the operation. We would normally meet at *Pete's* at 7:30 PM for a few drinks before dinner and then head off to some restaurant, most of which were quite good as well as interesting.

We had several fun evenings in Horta, usually a bit long as the wine continued to pour. On the 25th a thorough celebration of my birthday was made, complete with chocolate cake, gifts, cards, and a hearty singing of "Happy Birthday" by all fifteen sailors at our table. I was touched. The gang really made a big deal of it and I was both flattered and humbled. Later, one of the crew from *Great Escape* let me use his phone and I was able to speak to Lisa. It was a great birthday, this one being my 56th. It was one of my best.

We passed the days at Horta walking around town, checking out the coffee shops and stores, using e-mail cafes, buying gifts and mailing letters: all of the things tourists normally do. A few of us even took the ferry over to the island of Pico and walked up its 7500-foot volcano-capped mountain. The whole time we were at Horta a very strong northeast wind blew, which made us move the boat once and even delayed our departure by a day. On Friday, however, we re-provisioned and made ready to set sail. On Saturday morning, May 28, we left.

My watch-mate Tina had elected to leave the boat in the Azores. To fill her spot we took on David, a professional sailor who was on *Great Escape* for the first leg to the Azores. The second leg of the trip, 1200 miles from the Azores to Southampton, would be quite a bit more challenging and much colder than the first leg. David's expertise would come in handy.

David had sailed on scores and scores of boats and he had many stories to tell, some of them quite scary. I think we were fortunate to be on a safe and seaworthy vessel like *Skyelark*; many of the vessels David had sailed on—and many of the crews encountered on those boats—were poorly suited for ocean travel, the discovery of which was often made too late. I never felt that I was "cheating death" on *Skyelark*, but I think David had done so several times in his career as a professional sailor. Perhaps it's a fun occupation—certainly it can be at times—but being a professional sailor has its disadvantages and the riskiness of the job leads that list. I don't recommend it.

By the time we left the Azores the northeast wind that had been blowing strong for several days had simmered down to a comfortable ten knots. It still came "on the nose," and though the sea remained churned to "moderate," I was surprised when both Lenny and I once again began to feel the nausea of seasickness. We used my two remaining *Transderm V* patches, grateful that they again worked perfectly, and we had no seasickness aboard *Skyelark* for our second leg. (*Great Escape* had three people sick at the time.)

All too soon the full strength of the northeast wind returned and we found ourselves pounding into 10-foot waves. For two days we battled our way on the port tack, the boat leaning way over to the right. Cooking became a particular challenge with the hot contents of the stove threatening to fly across the cabin each time someone tried to open the oven door. Even using the galley lockers presented a problem as the spices, dishes and cutlery all had to be held in place each time one of the cupboards was opened. We sure learned why the port tack is called the "uncomfortable tack."

Dan continually monitored the wind predictions on GRIBS, a system of which I was starting to become a believer. By this time we no longer had shore-based weather advice, but with his keen expertise and the help of GRIBS, Dan was able to identify a small area of high pressure several miles north of us. We made a "tactical move" and switched to the starboard tack—Thank God!—finding a south wind half a day later that allowed us to run "goose-necked," level and peaceful.

During this time Dan got word that the sailing yacht *Tangarera*, one of the several yachts he was having delivered to Europe at the time, had encountered extreme weather with the northeast gale that went by when we were at the Azores. The boat had sustained significant damage and the captain was now contacting the boat's owner to gain permission to "cut down the mast." Other yachts had trouble too: One suffered a knockdown (mast in the water, cabin half-filled with water); another was hit by lightning. Closer to home, our own *Great Escape* with Dan's wife Emily on board ripped both the boat's mainsail and its genoa, lost use of its generator and water making ability, and even broke a steering cable.

It's comes as no surprise, the troubles that can be encountered at sea, either by the elements themselves or simply because of lack of vigilance and intelligent seamanship. I saw a potential disaster on our boat: David, a smoker, had convinced several on board to take up the smoking habit, and one morning I noticed him and Mark sitting on the aft-deck with a gasoline can between them, joking away and "having a fag." I mentioned the hazard to them but they remained unconcerned and I had to involve the captain before I could get the gasoline moved to another location on the boat.

One can only imagine the disaster waiting to happen at that time. I still can't believe these two sailing professionals were so careless of the obvious hazard, even when I brought it to their attention. Perhaps it's because they don't use much gasoline in Britain (cars normally run on diesel) and they're unaware of how explosive it can be. Regardless, disasters do happen at sea: *Tangarera* and the others seemed to be having theirs; we could have had one too.

The south wind we had found by tacking north continued for a couple of warm, splendid days. Then, as GRIBS had predicted, it turned around and came again from the northeast, strong once again and this time biting cold. The sea roughened up considerably with impressive twelve foot seas and a most gorgeous dark royal blue color. Harsh, wild conditions were expected for the rest of the voyage, and Dan mandated that life-harnesses be worn "at all times from here on." The cold weather continued and normal clothing on watch became two shirts, a winter coat, foul weather bibs and jacket, wool hat, boots and gloves. By this time we were all well-acclimated, however, and we had no trouble taking the punishment of the ocean, especially if it allowed for fast progress toward our destination. We did, in fact, have three or four days of record speeds.

Earlier, I had made a mental commitment that I would never count down the final days of the voyage—"wishing away a great adventure"—but now I found myself doing just that. I was anxious to get in after a long voyage, one that was finishing up with several uncomfortable days. The boat was healed over significantly and pounding away noisily, my thumb still hurt considerably and the nail was now about to fall off. Also, during this time I was sitting in the cabin when a wave caused the boat to lurch and I went flying across the cabin, smashing my shin against the (very solid) leg of the salon table. (I was lucky I didn't break my damn leg!) I was done. Finished. Cooked. Much like you see on a Thanksgiving Day turkey, my button had popped out.

The voyage had been a terrific experience—everything it could ever be. It was a real "sailor's sail." It was lengthy enough: across the Atlantic Ocean and certainly not across the shortest route. It was difficult, not impossibly difficult, but sufficiently challenging—certainly not easy. And it was done right! It was definitely another "experience of a lifetime" and I wanted to enjoy every minute of it—"living in the moment"—never wishing away any of the experience at all. It was not to be, not quite. Though I would never give back even a moment of this great adventure, the "old countdown" began and I looked forward to the conclusion of the Voyage of the *Skyelark of London*.

Indeed, I wasn't alone: Mark, who was doing this trip for certification reasons so that he could do numerous future voyages, decided that it was all too much and he was going to pursue some other occupation. That's a big change of heart! "Too much," he said. "It's just too damn long and too damn hard."

Len was pretty tired of the trip too: The *Transderm V* was starting to wear off, resulting in a bit of seasickness (nothing serious) and he was very much looking forward to returning to his comfortable home (and girlfriend) in Switzerland.

You will also recall that Tina left the voyage in the Azores, and this, too, was because of disillusioned ambitions. There was also Chris, who had left the voyage before it even started!

It is a phenomenon I see in myself and in many others very, very often: We become disillusioned and at some point begin to wish away the very adventure we planned so long and worked so hard to begin. It's a real pity. It has become my goal to never wish away any of life's experiences, even the bad ones. One day all too soon, I'm sure I'll be wishing for just one more experience in life—any experience at all. What a pity it would be to wish away the very best of them.

So, along we went crashing through the waves, dressed up in all the winter clothing we could muster yet chilled right to the bone. I nursed my injuries and forced my spirits to remain as positive as possible. Early on Monday, June 6, we passed the Scilly Islands and soon spotted Land's End followed by Lizard Rock—all very well-known landmarks in British sailing lore. We were still a distance from Southampton, but this was reached later that morning, thus ending 10 days of sailing from the Azores and 27 days of sea time since sailing from Antigua. The total distance of the voyage was 3380 miles. We tied up at a dock and enjoyed an "English Breakfast" at a local pub, then returned and cleaned up *Skyelark of London*, making her all bright and shiny, and washing everything including the sails with fresh water.

That evening we enjoyed a celebratory dinner with all hands from *Skyelark of London* and *Great Escape* present. I was in bed by ten, but only for a few hours. At 3:00 AM I caught a cab for Heathrow Airport, and by 3:00 PM Detroit time I was back at home, safe and sound.

Chapter 3. The Voyage of *That Darn Cat*

I could have ended my sailing career after the voyage on *Skyelark of London*. Really! With *C'est si Bon* I had followed my dream, quitting my job and sailing off to unknown horizons. On *Skyelark* I had sailed clear across the ocean, braving its elements and challenges on a proper ocean-going yacht. Along with these adventures I had enjoyed almost twenty years of seasonal sailing on the Great Lakes—arguably the most wonderful sailing waterway in the whole world. I had accomplished all of the sailing goals I had ever dreamed of. Everything in the "Sailor's Dream"— the serene sunsets, the bikini-clad first-mate, the sailing to distant shores—I had enjoyed many times over. What would be the point of simply continuing on and doing the same?

These thoughts *did* occupy my mind and indeed, I *did* relinquish my foul weather gear at the end of the voyage on

Skyelark (it was too big anyway). "You don't have to do anything forever," my dad used to say, and I was thinking I would spend more time riding bicycles and skiing mountains, two cherished hobbies that had become somewhat neglected. I still belonged to the crewing network OPO, and still received their e-mails regarding future trips, but soon it was late summer—a risky, hurricane-plagued time for sailing in the North Atlantic. I read the e-mails with disinterest and simply waited for September when I would leave the annual OPO renewal fee unpaid and my membership would expire.

September did come and pass, but for whatever reason my membership was *not* deleted. I continued to receive e-mails, these getting slightly more interesting as the fall boat migration season came into bloom. Most boat transports in the fall are from the US eastern seaboard going south to the Caribbean, and by necessity these are scheduled during a narrow weather window between the season of hurricanes and that of winter storms. I really wasn't too interested in a heavy weather trip, and even in the best of conditions none of these trips would ever stand up to the voyage on *Skyelark of London*. I didn't think I would be doing a trip—not that fall, perhaps not ever.

This all changed when I read a notice regarding the boat *That Darn Cat*. It was October 17, 2011 (five months after the crossing on *Skyelark*) when I first received the OPO e-mail regarding Mike Stafford and the boat he had purchased earlier that year. Mike lived in Boston and he had purchased the boat in France and needed to bring it home. (Hmmmm... Another Atlantic crossing!) *That Darn Cat* was a 52-foot French-built Catana racing catamaran, set up for ocean travel and a veteran of four Atlantic crossings with her previous owners. Mike had already moved the boat from France to the Canary Islands and at this time he wanted to sail it from the Canaries to St. Martin in the Caribbean. He needed two people to crew for the Atlantic crossing, and for insurance reasons he needed at least one of them to have prior Atlantic-crossing experience. Mike would be paying the boat related expenses of the voyage (that's normal) including food (that's a bonus) and he would even pay the air fare for the person with the Atlantic-crossing experience.

This was an outstanding opportunity. Sure, I had already fulfilled everything in the Sailor's Dream, but this trip was Sailor's Dream Plus! Catamarans are incredibly spacious boats, allowing for superior accommodations and a much more comfortable experience. Also, catamarans don't have weighty keels like mono-hulled sailboats hence they can plane on top of the water and reach incredible speeds. And with the twin pontoons they don't even heel!

Then, there was the route of this voyage—downwind in the North Atlantic trades. Other than sailing in the islands of the South Pacific, this is the most sought-after route in the world. And all for free! This opportunity just couldn't be any better.

I responded to Mike's e-mail and applied for the position. I tried to make the best impression, telling him what a "team player" I was, how I knew how to care for another person's precious belongings (i.e.: a half-million dollar yacht) and what a great cook I was. These e-mails were always much like a job interview: I would try to convince somebody I didn't know to choose me over several other applicants and that he really could trust me to operate his precious boat in a huge ocean where anything could happen. It was always a tough sell for me; I can only imagine it was always a tough decision for the boat owner.

I made the "first cut." Mike wrote back stating he had received quite a number of applications for the voyage and that I was "considered." He had some more information about the trip, and he wanted to know who was "still interested."

Still interested? This was the trip to die for! You bet I was still interested. I wrote Mike back with these sentiments, careful not to seem overly enthusiastic. I also mentioned that "in order to move my name up on the list, please allow me to pay my own airfare."

Now, I didn't think Mike needed the $1200 I was offering to pay but I was hoping my offer would send a positive message, one that would get his attention. Over the years I had rubbed shoulders with a few wealthy folks and I hadn't met any that didn't understand both the value and the meaning of money. I was hoping my offer would demonstrate that I really was interested in helping with the voyage and that I wasn't doing this just for a free boat-ride.

Somehow it worked and I was picked. Mike wrote back and informed me of his choice, telling me of the initial airline arrangements. I should fly to Madrid on the Saturday of Thanksgiving weekend, his note said. I would meet him and the rest of the crew there in the airport. We would then all fly to Lanzarote (one of the Canary Islands) and board the boat there. I received this notification on October 27, leaving me about four weeks to get ready.

So, what must a sailor do to get ready for a month-long sailing voyage? Certainly there were many preparation tasks I did *not* have to do. I would not be doing any boat-work to prepare it for the arduous passage ahead, for example—no bottom sanding, no engine maintenance, no cleaning. I had no responsibility to ensure the adequacy of the safety equipment, the navigational electronics or any of the other critical systems found on an ocean-going sailboat. I would also have no role in planning the route, selecting the crew or acquiring visas. Best of all: I didn't have to worry about how all this was going to get paid for. I've heard it said: "Rank has its privileges." Well, let me tell you: Having the rank of "unpaid crew" has its privileges too.

Still, we all have lives to live, some of them complicated I'm sure, and it is only normal to have a home and a car as well as a few pesky financial responsibilities. All of which must be managed when one is away, of course, and it helps to simplify and automate as much as possible. I have a condo, for example, one that pretty much takes care of itself, and it seems to be a good living arrangement for an adventurer hitting the road. Regarding a car, certainly there are methods to store these depreciating rust buckets for lengthy periods, but for shorter durations like a month or two, if you top off the fuel tank and disconnect the battery you should be okay. Automatic deposits and bill payments do wonders for home finances. All in all, it's best to go to sea with zero worries of home responsibilities. I'm sure many people have a life more complicated than mine; sometimes simplicity, like rank, also has its privileges.

More on voyage preparation: I *did* need some new foul weather gear for this trip, so I got on Craig's List and found a great heavy weather set. (I took a light set, too, which was all the voyage required.) I also needed some replacement *Transderm-V,* some sunscreen, a new bathing suit... All small stuff!

Thanksgiving is a major holiday in the US, and preparing for the holiday occupied much of the last week before the voyage. The big Thursday night dinner was at Lisa's house and fifteen members of her extended family were present for the occasion. The celebration accomplished what will always be a very important part of voyage preparation: saying a proper good-bye to loved ones. Although Lisa had displayed ample enthusiasm when I went away on past adventures, being left behind was always painful for her. The days we spent preparing for the Thanksgiving meal allowed us to "get ready" for a few weeks apart.

I, too, had to become mentally prepared for the voyage, one that might not end exactly as planned. Recalling the risky experiences on *C'est si Bon,* I have often thought of an ocean voyage as a time when a sailor gets a bit closer to his or her own demise than one would normally prefer. Now, on *That Darn Cat* I didn't think I would be staring into the face of death, a condition one might argue to have been the case on *C'est si Bon.* And truly, with the safety devices on modern boats much of the risk of ending up in a life raft and eating your friends for survival is avoided... (Let's not even go there!) Still, if any one of several things were to go wrong, you could well be looking at the end of your days and that is *not* an exaggeration. For whatever reason, for me at least, going offshore always brought this possibility into conscious consideration. One might ask: Can I accept this possibility? Are my affairs in order? Is there somebody I need to apologize to? Have I hugged my tree? Am I straight with God?

Oh hell! There it is again: the God thing. And yeah, this factory rat from Detroit City—a confirmed atheist for forty-some years—will now tell you that during some of the more harrowing times at sea, well... (Oh this hurts!) Well, I found myself digging out those long-forgotten prayers I had learned in childhood. You may recall during the *C'est si Bon* voyage—and don't forget that was way back in 1989—I had a religious experience: The auto-pilot had blown a transistor and I needed God to step in and fix it. I prayed *really* hard. It didn't work. As I had come to say, "I ain't been back to church since!"

But the point is: I was praying! Shit, I hadn't done that since I was a kid! But far out at sea—and yeah, more than a little scared—I found myself praying away like the Pope. There just seems to be something about knocking at death's door that makes believers out of many of us, me included. (What was that saying?—"There are no atheists in the foxhole.")

I recall a big "aha moment" when I was at home lying in bed a week or two before the voyage, thinking of the time I'd be spending out at sea. I imagined I was on watch one night, all by myself with everyone else asleep. I wore a life-jacket and harness (we always do at night) but I had failed to clip the tether from the harness to the boat. In my imagination the boat lurched and I was thrown overboard. I yelled for help but no one heard me. In the blackness of the night I remained in the water, kept afloat by my life-jacket. I had no chance of ever getting back aboard the boat—I was going to die—and I realized this as I watched the boat sail away.

Still in bed imagining this scenario, I asked myself what my thoughts might be at the time. Would I be saying, "You know, I really don't believe in God?" Probably not! More likely I'd be praying to the good Lord to save my soul: "You and me, Lord. All the way!"

In prior times, I figured I was "cool with God." My plan had always been to be the best moral person possible and leave it at that. Sailing—and fearing for my survival while hundreds of miles offshore—taught me the hypocrisy of that plan. I learned to humble myself and get real about what I know and don't know, about what I believe and don't believe. Preparation for a voyage began to include preparing myself—mentally and spiritually—for the worst. It became important to make sure that I really was right with God. It was a mindset change for me—not total, but major. It was a change of attitude that in time would bring an improved inner peace, one that would surely come in handy while out at sea.

So, with all matters in all categories sufficiently secured, on November 28th I hopped aboard the first of three planes that would take me Lanzarote. The trip from home to boat would take about 24 hours.

Though the five of us making up *That Darn Cat's* crew were arriving from three different locations in the US, we were all scheduled on the same flight from Madrid to Lanzarote and had agreed to meet at the gate for that final flight. I was the last to arrive and had no difficulty picking out the other four red-eyed and not-so-young American sailors. They were seated together, heavy in conversation, laughing and carrying on like a bunch of teenagers. As I approached, one of them—Mike Stafford, the owner/captain—stuck his head up from the gang and recognized me.

I had sent Mike an e-photo of me, so he knew what *I* looked like. "You look just like me," Mike had told me after seeing the photo. "Just look for someone who looks like you do, but with less hair." (Off the record, I couldn't see the resemblance: His black hair, bald on top, wasn't like mine, and his short stature, thick middle and wide face—though I'm neither tall nor thin—would not describe my appearance either.) He was a welcoming, gregarious type, and he quickly got up from his seat and took several quick steps toward me with his right hand fully extended. His smile was full and real and his eyes were kind. He shook my hand eagerly, looking me in the eye and reciting his full name. "Good guy," I thought.

As Mike and I exchanged initial pleasantries, the three others remained seated, still absorbed in their own animated conversation. One of them, Julian I would learn, seemed to be intent on imparting some sort of story to the other two. It was a story about his past sailing exploits I started to hear, one that continued even after several attempts by Mike to introduce me to the others.

"This is my brother Walter," Mike finally interjected when Julian paused for a moment. Walter, the oldest of the group, looked up slowly, still grasping the details of the story Julian had been telling. He seemed to have trouble switching from one speaker to the other and he barely noticed Mike's introduction. "This is Mike Gemus," his brother Mike told him more directly, "our other crew." Walter was still confused.

"Hi," he said in a distant voice I could hardly hear. "Oh...," he said after a moment, finally realizing who I was and why I was being introduced to him.

"I'm George," said the last man, not waiting for an introduction. "George Tripler. I'm the other OPO member," his Brooklyn accent obvious to me by this time. Thin, wearing glasses, he was tall and lanky and stood bent over slightly, as if the air was too thin at his full height. He had a sharp objectionable voice and he spoke a bit too loudly, with vowels, especially, pronounced in a hard and obnoxious manner. We shook hands and I noticed he was missing a finger or two. He saw my facial reaction and explained: "Happened last year. I was putting a dock-line around a cleat and didn't get my fingers out in time. Lost two!" he said, and I winced as he held up what remained of his hand.

Julian, the story teller, was still seated but had at last ceased with the story and was paying attention. The captain introduced him: "This is Julian, Mike. Julian Cohen. Julian sailed with me before in the Bahamas."

He stood up partially as he extended his hand. He was clearly unfit and though I knew he was precisely my age, he sure didn't look it. He continued to straighten, and when he was finished he towered a full head and shoulders over me. A man that height would normally have about 30 pounds on me, but Julian was no lean machine. Hell, with the well-developed beer belly he sported, he probably out-weighed me by 100 pounds.

"Hiya," he said. "Glad ta meet-cha. Mike told me all about-cha."

The way he truncated the word "you" to "cha" struck me as strange, as did the content of his comment: I hadn't told Mike very much about me; hadn't had the chance. I couldn't imagine what he would have told Julian. I shook his considerable hand, obviously strong but smooth and uncalloused. He wore a large mustache, which did nothing to hide the deep wrinkles that surrounded his jaw. In fact, his whole face drooped as if it were made with too much skin.

"I'm glad to meet you too," I said to Julian. Then to the rest, "I'm glad to meet all of you." I noticed a few grunts and nods, which indicated to me that everybody spoke English but little more. "Everybody have a good flight?" A few more nods. "Did everybody's luggage make it?"

That seemed to cut the ice and we all sat down, the animated conversation gathering steam once more. Julian again seized Walter and George and continued his story—or perhaps it was a new one. Captain Mike Stafford and I chitchatted by ourselves, happy to get to know one another at last.

Mike, married to his wife Judi for 39 years and father of three sons, was a mechanical engineer by trade, he told me. He had owned his own business designing and manufacturing production automation, and had recently sold it so that he could retire. He loved sailing, he said, and already owned one full-sized catamaran. "It's a terrific boat, but I'd really like one that's on the cutting edge of technology," he said. "And super-fast," he added with a guilty grin.

It occurred to me that Mike was probably afflicted with a "Sailor's Dream" of his own, and no, I don't mean that in a critical way. "Follow your dreams," it is often said, and if Mike's dream pointed him toward a million dollar boat— or two as would be the case—who am I to suggest otherwise? As a business owner, surely he had spent much of his adult life working long and stressful days. "We once went two years without a nickel taken as salary," he told me. Certainly he paid his dues with his work, and as he told me at one point, his priority had always been to love and support his wife and the family they raised. Why, then, shouldn't he be allowed to follow his dream, even if it seemed—at least to the less affluent—somewhat extravagant?

But let's be real: Mike was acting on a fantasy. It might not have involved the bikini-clad first-mates of *my* dream, but it was still a yearning of sorts: of serene sunsets, of distant shores, and in Mike's case, of speeding along faster than any of his friends could imagine. It's a wonderful dream—at least at times. And it does come true—at least in part. But it's a dream. It's the "Sailor's Dream."

Julian rambled on: "Then I rowed my sinking dinghy over to the anchored boat, and a chick in a red dress came up on deck and..." He was telling this to George as the two of them sat across from me. Poor George: It is said that every actor needs a *captive* audience; Julian had a *captured* one in George, sometimes even grabbing his wrist or putting a hand on his shoulder, just in case George was planning an escape. George had a vast amount of sailing experience—he had completed a particularly stormy delivery only a week prior—and I was sure he had run into long-winded bragging sailors before. Still, Julian presented him with an uncomfortable challenge, and I saw his eyes darting left and right, hoping for a way out. (Later, I would frequently be a similar victim and would recognize the same darting from left to right of my own eyes.)

Walter—Mike's brother—sat still and quiet. An old ex-hippy, he sported a beard and ponytail, both grey and grown well past his shoulders. Staring off in the distance, he appeared uninvolved as conversations and other activities progressed around him. He spoke sparingly and answered questions with single words, and it became clear that Walter was never going to be the life of any party.

Though he had worked as a process engineer for much of his life, Walter would be best described not in terms of his work, but of his knowledge of details (some trivial, some not), his inspired philosophical nature, and his eccentricities. He was the strange one who kept a special toothbrush at the galley sink so that he could properly clean fork prongs. He was the only one among us with enough patience to painstakingly clean salt corrosion out of electrical fittings so that we all could enjoy the helm navigational instruments. He argued that the world was indeed fair: "What else could it be?" he challenged. None of this came out of Walter in the airport, but by constantly engaging him, over time the rest of the crew and I were able to convince him to open up. As we sat waiting in the airport, however, we barely got a word out of him.

"Cha wouldn't believe St. John in the nineties, nope cha wouldn't...," Julian continued, this time to me.

"*My God, he talks a lot,*" I thought.

Coincidentally, Julian had "taken off" in search of the Caribbean sun two or three years before I did on *C'est si Bon*.

91

In fact, like me he had first gone to St. Thomas and was probably one of the "have nots" Ian and I had seen at the *New York Bar* where Maggie worked.

"Yah, I stayed at St. Thomas for a while," Julian told me, "but it was too crowded. Yah, too crowded. I went to St. John. Much better there."

Julian lived as a Caribbean drifter for twenty years. He owned and lost a boat or two of his own, lived aboard and delivered several boats owned by others, flirted with many a woman, and drank many a beer. Several times he found himself offshore on an unseaworthy boat, lucky to survive. For lengthy periods he was homeless, sleeping on the beach. Some might say he lived an unproductive, wasteful life; others might say he simply lived a happy, carefree life, the aspiration of anybody living the "Sailor's Dream." Regardless, if I ever wondered how I might have turned out had I stayed in the Caribbean on *C'est si Bon*, Julian was the answer. I was again grateful for the decisions I had made.

So, it was in this social environment in the Madrid airport that the five of us got to know one another. Mike immediately became the gracious host. Julian told his stories; Walter did *not*. George and I—the newcomers to the group—did our best to follow the conversation by talking or keeping quiet, whichever we thought best. It was an important time of bonding and of establishing trusting relationships: Each of us would soon be taking solo watches with the others totally under our care. Any wayward behavior, from poorly steering the boat, to not reacting to a squall, to unsanitary food handling practices, to allowing oneself to be injured or lost overboard would affect the rest of us thoroughly. We were five adult men with five personalities and five egos. We each had our strengths, weaknesses and quirks, and we would all be together on a small boat, on a big ocean, on a long passage.

It was about noon, Spain time, when we hopped aboard our plane bound for Lanzarote, and about three in the afternoon when we disembarked. Mike rented a small car, and after we packed it full with our gear and ourselves we headed off to Marina Rubicon on the south end of the island. Marina Rubicon was much more extensive than I had imagined with several hundred fishing and sailboats, all made for the ocean. It was a good quality marina with ample security and full boat hauling and repair facilities. It also had a ship's chandlery and gas dock and, as I would come to learn, comfortable showers and bathrooms. The marina itself was surrounded by a small village of shops and restaurants as well as a few bars with live entertainment. Mike and his wife, Judi, had been at Marina Rubicon just two weeks prior provisioning *That Darn Cat* and Mike knew the area well. He parked the car near the boat and we all approached it with much anticipation. We were made to believe that *That Darn Cat* was a pretty special boat. We were not to be disappointed: *That Darn Cat* was absolutely gorgeous.

At 52 feet long, 28 feet wide and weighing 40,000 pounds, *That Darn Cat* was a big, huge boat. Immediately apparent was the ultra-high-tech carbon fiber mast that identified *That Darn Cat* as a serious racing machine, not your family cruiser. I noticed the huge flat foredeck with its extensive trampoline; bikini-clad sun-tanners (see Sailor's Dream) would need nothing more. Right away *That Darn Cat* made a statement: This is the big league. Amateurs need not apply.

The boat appeared to be in good shape. Salt water is very hard on a boat, and with *That Darn Cat* being six years old—all of this time spent in salt water—you would expect some significant signs of age. This was not the case. The outside fiberglass, though perhaps in need of a good waxing, was clean and well-conditioned. The cushions, inside and out, all appeared new. The stainless steel had no saltwater stains, usually a tell-tale sign of an ocean-going boat. I saw no damage anywhere and the entirety of the boat was maintained in "newer" condition: clean, organized, well finished and tidy.

Upon boarding *That Darn Cat*, I couldn't help but take note of the extensive outer salon. Located toward the rear of the boat and separated from the interior by a large window and two full-sized patio doors, it was about ten feet deep and ran the full width of the boat. It was a back porch as fine and relaxing as any ocean-facing patio you might see on TV. It sported numerous couch-like cut-outs all around, allowing those so motivated to sit and stare out at the ocean, something we, the crew, would do *ad infinitum*. The outer salon also featured a large teak dining table with seating for eight—the most exquisite setting for a summer dinner party.

Also part of the outer salon, and toward the terminus of each of the two pontoons, one would find the twin helm stations. Each helm station had a form-fitting cushioned chair for the helmsman (or woman) with a steering wheel and controls for an engine and an auto-pilot. (*That Darn Cat* had two diesel engines and two auto-pilots.) There was also a compass at each helm station, along with some GPS related navigational electronics. (Wind instrument displays were *not* at the helm stations but were placed in three strategic locations surrounding the outer salon, allowing viewing from any location.) Behind each helm station was a set of stairs and these led to the twin swim platforms near the water. In the space above and between the pontoons, suspended by powerful davits, was a 16-foot rigid-bottom inflatable dinghy with a 50 horsepower Mercury outboard engine.

Designed as a racer, *That Darn Cat* had some pretty fancy racing sails in its inventory. The mainsail had two or three laminations of Dacron with carbon fiber bands between the laminations, all of this to preserve precise sail shape. The sail had full-length battens and was designed with a huge rule-beating roach (extended sail material off the back of the sail), which made for an impressive, but very expensive, high performance sail. The boat had two headsails—a large genoa and a smaller staysail or "solent"— each on its own Pro-furl roller furling system. We also carried a spinnaker, which on a 52-footer would be a very large and unwieldy sail indeed. The spaghetti of lines to control these sails was extensive but the chaos the lines created was nicely handled with numerous strategically placed rope lockers. Being on a large boat with big sails, the tensions on the lines would be extreme, but the dozen or so good-sized Harken winches—five of them electric—would handle this problem adequately.

Inside the boat there were duplicate wind and boat instruments as well as the real navigational gear. Here we had a computer chart plotter, which contained charts of the entire North Atlantic. We also had GRIBS, the weather forecasting system; AIS, the system which identifies any boats in the area; two satellite phones, and an EPIRB emergency beacon. I counted three laptop computers aboard and half a dozen GPS receivers, counting everybody's personal one. The electronics were six years old—and Mike said he couldn't wait to update them—but they seemed much more than adequate to me.

The boat also had all of the amenities required for safe, extended cruising: tanks for 200 gallons of water backed up by a desalination system, 250 gallons of diesel fuel, two generators (each capable of 12, 110 and 220 volt electricity), a life-raft, ocean ground tackle, life-harnesses, and man-overboard gear.

The interior of *That Darn Cat* was truly spectacular with extensive cherry-wood, well-crafted joinery, and a sparkling finish. As on all other large catamarans, the main salon was elevated with windows all-around and a spectacular view outside. One's eye was immediately directed forward and to starboard where an eight-foot dining room table was located—a gorgeous example of craftsmanship surrounded by upholstered seating for eight. Also forward but on the port side, a no-nonsense

95

navigational station had been set up, and with its computer screens, radios, and numerous dials and gauges, it appeared more suited for an airplane than a sailboat. The full galley—not meager by any means—took up a third of the main salon, and included a propane oven and stove, a good-sized refrigerator and separate freezer, and also a microwave oven, a coffee maker, and all the pottery, dish-sets and utensils with which we were to cook up many a fine meal.

On either side of the main salon, and down three or four steps, was the entrance to each pontoon—each in itself the size of a large mono-hull sailboat. Aft in the starboard pontoon was the "owner's quarters" with a queen size bed. Forward of this was a washer and dryer and a huge shower and bathroom, the latter much too extravagant to be called a "head." The port side pontoon had two cabins, one forward and one aft, with a bathroom (you *could* call this one a "head") and a separate shower room between the cabins. The front cabin had a twin size bed, and Julian was assigned to this cabin. The aft cabin, which George and I shared, was large and airy with a couple of windows and two single beds separated by an aisle. By this time George and I had each done our share of cruising; both of us regarded this cabin as the best we had ever seen.

That Darn Cat was also well provisioned, the result of the visit Mike and Judi had made to the boat two weeks earlier. They had spared no expense, and the refrigerator, freezer and pantry lockers were all stocked full—you would think we were an army going to war. Judi had created menu suggestions for two full weeks, and the food stores were procured accordingly. To supplement this, we went to a supermarket before cast-off and Mike encouraged all of us to pick out anything we wanted. It was wonderful and generous hospitality and Mike paid for it all. Indeed, Mike paid all expenses of the trip, including meals we ate while ashore.

It would be only 24 hours that we were on Lanzarote, but we sure packed in a lot of activity in that short time.

After touring the boat and unpacking all our gear, the five of us walked and found a near-by restaurant with an outdoor patio where we had "paella for five." We then went to the town's grocery store and stocked up on produce and other perishable goods, returning to the boat afterward for a very welcomed night's sleep.

The next morning Mike took us for a car-tour of the island, which included a guided hike of some underground caverns. The island of Lanzarote was very interesting, for sure, with its black lava soil and its white houses with flat roofs, the exclusive architecture on the island. After the tour we found the Customs office and got proper clearance to leave. We then dropped off the rented car and returned to the boat. It was time to get underway.

It didn't surprise me when Mike and Julian began a discussion regarding our readiness for the voyage; we probably should have had the discussion some time before. It *did* surprise me, however, when Julian stated, "We're *not* ready. We can't go."

At the time I didn't really understand Julian's role on board. In an e-mail I received from Mike a week before the voyage, Julian wasn't even on the crew list. Mike later mentioned that a friend of his (Julian) was "also coming." I was aware only that Julian was an invited crew person like me. I thought he must have discovered something of major consequence to make a statement such as, "We're not ready. We can't go."

He had been fussing with the boat's navigational electronics, trying to predict the best course across the ocean and entering into the plotter the various GRIBS wind predictions to do so. Julian's issue, as it turned out, was that the navigational electronics had not been fully tested— which really wasn't true—and that his GRIBS developed mid-ocean waypoints for the voyage had not been entered into the boat's GPS. Mike and Julian discussed the matter at length but without any conclusion. Neither Walter nor George said anything one way or the other (probably a wise move), but in my naïveté I stepped into the conversation, which in hindsight was an error, no doubt.

Quite simply, I didn't see the problem Julian was identifying. I thought of "worst case scenarios" and "what ifs" and I didn't see any scenario that could sufficiently affect the voyage. (Even with no electronics at all, we still had paper charts and we certainly had redundant GPS capability. And as far as GRIBS weather predictions go, they're just that: *weather predictions*. And I'm sure we're all familiar with the poor reliability of weather predictions.) I thought it obvious that we *should* go. The electronics had indeed been tested on the passage over from France, and the waypoints... Well, I couldn't see why you would enter mid-ocean waypoints anyway. I verbalized some of this, but thankfully, not all of it.

My error was thinking that the conversation was solely about sailing and electronics. In reality, it was much more about rank on board, power, and good old-fashioned ego—things like that. Had I realized this, I would have stayed clear and let Mike and Julian "do their thing." As I mentioned, I thought Julian was an "also coming" member of the crew. That's what I had been told. As it happened, we were several days into the voyage—several hundred miles offshore—when Mike first referred to Julian as "the captain." It was a casual statement and it completely surprised me: *When did this promotion from "also coming" to "captain" occur? Why is the owner not the captain? Why is this being announced so casually and so untimely?* It was an astonishing development, but it wouldn't be the last time I would be on a voyage when an unexpected promotion occurred. From Mike's comment about Julian being "captain," I understood all that was going on during the discussion on readiness: Julian was establishing his command, his authority in relation to the owner. I was way out of my league.

Still, it was absurd that Julian voiced so assuredly that we couldn't go. He didn't say, "Before we go I need to do this, this and this." He said, "We're not ready. We can't go." It was an impossible non-solution. Of course we were going. We *had* to. And we did.

At about noon on Thursday, December 1, we untied the dock lines and Mike motored *That Darn Cat* out of its slip and over to the fuel dock. We fueled up, bought an extra chart of the North Atlantic, and motored out to a bay so Mike could jump in the water for a last minute bottom inspection and a quick brush of the propellers. All assured, we set off, "sweating up" (hauling by hand) the mainsail as much as we could and winching it what we couldn't do manually. Next, we unfurled the genoa and trimmed it using the massive primary (and electric) winch. *That Darn Cat* took off in a rush, accelerating to fifteen knots with little trouble. We headed south around the island of Fuerteventura, the easternmost of the Canaries, then out into the great expanse of the Mighty Atlantic. We were bound for St. Martin, 2800 miles away, west by southwest.

This was sailing in the Trade Winds, a wonderful phenomenon, wonderful at least for any sailor sailing east to west in tropical latitudes of any of the earth's oceans. Let me explain how they work:

The Earth spins from west to east with points on the equator moving about a thousand miles per hour. Pretty fast, especially near the equator. The air above the surface doesn't quite keep up, resulting in a wind that flows from east to west. Called "*east* winds," they are so stable and reliable that they came to be known as the "Trade Winds." They are heaven for a sailboat and sailors seek them out fully. These east winds are able to circle back and head eastward nearer the poles where the earth's rotational speed is a lot less than it is near the equator. Eventually a circular flow of air forms over each ocean, clockwise if in the northern hemisphere and counterclockwise in the southern hemisphere. In the center of each of these rotations, an area of high air pressure with very little wind forms. Sailboat operators might want to avoid these areas. Also, in the westerly wind belt far south in the southern hemisphere, the wind circles the globe unimpeded by land, resulting in the infamously strong winds and huge waves of an area called the "Roaring Forties." Sailors might want to avoid this area as well. Even picking the wrong season in a particular area can make for an unsafe or uncomfortable passage. Above all, you don't want to sail in an area when hurricanes or other severe storms are likely.

Knowing the expected weather and wind conditions for an area, and scheduling a passage during the months of the year when the best conditions are normally experienced, is one of the most important trip planning decisions to be made. There is a wonderful, if not imperative, resource book called *World Cruising Routes*, written by Jimmy Cornell, and it is dedicated to this very objective. As the title implies, *World Cruising Routes* describes all of the normal ocean passage routes, identifying the best (and worst) times that they should be attempted. It is because of information found in Cornell's guide that our passage was planned for December, not say, October.

For this reason too, I've always been alarmed to see boats—even organized groups of boats—leaving the US east coast bound for the Caribbean in early November, still in what is labeled Hurricane Season. George Tripler—the same George Tripler presently aboard *That Darn Cat*—had just finished such a delivery and he gave us a first-hand account of the rough and stormy the passage endured by all. (Well not "all." Several boats withdrew before the start; some started but didn't finish.)

On the other hand, largely because we were in a much better area, but also because we left after the November 30 hurricane boundary, we on *That Darn Cat* were expecting mild "shorts and T-shirt" weather the whole trip with very low risk of winter storms, tropical depressions, hurricanes, or even rough weather. This was a big reason why I was so eager to join this voyage: We were to be sailing in those trade winds of which sailors are so fond, and we were to complete the voyage well within the recommended season. The trip planning was sound.

So, in a northern ocean like the North Atlantic the wind pattern is clockwise, and at the Canary Islands the wind is still largely from the north, getting ready to make that right turn across the Atlantic. The question becomes: Should mariners on boats like *That Darn Cat* head straight across the ocean toward St. Martin, or should they sail south a few hundred miles off the *rhumb-line* (the shortest distance between points) and follow the wind pattern?

Questions such as this create the topic we call "sailing tactics," and there is bound to be differences of opinion. The years I spent sailing the Great Lakes of Michigan taught me a simple rule: Don't veer too far from the rhumb-line. Violate this rule and you'll often get caught far off course when the wind on which you were depending either changes direction or dies altogether. We Michiganders tack and jibe often and *never* go chasing a wind predicted by some weather forecast. The winds in the Great Lakes are just too undependable. You sail what you have and take what you get. That's the normal tactical strategy.

In the ocean, apparently it's a bit different. Mike and Julian thought best to head south where the winds were expected to be stronger and more easterly. I expressed my rhumb-line opinion as humbly as possible (not my strong point) and they heard me (not theirs either) and then we did it *their way*, heading south. Later, we heard that boats taking the northern rhumb-line course—the one I recommended—experienced a lot of light winds, requiring several hours of motoring. We, on the other hand, experienced mostly non-stop winds of 20 knots or better. Indeed, we made the right decision on *That Darn Cat*. It sure seemed wrong at the time, heading hundreds of miles off course, but it *was* the textbook answer and the textbook was sure as hell right this time. It was a new lesson for me: Oceans are prone to obey fundamental principles, certainly more so than in the Great Lakes. Ignore these principles at your own peril.

Hence, we initially headed south, with the wind coming from behind us, and with the expectation that we would eventually turn west as the wind also changed, thus providing us with a following wind for the entire crossing. This brings up a second sailing performance-type question, one that was left answered until the very end of the voyage:

No boat can sail directly into the wind. We all know that. But less known is the fact that most boats sail poorly directly downwind as well. To alleviate this issue, if needing to sail directly downwind a sailor will turn the boat upwind 30 degrees or so and sail a "broad reach" on one tack for a while, then turn straight downwind plus another 30 degrees to jibe the boat and come about on the other tack. This repeated jibing results in a see-sawing course, a bit longer than a straight-line course, but safer and faster and—as it turns out—the obvious alternative. The problem is determining how high into the wind you should steer on each tack: The higher upwind you go, the faster the boat goes but the farther off course it goes as well. On mono-hulls, especially when using a spinnaker, it is important to remain patient and "keep the boat down." Turning upwind too high shows lack of finesse and will cost you plenty of time. On multi-hulled boats such as *That Darn Cat*, the increase in speed observed as the boat is pointed higher into the wind is much more pronounced, critically altering the equation and making appropriate a higher sailing angle to the wind. George and I, a couple of mono-hullers "with lots of finesse," would normally keep the boat off the wind, sailing with an apparent wind angle of 130 degrees or so, extremely high in our experiences. Julian, on the other hand, would sail quite a bit higher still, between 115 and 120 degrees apparent. He would go much faster but farther off course. The question becomes: What is the optimum sailing angle that will get you to the destination quickest?

The question brings up the concept of "Velocity Made Good" or VMG. VMG is the speed of a boat reduced by the angle sailed off the rhumb-line, a difficult calculation I'm sure, but a rather simple one for any sailing GPS unit. Unfortunately, the reading on every device I had seen varied considerably as it was being displayed, and I mean *quite* considerably. Very much required is a VMG device with a dampening feature, and if such were to be mounted within view of a helmsman, he would always know the fastest course toward his destination. Until then we're really just guessing, and guessing is what we did, all the way across the ocean—Julian sailing his method, George and I sailing ours, and everybody else probably somewhere in between.

So, away we went: around Fuerteventura and off into the great expanse of the Mighty Atlantic. The trade wind blew true, and with a full main and genoa *That Darn Cat* took off *with a bone in her teeth*, roaring away on a broad reach, approaching 20 knots. This was my first time sailing on a full sized catamaran, and I found that kind of speed incomprehensible. (I would never have believed that a 20-ton boat, powered only by the wind, could plane on top of the waves but that was exactly what we were doing.) From the foredeck you could watch the pontoons slicing though the sea—quickly, easily and with a soft and clean "ssssss" sound. Off the back you could sit in the outer salon and watch the two sterns snake through the water, leaving a big long whirlpool and making a deep "shhhhh" roar that never ended. I think I could easily spend the rest of my life enjoying those two sensations. Mike Stafford, proud owner and operator, sat at the helm and I swear his smile was sticking out over the gunwales.

Julian took over at the navigation table, plotting our course and checking over the extensive collection of electronic devices we had aboard. He also devised a system of watches which he discussed initially with each member of the crew and then posted on a white-board in the galley.

You will recall that on *C'est si Bon*, Ian and I adhered to the challenging watch schedule of "four hours on and four hours off." Slightly different, Captain Dan Bower on *Skyelark of London* set up two-man watches with four-hour tricks during the daytime and three-hour ones at night. On *That Darn Cat* we left just one sailor on watch, figuring to use the auto-pilot extensively and to sail the boat conservatively, especially at night. (We planned to jibe, reef and do other complicated sailing tasks as a team when required.) With this in mind, the watch schedule became "three hours on, twelve hours off," a wonderfully restful and casual existence. On other boats, when not on watch you normally needed to get your butt in bed to catch up on much needed sleep; on *That Darn Cat*, if you stayed up too late watching a movie, reading, or listening to one of Julian's long stories, you could simply complete your short three hours on watch and then you had twelve full hours to catch up on anything you desired. I was a bit concerned that a single person wouldn't be able to react to emergencies (i.e.: squalls, man overboard) but the system worked perfectly and it sure made life enjoyable.

Cooking the evening meal was done on a volunteer basis and I decided to be the chef that first evening at sea. Toward the beginning of the voyage we largely obeyed the menu suggestions Judi had created; that first night "spaghetti and Italian sausage" was scheduled. Lisa (my girlfriend) is Italian and I thought of the delicious Italian sausage I'd often enjoyed at the dinners she prepared. Mike and Walter are Polish and I was drooling as I thought of the Polish kielbasa I'd eaten in Hamtramck, a Polish area near Detroit. Indeed, there *was* some good Italian sausage aboard *That Darn Cat*, but that wasn't what I picked for dinner that night. What I picked was some breakfast sausage that, well, should have been left for breakfast. I over-cooked the pasta (and I *never* over-cook pasta) and cooked the sausage very thoroughly, hoping the "charred effect" might help. It didn't. Not my best meal. Nobody complained (thanks!) and I made a mental note for improvement next time. We had some very fine meals aboard *That Darn Cat* but this one wasn't our best.

At any rate, George cleaned up the dishes, and the watches rotated with Julian going on, followed by Walter, then Mike, then George. Finally, at 5:45 AM George whispered softly in my ear, "Mike, honey, your watch."

Actually, George, who would be calling/waking me every 15 hours for the duration of the voyage, scared the shit out of me with his yelled "Mike, your watch!" all the way from the helm.

Every watch period—and at three hours each, there were eight of them each day on *That Darn Cat*—had its beauty and its distractions, but the 6-9 AM watch finished off the night and caught the sunrise. It was always one of the very best. That morning the wind and point of sail were unchanged since the previous afternoon, and I had my first experience steering a 50-foot-plus catamaran surfing away at 20 knots. The swells were 10 feet or so, moving slower than the boat, and *That Darn Cat* would fall off one swell and accelerate fully so that it appeared as if the bows were going to dig into the next, threatening to flip the entire craft end-over-end in the process. I had never before sailed faster than the speed of waves—not even close—and it sure looked pretty dangerous to this middle-class factory rat from Detroit City. I steered *That Darn Cat* first one way and then the other, trying to slow the boat down and avoid the riskiest waves. Finally dawn came and the others woke up, confirming in unison that the conditions and speed I found so alarming were all quite normal and safe. The speed never seemed so disturbing to me after that—and this I can't explain—but at the time I was sure spooked.

Also on that first watch of mine, right near the end of it, I spotted perhaps a hundred dolphins coming over to meet us. I called for the rest of the crew to come and see them and everybody came out, camera in hand. We watched the dolphins for a good twenty minutes while they played their game of "chicken" with the bows and performed all their other normal acrobatics. One jumped up fully, straight out of the water, flapping his flippers, clearly communicating to us, "Hey look over here! Look at me!" Then, as quickly as they came, they took off for other adventures and were gone.

Dolphins sure seem to have a lot of fun. Someone once asked me what I would like to be if I were ever reincarnated. Without hesitation I answered, "A dolphin!" Hey, dolphins rock!

Along we went as we finished our first 24 hours at sea. We jibed once to starboard and then again back to port. By noon we had already traveled 230 miles, a remarkable distance. I left the window over my bunk open allowing my bedding to get a bit damp, which I then hung out on the lifelines to dry. Such is life at sea. Lisa had prepared a card for me "to be opened out at sea" and I read it, already missing her entirely. I was back on watch at 9:00 PM and I watched the sun cross the horizon for a second time. It had been a great day. This was going to be a great voyage. I felt very fortunate indeed.

The next night, our third night out at sea, I came on watch at 3:00 AM, sailing the boat straight south and getting within 20 miles of the coast of Morocco, Africa. We were using the port steering station at the time (Recall that *That Darn Cat* had two, one on each side.), and the port-side auto-pilot didn't work so well. *That Darn Cat* was a bit of a bear to hand-steer—I never understood why—but it took some muscle to keep her on course. I recall my back muscles were getting pretty tired as I was trying to keep a keen eye out in case we came up on the coast unexpectedly. Suddenly, I saw a boat off the port beam with a huge (illegal) white light on it, the boat appearing to be heading our way.

Now think about it: we were off Morocco, a place that has had its violent times. (Joshua Slocum, in his book *Sailing Alone Around the World*, told of being chased by pirates in this same area.) I didn't think there was a problem (I mean,

106

who *really* has seen a pirate??) but I wasn't about to take this one on alone. I woke Julian (standard procedure: he wasn't "captain" yet, but he was next on watch) and we both watched the boat and its stupid light (probably a fishing boat pulling in a catch) disappear behind us. Geez!

Off watch and in bed at 6:00 AM, I slept well until noon, getting up just in time for the boat to lurch, sending the coffee pot flying. The glass decanter broke when it hit the floor, sending glass everywhere, ready to cut someone's foot. I cleaned up the mess, and with this done Walter set about in his patient "fix it" mode and made a couple of "tea bags" (with coffee in them instead of tea), using a stapler and the now obsolete coffee filters. This worked okay until Julian found a French Press coffee maker, which we then used until that too broke a couple of days later. Coffee, my confessed addiction, was not our strong suit on this voyage.

Going off watch at 6:00 AM meant I was back on at 6:00 PM. Just before I went on, however, I heard a call from George at the helm: "All hands on deck!" The rest of us all dropped whatever we were doing and rushed out to the outer salon. A squall had hit us and I could hear the gale-force wind howling in the rigging. Sheets of rain sped by horizontally and George was leaning his body into the steering wheel, using all his strength and weight to fight the "weather helm" and keep the boat from rounding up into the wind.

Weather helm is normal on a sailboat. Because a sailboat's sails pull forward and are off to the side, and the hull (or hulls) drag aft and are *not* off to the side, a sailboat will tend to head up into the wind—that's weather helm. Stronger winds increase the weather helm and when extreme, the boat rounds up fully out of control in what is called a "broach." On mono-hulls especially, a broaching boat can roll over on its side, and if the companionway hatch is open, a solid flood of water can fill the boat, sinking it immediately. (It has always been my opinion that this is what happened to the boat of restaurateur Chuck Muer in

1993 when his boat, probably with all hands tethered with their life-harnesses, vanished in the "storm of the century" without a trace of boat or crew.)

We didn't broach on *That Darn Cat*, largely because George had correctly assessed the excessive weather helm and called for help. With all of us working together, we were able to put two reefs in the mainsail and replace the genoa with the solent, the smaller headsail used for heavier winds. With the smaller sails, the excessive weather helm became normal once again and the boat was easily steered on course. Before long the squall passed and nobody could remember what all the fuss was about.

That night, an hour or so before midnight, just as I was dreaming of the girls in grass skirts we would no doubt meet once we got to St. Martin, we heard a loud "bang." We had hit something! Everyone got to work pulling up floor boards and looking for water that might be flooding the bilge. We never found any damage of any kind. We had hit something, that's for sure, probably some floating debris of some sort. Thankfully, it wasn't a huge barrel or one of those offshore shipping containers. Something like that could sink a boat like ours.

And I never dreamed of those girls in grass skirts again. Darn!

Over the next several days, a normal and comfortable sea-going rhythm developed aboard with each of us taking turns cooking, eating, sleeping, reading, and going on watch and off. The weather was absolutely gorgeous each day with perfect T-shirt wearing temperatures non-stop. The wind always came from behind us, normally at 20 knots or so. For a day or two it decreased quite a bit and we all started estimating that it would be "sometime next summer" when we would get in. As would be expected, however, the 20-knot ENE wind *did* come back and stuck with us for almost the entire voyage.

For the first few days we struggled with the port side auto-pilot that didn't work so well. On the sixth day, however, somebody (probably Walter—that was his specialty) got the starboard auto-pilot working and this steered the boat beautifully for the rest of the voyage. The starboard helm station also had the *Hummingbird*, which was actually a fish finder with a GPS built into it. We were able to use this device—which we named "Wilson" after the volleyball character in *Castaway*—for navigating at the helm. Thereafter, we rarely touched the steering wheel. We even stopped using the steering compass, covering it at night to save our night vision. It was a peaceful time.

Well, not perfectly peaceful. Shit *did* happen. Indeed, things will *always* happen on a sailboat crossing the ocean. I know you want to hear all about it, so for the sake of completeness, let me tell you about the Things Gone Wrong (TGW's) we experienced on *That Darn Cat*:

I've already mentioned the broken (glass) coffee decanter incident, which was our first TGW. Glass items such as beer and liquor bottles, jars, glasses, dishes and picture frames don't belong on a sailboat. With complete certainty, something *will* break, and the resulting mess is impossible to clean up adequately. A cut foot is likely to follow and who needs that? The galley floor on *That Darn Cat* was pretty solid and contained, and I *did* clean up the glass as thoroughly as possible. Several days later, however, I found a wayward piece of glass, just begging to do damage. It's just one of the ways that "shit can happen" on a boat.

The second TGW was the "bang" we heard the fourth night out, probably the result of hitting some (small?) object in the water. Next to falling overboard, I think hitting another boat or some object in the sea is a sailor's worst nightmare. (Aboard my last voyage on *Skyelark*, the captain spoke of nearly colliding with an abandoned boat in the very same area of the ocean that *That Darn Cat* was sailing.) Sailors have reported hitting whales, offshore shipping containers, fishing buoys and nets, logs and just about anything else you can imagine. A good look-out will help, but especially at night, you're really at the mercy of Lady

Luck. When you suspect any sort of collision, you immediately inspect for flooding and damage, which is what we did on *That Darn Cat*. Fortunately, things were fine.

There were also a few breakages on *That Darn Cat*. A couple of minor things happened indoors: the fiddle for a shelf in the cabin that George and I shared broke, as did the flashing on the door to our cabin. Also, the hinges to the toilet seat in the port-side head broke. Outside, a piece of a lifeline came off and was lost overboard. These were all minor things, for sure, but it was a shame to leave Mike and his family with these damages. We had started with a perfect boat; we all wanted to leave with the boat in original condition.

We also had a few more serious failures:

1. The mainsail, a beautiful and very expensive fully battened Dacron and carbon fiber racing sail, basically disintegrated on us. First, a couple of large brackets that hold the furled sail in place on the boom broke clean off. Then one of the battens broke, followed by five or six others. Finally, the Dacron/carbon fiber construction of the sail began delaminating. Geez!

2. The spinnaker ripped along its foot (the lower edge) after about two hours of use. Spinnakers, those big colorful sails used for going downwind, are not that great for ocean cruising: they can be unwieldy and hard to handle, they're prone to "twisting"—now there's a wonderful experience—and they're soon over-powered if the wind kicks up. (Think: "broach!") Still, we *did* do a lot of downwind sailing and we could have used the spinnaker.

3. Late one night—TGW's always seem to happen at night—we heard another "bang." This time, the large and substantially strong grommet at the clew of the genoa (The "clew" is the aft corner of a sail, the one you pull in to trim the sail.) came clean out of the sail. We then had no way to trim the sail and it just

110

flapped in the wind. Julian was on watch and he furled the sail to prevent further damage, but that sail was a "goner" for the rest of the voyage.

Minor problems continued to occur as they seem to occur on any boat: The Hummingbird stopped working, which Walter was able to fix; the 220V electrical system kept blowing a circuit breaker, this problem traced to water spilled on the toaster causing a short; a few leaky windows identified themselves; a leak in the water pressure system developed—all minor stuff.

Then, about mid-day, mid-voyage (December 10) and mid-Atlantic, Mike and Walter both noticed a significant amount of water coming out of the port-side shower room. This turned out to be a broken hinge on a knee-high bathroom window. ("Knee-high" on the inside of the boat equated to "water level" on the outside.) It was such a cute little window; it was astounding how much water could come in through such a cute little window. Now, this was a bit serious: we were indeed "in the middle of the ocean" and we had significant water coming in the boat. (Well, not as long as Walter kept holding the window in place.) And who the hell carries spare hinge parts on a boat? Still, I was a bit surprised when Mike optimistically stated, "I think I can fix this!"

I said to myself, "Of course you can fix this. You can fix anything! Besides, what other option do we have?"

Actually, Mike *can* fix anything. He was an engineer-type person and that clearly showed in his problem solving efforts. For me, a problem is always a *big* problem, something to get emotional about. For Mike, it was always "just life," and solving mechanical problems was what he had been doing all his life. A broken batten requires a replacement. When all of the replacements are broken, you splice all the pieces together and make a new one. Different sizes? No problem: just file, cut and chisel the big ones down to fit the others. Broken window hinge? No problem:

111

"Walter, you hold the window in place and I'll make a new hinge."

To watch Mike and Walter fix something together, as they did with the broken shower room window, was very cool. Hooking up Walter's tenacity and ability to focus with Mike's big-picture analytical and problem solving skills created a synergistic excellence that only these two brothers could provide. They were great to watch. Hey, those guys rocked!

There was one problem, however, a problem with personnel, that neither Mike nor Walter could solve. It's a bit embarrassing to mention, but those of you who have stayed with me this far deserve a full story. It involved Julian and me. It was no one's fault—well, I'll accept responsibility—but it *was* a problem and it needed to be resolved.

I don't regard myself as being either particularly boisterous or quiet, but if I've got an inspired thought or good idea in mind, I generally like to share it. At the beginning of the voyage, for example, Mike and Julian were charting the normal trade wind route to St. Marten—which began with a detour of several hundred miles—and I mentioned my idea of sailing closer to the rhumb-line. It was simply an idea. I figured to put all ideas on the table and pick the best one. Sometime later, we started that whole discussion regarding the best downwind sailing angle and Velocity Made Good (VMG). It was an important consideration and a disagreement we never settled. There was one morning, too, when we debated the idea of steering based off the compass, the auto-pilot, or the GPS—all of which disagreed with each other. We also discussed true bearings versus magnetic, this too without resolution. These are all things sailors like to discuss. They're interesting and somewhat complex sailing topics and heck, we were sailors! I was simply trying to offer good suggestions. Apparently Julian thought otherwise. Perhaps he feared that I was trying to usurp his authority as captain.

Maybe he thought I was trying to argue with his knowledge, which was indeed extensive. I once suggested, asked really, if we should try sailing with the genoa alone, a set-up I had often used with great success for downwind work. It was a suggestion that Julian clearly did not enjoy. (And he was not very kind in letting me know it.) Then, sometime later, I think I *did* step on his toes when I took to offering Walter some steering suggestions. Things were not good: Julian was pissed and so was I. Julian's smile, a real mainstay, was gone. We were no longer friends, so it seemed. He spoke in one-word sentences. His stories, normally numerous, were gone too. I wasn't happy either. My content and easy-going mental disposition—my most valued possession—had soured. I was feeling bitter.

I do believe that deep personal differences do not need to be resolved on a boat out on the ocean, but surely everyone must get along for the duration of the voyage. Somehow, a void had developed between Julian and me, and that void needed to be filled. It was threatening to ruin our wonderful voyage, and besides, I had no business being at odds with the captain.

I didn't know what I was going to do—and it's not as if I stopped to make a plan—but to make amends, here's what I did: I went over and sat next to Julian, snuggling right up "in his space." I told him quietly and privately that I really didn't want to step on his toes or usurp his authority. I told him I would keep my suggestions to myself. I said that I would let him captain the boat and that I would re-double my efforts to simply be the best and most helpful crew person I could be. My unrehearsed words were real and sincere. I was humble but unapologetic. I held out my hand to him and he shook it. And then he thanked me. And when he thanked me I knew I had reached him. I still had to prove myself by doing what I said I would do, but I knew I had bridged that void between us.

I had no idea, however, how completely my effort had worked. Immediately Julian's smile returned. His started telling his stories. We were once again "good buddies" and from that point on we worked well as a team. The fix was immediate and complete. It was great. I couldn't believe it. What a success! My own content and easy-going mental disposition returned as well, and that, of course, was great too. Much later in the voyage, with all bitter and otherwise unhealthy thoughts long forgotten and with my mind clear and at rest, I thought to myself, "Damn! I sure am glad I was able to fix *that* problem."

On the morning of December 11, 9-3/4 days out of Lanzarote, we reached the halfway point of the voyage. This virtually assured that we would all be home for Christmas, really the only reason any of us should have been anxious to get in. You may recall on my previous voyages, especially that of the *C'est si Bon*, I described the unfortunate human tendency to start the "old count down" at times like this, living in anticipation of the end of the voyage and wishing away what really is one of the best experiences of a lifetime. On this trip, though I wasn't able to avoid the "old count down" completely, I really was having the time of my life. Voyages like this should go on forever.

One thing I was able to do during this "halfway" point was to call Lisa on the satellite telephone. Knowing her normal schedule, I called her at 9:00 Sunday morning, Detroit time, and I was relieved to get her. (*That Darn Cat* had left the dock quite quickly at Lanzarote, and when I called Lisa to say goodbye I was only able to leave a message.) I had missed her, without a doubt, and she had missed me too. She was glad to hear from me but I detected sadness in her voice, something that made me start to re-think the appropriateness of me being away for these lengthy sailing escapades of mine. Lisa's love was real and thorough, and I was lucky to have her in my life. Our conversation reminded me that I needed to never take that love for granted.

Since we were moving westward across the globe, we were observing dawn and dusk later and later in the day.

At this point of the trip, we were getting first daylight about 9:00 AM ship's time. "Ship's time" is whatever time the clocks aboard read, and it really shouldn't matter at which time zone they are set. Ours were set at the Lanzarote time zone, one hour behind Universal Time. Again, it shouldn't matter where the clocks are set, but left alone, we all like to get up, more or less, with the sun. Since getting up at 9:00 didn't seem to sit well with our human instincts, we figured we'd reset ship's time. One problem was that altering the time would cheat somebody out of his sleep time, which being as ample as it was, shouldn't have caused much concern. After quite a bit of discussion, we figured we would change the clocks by three hours, a full watch. Still, we couldn't agree upon when we would actually change the clocks, or what time zone the clocks were already set, or what time zone St. Martin was on. In the end we could only figure out how to change half the clocks aboard anyway. What a nightmare! Nevertheless, we pushed the clocks back three hours. Or was it two hours? Or was it "pulled ahead?" Hmmmmm... And in the end, all of the clocks were different.

We caught a fish. Actually, we caught several fish, the first one back on December 6. Mike had a couple of no-nonsense fishing poles aboard, and we normally had them both rigged, each dragging a line aft with a plastic lure that resembled a squid. I recall catching the first fish: We were, of course, in the middle of a jibe when one of the reels starting whizzing away and someone yelled out, "fish on!" While the rest of the crew finished the jibe and reduced sail to slow the boat, Mike positioned himself in the fighter's chair and put on one of those gizmos that allows you to pivot the rod in your lap without spearing yourself. The next half hour was spent reeling in the fish, a few feet at a time, which proved to be a good amount of exercise. Finally, we had our prize aboard: a three-foot-long mahi-mahi. (The fish that's so good, they had to name it twice.)

We had a bottle aboard that said, "*pour poisson*" (for fish); it was actually gin and it was meant to subdue a large fish for killing. With the fish aboard, we poured some *pour poisson* into its gills, but the fish still flopped about violently, not at all subdued. Walter brought a huge knife from the galley, and at great risk of losing a finger in the process, Mike chopped off the head of the fish, which, by the way, subdued it completely. He then fileted the fish, getting blood everywhere. (We called our method of fishing "filet and release.") Using my Buddhist leanings, I said a prayer for the fish, which didn't seem to work—at least as far as the fish was concerned.

That fish fed us for two nights, the second via a wonderful fish stew that Julian concocted. Mahi-mahi, fresh from the ocean, is terrific. We caught four more over the course of the voyage, giving me lots of opportunity to refine my cooking. Rolling pieces in salt-and-pepper-seasoned flour and frying them (not too much) in olive oil ("a la Mike Stafford") was the best we came up with. Julian's stew was equally fantastic and I made a mental note to find out how to make "fish stew." We also caught two tuna, and none of us could resist grabbing a chunk of raw tuna meat and putting it into our mouths. The best sushi! We sure had some good fish aboard *That Darn Cat*. I finally experienced what offshore fishing really could be. Ian would have been in heaven.

Since the wind was always behind us, and since sailboats, especially catamarans, don't sail well directly downwind, we on *That Darn Cat* would have to spend significant time on both tacks to complete our crossing. Normally one would jibe often to do this, but GRIBS was forecasting a wind shift to the SE on the 13th, and this expectation kept us on the starboard tack since December 9th. At the time I was still not a great fan of GRIBS, and even if I was, I wouldn't recommend delaying a jibe for that length of time, especially based on a wind shift forecasted four days hence. I had to bite my tongue as we sailed north, far off the rhumb-line and crossing the Tropic of Cancer for the second time. This was the point in the passage when I started getting impatient and I had to fight myself to maintain a good attitude. Life could be a whole lot worse than being adrift on a luxury catamaran like *That Darn Cat*, but as the wind died and we began making some very meager watch-to-watch advances, I started wishing a speedy end to the passage and blaming everybody on board for not allowing it to happen. (Thank God one's thoughts can be kept private.) Finally, just before noon on the 13th, the wind *did* clock to the SE as forecasted, and it came on with some good strength to boot! We jibed over to the port tack, and sailed straight toward our target, making a respectable 10 knots. The next morning, however, the wind clocked further, coming from the south, and this sent *That Darn Cat* once again sailing north of our desired course. Sometimes you just can't win.

This south wind was also forecasted by GRIBS, as was a total 180-degree shift of the wind (i.e.: to come from the north), expected for the morning of the 15th. GRIBS showed a most interesting phenomenon: arrows showing a south wind, drawn directly over arrows showing a north wind—as if the wind would come from two directions at the same time. Clearly, a severe wind shift was forecasted, and with it, the arrival of a significant cold front. Being December, I wondered what kind of a winter storm might be approaching.

The night leading up to the change, the 14th/15th, passed with anxious anticipation. Storm clouds were all around, and lightning was everywhere. It rained off and on all night. *That Darn Cat* sailed on, making good speed but heading well north of what we wished. The morning brought fairer weather but no change in the wind direction, which was forecasted to come along several hours prior. I handed the helm over to Julian at 9:00 AM, leaving him for the second time in a row with rotten weather, this time with a huge black line of clouds (storm front?) directly over us.

It wasn't five minutes later, however, when he yelled out, "Ready to jibe!" The dark line in the clouds was actually the wind shift. The wind reversed direction, the sun came out, and *That Darn Cat* surfed away directly for St Martin.

We continued as such for three more days until we approached the Windward Islands of the Caribbean and the island of St Martin. Still a few hundred miles out, a couple of very tame barn swallows landed aboard, but they died a day or so later. The wind eventually went back to its old reliable ENE, leaving us running downwind and not quite able to make the course we wished, but hey, close enough. On the 16th of December we once again crossed the Tropic of Cancer and we continued to enjoy warm temperatures and pleasant trade wind conditions.

We jibed two or three times during this time, and with each jibe it seemed we broke a batten or two, each threatening to poke a hole into the mainsail. We took down the main a couple of times, at first exchanging broken battens with unbroken ones, and then later splicing pieces together once the supply ran out. During these repairs with no main and only the little Solent up front (Recall that our genoa was unusable at this time.) we'd be pretty much dead in the water. At one point we elected to turn on one of the engines, which was run for about an hour. Since we were not in a race or constrained from using the "iron genoa," running an engine would be considered quite normal at such a time. Nevertheless, it was the only time on the voyage that we propelled the boat other than with the wind, and it really wasn't necessary. No one said anything at the time, but I think we all regretted the use of the engine afterward. Chances like this only come along every so often, and to cross the ocean without using the engine even once would have given us serious bragging rights.

It was also during this time, actually our last full day at sea, that we finally came to some resolution of the Velocity Made Good (VMG) issue. Julian showed me his hand-held radio that happened to have a GPS with a feature

118

called "Time to Go" (TTG) on it. TTG is really VMG in reverse, and this feature *did* have at least a partial dampening effect to it. From this I could see that, in fact, I was steering too far down wind and that reaching higher would have given us an improved VMG. Yes, Julian was right again (though I still think he steers too high) and he was equally right (though a bit unkind) when he said that I should get on a Hobie Cat (a small racing catamaran) and I'd see the folly in my ways. This is actually a well-known sailing truth: if you want to learn what works best on a sailboat, you'll find it by experimenting (i.e.: racing) on small boats. One day soon, though, a properly dampened version of VMG will be available on sailboat helm instruments, and then we'll all be properly enlightened.

Since we did have a satellite telephone aboard, and since none of us had airline tickets to get home, Mike called his wife Judi to see if she could schedule us some flights. Several communications—via satellite phone to us, then via landline and the internet to a booking agent—were necessary to transfer all of the required information for five international flights and to complete the bookings. It was a frustrating and exhausting process, one that that kept Judi up good and late into the night. We were all grateful that she persevered and got the job done.

The next day when I got my flight information, however, I noticed that the flight was for a week later than expected, a couple of days after Christmas. Another call to Judi confirmed that all of the tickets had the same error and would have to be re-scheduled. Thank God for 24-hour re-scheduling windows.

Land Ho!! At 8:50 AM on December 19, George, with his uncanny ability to see things on the horizon, spotted several of the Windward Islands, St. Martin included, still almost 40 miles away. Mike Stafford, proud owner and operator, took over the helm and hand-steered *That Darn Cat* the rest of the way. Upon reaching St. Martin, we took down the main at four o'clock that afternoon—18 days, 2 hours out of Lanzarote. ("Very respectable," opined Julian.)

We came in paralleling the north side of the island, the French portion which is called "St. Martin." (The other half is Dutch and is called "St. Maarten.") We entered a large natural harbor called the *Baie de Marigot* and meandered around the dozens of other boats that were already at anchor. We dropped our own anchor in a good sized clearing about a quarter of a mile from shore, and backed the boat up firmly to make sure the hook had set properly.

We knew Customs closed at five, so we lost no time lowering the dinghy from the davits and getting ready to motor in. All showered and looking our best, we locked up the boat and loaded ourselves into the dinghy. In a moment of inattention, we untied the painter (dinghy line) and set the dinghy free, an act we regretted a minute later when the engine wouldn't start. (And of course, we hadn't taken the time to bring paddles.) We *did* get the engine running— Thank God!—but between the cantankerous engine and having to return to the boat for some required but forgotten documents, we arrived at Customs five minutes after closing. Thankfully, the kind Customs officer let us proceed ashore to enjoy our night on the town, making us promise to "be here promptly at 8:00 tomorrow morning." (Editor's note: Nothing happens promptly in the Caribbean, except perhaps closing time. Still, we were very thankful.)

Straight away we stopped into a bar, of course, so that those so inclined could whet their lips. Walter had honeymooned on St. Martin some forty years prior, and rather than spend time in the bar, he was much more interested in walking the town and reminiscing a long-ago time that was surely special to his heart. George and I—two non-drinkers—were dispatched to find a suitable place for dinner, and after investigating all options, we settled on a quaint outdoor French restaurant called *Oplangeur Bistro*.

Arriving for dinner a few hours later, we chose an inviting outdoor table, pleased with the attractive rattan place-mats and the "real linen" napkins. Though small and unpretentious, *Oplangeur Bistro* proved to be a comfortable place to dine with a surprisingly extensive menu. Mike chose the scallops, while I had the seafood platter; the others all went for a steak. The meals were all fantastic— the food, yes, but also the exquisite presentations of the dishes which the French always do so well. We dined slowly, taking ample time to enjoy a relaxing celebration of a superb Atlantic crossing. With his usual generosity, Mike paid for everybody's dinner—just one more item to put the voyage in the "extra-special" category.

Content and satiated on all levels, we returned to the boat via the dinghy which, without paddles, lights, or life jackets, scared us all silly when it stalled half-way back and re-started only after much coaxing. Back aboard, I was in bed and asleep immediately and didn't stir until late the next morning. Upon rising, we all had a bit of breakfast then cleaned the boat, leaving it in the best condition possible. Mike rented a car and the entire crew drove to the airport where I was the first to depart. Smiles, hugs and farewells were freely shared, all of us agreeing, I'm sure, that the Voyage of *That Darn Cat* was one that might never be paralleled.

Chapter 4. The First Voyage of the
Allegretta

The completion of the voyage on *That Darn Cat* brought to an end the year of 2011, a year that, for me, provided two Atlantic crossings. That was a lot of good sailing! Was I being over-indulgent? No, I don't think so. I would argue that I was simply enjoying what life had to offer. Done well? You bet. Overly done? Hell no!

Nevertheless, it occurred to me that I should spend some time at home, taking care of myself, yes, but also those close to me, the most important of whom is, of course, Lisa. You remember Lisa, don't you? Yeah, she's that best friend of mine, the one who stole my heart. She was my girlfriend, my loving partner.

We celebrated Christmas together, Lisa and I, and then New Year's Eve. We took a short trip to Collingwood,

Ontario for a few days of skiing, and I also spent 10 days in Colorado, skiing with my good friend Tony. Between those outings I spent my time close to home—making daily visits to the gym, spending time with family and friends, and wooing Lisa, trying to get her to love me even more.

Regarding sailing, since I had completed two Atlantic crossings, one of them particularly lengthy, my plan was to participate in the shorter and more common boat deliveries between the Caribbean and the US eastern seaboard. These deliveries center around the spring and fall migration seasons: Fall migrations move boats from New England to the Caribbean; the spring migrations return the boats north.

I mentioned previously that the fall migrations can be particularly nasty. Hurricane season extends until the last day of November, with October being a particularly bad month for these horrible storms that *must* be avoided. October also marks the beginning of winter storms, the nor'easters, and these become more frequent and intense as winter progresses. The conventional wisdom, though it doesn't seem too wise to me, is to leave New England in early November—still in hurricane season and well into the nor'easters. The trip south is bound to be unpleasant, healed way over and pounding into waves the entire distance. Storms, some of them fierce, are likely. You *will* get hit. Not surprisingly, I had little interest in participating in these fall migrations.

A boat delivery in the spring promises a much better experience. May is the best time to leave the Caribbean, in my opinion, although many boats seem to leave in April. In either case, you leave the islands when the weather is at its best, and the rise of spring follows you as you proceed north. Storms are rare during these times and hurricanes are non-existent. If you're lucky you'll catch beam reaches most of the way. It was in these spring migrations that I planned to focus my sailing.

For me, though, participating in the 2012 spring migration was out of the question. I really *did* need to spend some quality time at home, and Lisa's daughter was getting married in June—a huge family event. So, with spring 2012 "out" and fall 2012 "undesirable," I figured it would be a year and a half between the trip I did on *That Darn Cat* and the next one I might do.

Now, the above horror story of the fall migrations would apply only to deliveries between the US east coast and the Caribbean. Other passages, most notably the east-to-west trans-Atlantic crossings such as the one I did on *That Darn Cat*, enjoy perfect weather starting in late fall. So, while I *couldn't* take part in any voyage in the spring of 2012, and I *wouldn't* hop on any boat leaving New England in the fall, I *did* keep the time available and a keen lookout for a safe but rather sensational trip, thinking I would apply if one were to come along. It would have to be something special, as I had no interest in simply repeating the past. I didn't think it likely that a voyage meeting my requirements would come up, but I read every OPO e-mail that came my way—just in case.

On October 23 (2012) I received an OPO e-mail describing a request for crew from a Brian Matroka of the sailing yacht *Allegretta*, a gorgeous 62-foot French-made Dominique cutter-rigged sloop that Matroka chartered. The voyage would start in Gibraltar (near Spain, not the one in Michigan) and would go to St. Thomas in the US Virgin Islands, the same destination I had on *C'est si Bon* in 1989. There were planned stops along the way, the e-mail said: perhaps in the Canary Islands, perhaps in the Cape Verdes, perhaps both. The voyage would start in early November and would take about four weeks.

The expense obligations for this trip were identified: Boat expenses including food were covered; air fare was not—both very standard—but the e-mail also stated "the crew might be asked to contribute to food costs if improved food is desired." A bit peculiar, I thought—I had never heard of such a thing—but I spoke to OPO owner Hank Schmitt, and he commented that *Allegretta* was a "very

124

plush ride" and that a trans-Atlantic passage on such a fine vessel for a little bit of food cost was still a very good deal.

Being a luxury charter boat, Matroka had created a website for *Allegretta,* one that included descriptions and pictures of the yacht, her captain and crew. I'll tell you, it all looked quite impressive. The yacht was sleek and modern—"sexy," I'd call it—a luxurious toy that only one of considerable wealth could afford. The captain and first mate made a handsome couple: he well dressed, lean and bearded; she blond and pretty. The website contained biographies of the two of them, describing the extensive sailing experience and varied "artsy" backgrounds of each partner. (He used to be a professional ballet dancer, a Rodeo Drive store owner, and a NYC real estate developer; she was a geriatric nurse, a restaurant owner, and a care giver for the underprivileged.) What a boat! What a crew! What a voyage! What could go wrong?

Of course, plenty could go wrong, and I intended to ask sufficient questions to be assured of the seaworthiness of the whole operation. But in regards to his competence, what can you ask a captain who has been sailing for 40 years—without insulting him? What, exactly, could I ask this couple to make sure that their eighth crossing of the Atlantic together would be planned and executed as safely as each of their previous seven?

In fact, there was always precious little I could do to ensure the integrity of any OPO voyage before arriving at the boat. Any OPO introductory e-mail would normally describe the boat's safety features, the captain's experience, and the sailing route. Generally too, an exchange of a few additional e-mails would be necessary in the planning process, and these would provide clues as to the captain's demeanor. Other than that, however—and all of this would be dependent upon the truthfulness of the information provided—the true essence of the boat, the captain, the crew, and the integrity of the planned voyage would be identified to me only after I arrived on-site.

The OPO guidelines state that when accepting a crewing position (done via e-mail, long before seeing the boat), a sailor is promising to at least show up at the boat at the agreed upon time. With this obligation observed, however, I had always assumed that if I arrived at a boat and found something that would make the planned voyage unsafe, I would simply hop on a plane and go home.

That didn't seem to be at risk with *Allegretta*. I did more research on this trip than I had done on any of those previous, and everything indicated that this was another "experience of a lifetime," perhaps the best voyage that would ever come my way. I was a bit alarmed when I learned that only four people—the captain, the first mate, and two OPO members—would be on board. And yes, the food cost thing was a bit unusual. But it was a fine boat and the sailing experience of the captain and first-mate was exceptional. Again, what could go wrong? I applied for the position. The next day I received an e-mail saying I was accepted.

The next-day acceptance note concerned me. It was too quick. The captain could not have checked my references in the single day since he had received my application. I knew that my own sailing abilities were adequate, but I feared that such haste could have him choosing other candidates that did *not* have adequate skills. Nevertheless, I was happy to be going sailing again—and on such a nice boat. "We will be glad to have you aboard," Matroka said in one of his subsequent notes. "Fly to Gibraltar. We'll meet you at Queensway Quay Marina." I forgot my concerns and bought a one-way plane ticket: $1800. Plane fares had gone up.

On Wednesday, November 7, Lisa drove me to the airport, leaving me there as I prefer: three hours early. Flights to Europe are awful endurance contests, but as for me, I learned some time ago to simply shut down my mind—"let it go"—and patiently wait for the ordeal to reach its end.

This idea of "letting it go" was to be one of my mental objectives for the trip. One of my faults is that I have always tried to control things, concerned that events won't go as planned if I don't make sure of it. I step in and "manage" things, often only managing to screw things up, pissing people off all the while. (Recall, if you will, my experience with Julian aboard *That Darn Cat.*) On this trip with *Allegretta*, I wanted to leave the successful execution of events to those who were legitimately responsible. I wanted to "let it go."

I was able to test the idea as the plane was attempting its landing at Gibraltar. The "Rock of Gibraltar" is, in fact, a 1400-foot mountain, and about as prominent as could be. We circled around "The Rock" clockwise, approaching the landing strip into the teeth of a significantly strong east wind. The plane bucked like a bull as we came in and I pulled my seat belt a little tighter, realizing fully the futility of this action if a crash were to occur. The plane dropped into an air hole and I thought we were going down for sure. The elderly woman next to me grabbed my forearm so tightly her knuckles turned white. I heard several passengers gasp and I thought I heard a scream from the back of the plane. I'm sure more than a few prayers were being said. Me, I made a conscious decision to "let it go"—not that I could do anything else—distancing myself from the obvious threat and letting the pilot do his job. Which he *did* do. Thank God! (Er, I mean, the pilot.)

Apparently, *Allegretta* didn't understand the concept. When I arrived at Queensway Quay Marina, there was the boat: Gone! I lugged my 50-pound bag around the marina and finally found an attendant who informed me that *Allegretta* was expected the next day. Hmmmm... Planning for a simple delay, I got a room, ate dinner in town, and found an internet café. I had an e-mail from Brian. He said they had been delayed in a storm and were in Estepona, a port in Spain 25 miles from Gibraltar. I should go there, he said.

"Let it go," I was thinking the next day as I walked across the border to Spain and hopped on an *autobús,* thankful I knew a bit of Spanish. The bus was clean and comfortable—oh, if only we had Spain's bus system in the US—and I thoroughly enjoyed the meandering 90-minute ride through the hills of Andalusia. All too soon Estepona presented herself, and after a half-mile walk along the sea I came to the municipal marina where I would eventually find the *Allegretta.* It had been a long journey over, yes, but I arrived fresh and rested and with a tranquil mind. "Letting it go!" It's a great concept.

Of the hundreds of sailors that were bound for the Caribbean at the time, most had a much more difficult time than I in getting to their voyage starting locations. On the US eastern seaboard, hurricane *Sandy* hit toward the end of October, followed by the snowy nor'easter *Athena* in early November. Most boats in the fall migration I mentioned earlier—be they independent boats or those in the organized Salty Dawg or NARC rallies—endured one or both of these storms in port, a harrowing experience, no doubt. Quite a number of boats left after *Sandy* and were out at sea when *Athena* hit, receiving its full fury offshore.

Things were tough on the east side of the Atlantic as well: The storm that delayed *Allegretta* was part of a whole mess of stormy weather that battered the western Mediterranean for over a week. *Allegretta* and all of the other European boats bound for the Caribbean had to struggle with these hardships on their way to Gibraltar.

All of these troubles were far from my mind, however, when I arrived at the lovely town and port of Estepona on Friday, November 9. It was a beautiful sunny day, and one would find it difficult to imagine that foul weather had ever visited the area. I picked up a swipe-card from the security office at the marina and was directed to the large and beautiful *Allegretta,* tied-up broadside at the end of a pier. Standing beside the boat, facing somewhat away from me and focused on a frazzled dock-line he held in his hands, was the man I presumed to be the boat's captain, Brian Matroka. I walked up the pier, feeling the fatigue from carrying the heavy duffel but enjoying the private moment I had to examine my new colleague standing next to his boat. He didn't notice me at first, and I was fairly upon him when he heard my steps and turned to face me. I watched as I saw a smile start to form, first with his mouth and then with his eyes. Finally, his entire face came to life as he realized his crew from America had arrived.

He was probably in his seventies, and though lean and appearing fit, a slight stoop in his stature told me his age. The drooping outside edges of his dark brown eyes portrayed compassion and understanding. He had an easy, soft demeanor and a kind smile, the latter obscured by a thin grey mustache. He wore no shoes and his clothes were plain. Both his hair and beard could have used a barber.

"Ah, Mike!" he said, the quiver in his voice indicative of his years. Still holding the dock-line, he shook my hand with both of his. We exchanged a few pleasantries, sizing up each other for the first time. He spoke softly, conveying an inner confidence. He had a pleasant accent, though one I couldn't place. He was a person at peace and in control. A leader, I imagined. He was as I had hoped. What else could be expected of a USCG licensed captain with 40 years of sailing experience and seven Atlantic crossings? I was pleased with my choice.

Lucille (Marceau), first-mate on board and Brian's significant other, was inside the boat but came out to join us when she heard us talking. A good-looking woman— handsome more than beautiful—she appeared to be in her sixties and wore her blonde, curly hair in an age-appropriate style. Somewhat tanned and smiling, she reminded me of the female half of the host and hostess couples you often see in the charter-boat advertisements in sailing magazines. A French-Canadian (like me) from North Bay, Ontario, she had been with Brian aboard *Allegretta* for four years, completing all seven Atlantic crossings with him.

She smiled as she shook my hand, and though she seemed happy enough, I thought I saw some trepidation in her smile. I soon learned why:

Brian and Lucille were among those who had experienced a difficult time in the past week, they with the storm that blanketed Western Europe. They had been chartering *Allegretta* in the Mediterranean over the summer, finishing up in Malta, Sardinia, and finally St. Tropez, France. They had left St. Tropez a week before I met them, bound for Gibraltar and eager to get ready for the Atlantic crossing of which I would be crew. As they passed Barcelona, however, the weather turned sour, becoming increasingly stormy as they progressed south. They battled the elements for several days, mostly motoring along their course. *Allegretta* was a large and sound boat with a powerful engine; if the storm didn't get too bad, motoring through it would remain a good option. By the time *Allegretta* was twenty miles from Gibraltar—just outside of the port of Estepona—conditions were particularly nasty, with 50-knot west winds that prevented any forward progress of the yacht.

With Brian's experience, he surely would have understood the numerous heavy weather tactics that were available to him at the time. For example, he could have simply motored into the wind, unconcerned with progress until the squall passed, probably within an hour or two. Or he could have drifted along with the wind "under bare polls"—not an unpleasant sleigh ride going downwind. He knew, too, that what he *did* choose to do—laying anchor in open water—was not recommended.

It really wasn't the *last* option; it was a *non*-option. You just *cannot* anchor in unprotected waters in a storm. Brian later tried to explain to me the reasons for doing what he did, but I couldn't see the logic. It was simply a poor decision.

Getting battered by the elements, Brian and Lucille eventually had to let go the anchor and chain, tying a piece of line to it and marking its position with a buoy. They then went into the harbor at Estepona and tied up safely—which may or may *not* have been a safe option earlier. In the meantime, quite a bit of damage had occurred to the boat, which eventually cost over $10,000 in repairs and delayed the start of the voyage for two weeks.

Not to dwell, but there's another aspect of the experience that is important to understand: It was Brian the captain—not Lucille—who made the decision to anchor out, unprotected in the storm. That's the way it goes on a boat. Lucille's only option was to support Brian's decision, and she would experience the consequences—good or bad. Now, with me being on his boat, I would be subject to the consequences of Brian's decisions as well. My personal safety—perhaps my survival—would be dependent on his ability to make good decisions.

So, it was with this most unfortunate experience in the recent past that Lucille greeted me with a smile that seemed a little forced. We recited a few pleasantries, and then she went back below into the boat to finish up whatever chore she was doing before I interrupted. I was left again with Brian, and he took me for a tour of my new home:

We first went below, and though the boat matched the pictures I had seen, I found it difficult to believe a boat could have such opulent luxury. As tastefully tricked out as you can imagine, the interior was a carpenter's dream with beautiful teak woodwork everywhere. Unlike most "classic" boats, everything on *Allegretta*—from the present-day windows, to the brushed nickel hardware and wall-mounted movie screen—identified the boat as ultra-modern. I had never imagined a boat could be so fantastic.

The main cabin of *Allegretta* occupied at least half of the boat, creating an open and airy interior. Most impressive in this area was the huge round dining table, surrounded by smartly upholstered seating that would accommodate eight or ten diners. Also in the main cabin, there was an ample galley, a navigation station, and even a second smaller dining table, presumably to be used for less extravagant dinner affairs.

Four sleeping cabins completed the lay-out below decks. Of these, one was aft, and as on most boats, this would be reserved for the owners. Two others were located slightly forward of the main cabin, one to starboard, the other to port. Finally, forward of these was the "milkshake room," a wonderfully spacious cabin, but because of its forward position, the motion in this cabin would be excessive out at sea.

Through the toss of a coin, I was assigned the cabin on the starboard side, a most wonderful cabin, indeed. Beautifully finished with teak, it was sufficiently large with a double bed, a good-sized closet, several drawers (lockers) throughout, and a bookshelf with several books. As with all of the other cabins, mine had the uncommon luxury of its own bathroom and stand-up shower. It was a terrific cabin. One couldn't hope for more.

I quickly unpacked, then set about familiarizing myself with the boat, thoroughly impressed with the rigging and spars of the huge cutter-rigged sloop. (The term "cutter-rigged" means the boat has two sails up front: a large "genoa," which is the principal driving sail, and the inner and smaller "jib." These sails can be used separately or together to adjust for different wind strengths.)

By and by, Brian and I found ourselves standing on the dock beside the boat, talking away as a couple of ocean sailors would. We chatted well: quietly and unhurried, unpretentious, friendly. We were just getting to know each other but I already felt a sense of trust. This was a quiet, gentle man. Good guy!

It was during this time, just an hour or so after I had first arrived at *Allegretta*, when a man in his sixties walked up and made his presence. Looking at me, he made a comment or two about the boat, as if I were the owner instead of Brian. I was trying to correct this embarrassment

132

when we all came to realize that the man was "Drew" or "Don" or "Rolf," the other OPO member who, like me, would be crew for the voyage.

The confusion of the man's name was his own making: His full name was Drew Rolf Dickerson, but he complicated the matter by using a smaller case "d," apparently the practice of some Hollywood personality. In e-mail communications, Brian thought "drew" was either misspelled or not even a name so he changed it to "Don" at times and used the middle name, Rolf, at others. One of the first questions I had was, "Okay, man, exactly what is your name?" to which Drew gave a very long-winded and uninspired (Can you say boring?) explanation.

Drew was sixty-eight years old, looked all of it, and was wearing a silly floppy hat, mountain climbing sun glasses, Bermuda shorts and long rubber sailing boots. He was a funny looking dude, quite over-weight, and his outfit made him look absolutely bizarre. Finished, finally, with the aggravating story about his name, Drew immediately launched into another long-winded account, this one of the difficult journey he had to where he stood now:

Drew lived in Manhattan (walking distance from Ground Zero), and with that he experienced first-hand the effects of hurricane *Sandy* and snowy *Athena*. In fact, it was snowing fiercely in New York when Drew was trying to get from his home to JFK Airport, eventually to get to the boat. (It was because of the snowstorm that Drew was wearing sailing boots, figuring that he would be walking a fair amount in deep snow.) Drew took a taxi, as many New Yorkers do, and the combination of the rush hour timing and the several inches of falling snow brought traffic to a standstill, even more than normal. The flat tire the taxi experienced was only icing on the cake.

The taxi driver said that he could fix the flat, and since it's difficult to get a taxi in New York, especially in a snowstorm, Drew waited, watching the lateness for his flight develop. 45 minutes later the taxi driver admitted that he could *not* fix the flat, so Drew *did* get another taxi, arriving at JFK good and late.

"No problem," said the airline person. "The plane is still at the gate." Drew then boarded the plane, only to sit at the gate for seven hours as airport workers tried to get the de-icing system working, equipment that hadn't been used since the previous winter.

Of course, he missed the connector flight in London. The airline put him in a hotel for the short, 4-hour night, then flew him, but not his luggage, to Gibraltar the next day. Unlike me, Drew *did* receive the e-mail stating that *Allegretta* was in Estepona instead of Gibraltar, but just in case he wasn't completely frustrated, the airline personnel in Gibraltar stated that since he was going to be in another country, they wouldn't be able to deliver his luggage if and when they found it. (He *did* go and get it a couple of days later.)

So, there Drew was: with Brian and me, sporting sailing boots and shorts, no luggage other than his carry-on, and very tired after his 48-hour marathon journey. He accepted the beer Brian offered him and we settled into the main salon of the boat, Drew continuing to digress into one story after another, a pattern that never seemed to go away.

Drew was shown his cabin, the one like mine but on the port side. Like me, he was very pleased with the accommodations. (Who wouldn't be?) Later, though both of us were tired, Drew and I left the boat and walked into town to have dinner, Drew telling me he would have to borrow some euros because all he had was American cash. (Hmmmm...)

Estepona is a darling pueblo, one of the "White Cities of Andalusia" found on the western stretches of the Spanish *Costa del Sol* (Sun Coast), half way between Gibraltar and Málaga. It's small and unhurried, clean and tidy. The architecture is clearly Spanish, and the ubiquitous white houses are evidence of the moors that inhabited the area until the time of Columbus. The beaches are a favorite of the area, no doubt, but there are also several art museums, a bull fighting arena, two downtown areas and more outdoor cafes than you've seen in your lifetime.

Drew and I didn't walk far that first evening: Of the several bars and restaurants that surrounded the marina, we found one with a flamenco motif and what appeared to be good food. We each selected a few tapas and enjoyed our dinner, enchanted by the authentic old-style flamenco tunes pumped through the restaurant's music system.

Drew told me about his physical challenges: He was bi-polar, he said—had been for some time. He took medication for it, and in the early stages of treatment when the complicated dosage schedule was being determined, he had an adverse reaction. His kidneys were 90% destroyed and he had to have dialysis treatment for several years. This, of course, kept him away from his beloved hobby of sailing. It also cost him his marriage, his law practice, and forced him into a disability retirement at the age of 50. A few years ago he received a kidney transplant, which freed him up a bit and allowed him to join OPO. He was much improved, he told me, physically and financially, though unwillingly alone and with a meager apartment: a single room with a mattress on the floor that rented for $250/month. In Manhattan!

What could I say to a guy with a story like that? I was embarrassed to have my own good health. Suddenly, those boring stories didn't seem so boring, and I felt I could endure a whole lot more from this poor man. Where was my sense of compassion? "I need to be more patient," I told myself, "more understanding, more accepting." I didn't know it at the time, but these concepts would soon be well tested.

After dinner I retired to my cabin (Oh, what a lovely place!) for a bit of reading. I slept well enough and woke up rested the next morning, smelling coffee as I opened the cabin door. Brian had already been out and had bought some fresh baguettes, thus beginning a wonderful peaceful breakfast routine of coffee, baguettes with jam or peanut butter, and sometimes cereal. Sometimes I went out for the baguettes, sometimes Brian. Very European indeed! Drew always seemed extra eager with his stories in these early morning times, and though I was trying to be more accepting, I often moved myself out to the cockpit of the boat to enjoy a little peace and quiet.

We needed to get the boat's anchor. Again, Brian and Lucille had let it go (with its chain rode) during the storm before my arrival. Marked by a buoy (one of the boat's fenders), it was now a fare distance outside of the harbor. We had heard that the fishermen were already eyeing the prize, so we needed to get out there and retrieve it as soon as possible. I was thinking we would do this right away, but Brian informed me that also as a consequence of the storm, the engine control panel had gotten soaked and the engine starter switch wouldn't work.

After a bit of discussion, Brian and I set about trying to diagnose and fix the starter switch problem. (For whatever reason, Drew did *not* get involved.) Sure enough, the switch was shorted in the "on" position, had been for some time, thus also burning out the brushes of the starter motor. The motor would need a rebuild, so I crawled into the engine room and removed it as Brian handed me tools. I got it out, but it being Saturday, we would have to wait until Monday for the rebuild. We installed a new starter switch, but that was about all we could do for the day.

We worked well together, Brian and I. We spoke little, but when we did it was quietly and with purpose. We didn't do "small talk." We were each sure of ourselves and quickly developed a sense of being confident with each other. I was being helpful with repairs aboard—always welcome on a boat—and together we were developing a comfortable, trusting relationship. Brian mentioned he was happy he had picked me as crew. That pleased me, of course. He also mentioned he was not so happy with Drew.

That surprised me: it was still very early for such a conclusion.

A fellow named Antonio came by the boat. Antonio ran a sail-maker's shop in town and he wanted to investigate the genoa roller-furler. The roller-furler, the apparatus that furls the large genoa when it isn't needed, was malfunctioning, another casualty from anchoring out in the storm. Antonio was hoisted up the mast and examined the apparatus, concluding that the best "fix" was to replace the furling system, a fix that would cost 6500 euros ($9000). The new system would have to be custom made and shipped from Sweden; installation time would be extensive as well. Antonio estimated that he could get us ready to sail in a week or so. (We were already a couple of days behind schedule.) He also had the genoa sail itself in his shop, as well as our Bimini awning, both of which were ripped and damaged in the storm. That storm, along with the action to anchor out fully exposed to it, was getting to be very costly, both in terms of repairs and delays. It still wore on my mind as to why such an action was chosen. It was a poor decision—we've been through that—but beyond that: why, exactly, was such a poor decision made?

A block away from the marina I found an internet café, a place where I could use the web and mail letters. (Eventually I found out that I could cheaply make phone calls from there as well.) I sent a note to Lisa, letting her know that I had arrived safely and that all was well. My note was a happy, care-free description of my new environment. As in most communications, I tried to minimize the problems that had come up, knowing that no problem later would seem as bad as it was at the time. It was comical, afterward, to read in a few minutes this note and those that followed. Seeing the bright and airy ones followed by ones that were not so cheery, one would think that the voyage never had any promise. At the time, however, though I had already seen a couple of issues, I didn't anticipate any major problems. Things were fine! We were hanging out in southern Spain, drinking coffee and eating tapas. Things could be a lot worse than being held up in Estepona.

Monday morning was an anxiously awaited time. Brian and Tony, a captain who managed a large powerboat next to us and who had a car, took the starter motor in to have it rebuilt. They returned shortly before noon, carrying the rebuilt starter which I re-installed right away. The engine started up easily and I regarded this as a huge milestone: we had several other things to attend to, but getting the engine running was major. We had a bit of lunch, then untied the dock lines and set off to retrieve the anchor.

I thought that retrieving the anchor would be a short, easy matter but I also realized that it would be the first significant task that we were to accomplish as a team. We sped out of the harbor and motored the half mile or so over to the buoy floating in the water, the one Brian and Lucille had left with a piece of line connecting the buoy to the anchor chain. Using a boat-hook we picked up the buoy and pulled in about 30 feet of line until the chain appeared. This task required the use of a halyard and some serious winching, and still we could only get a small portion of the chain to break the surface of the water. It was a 300-foot chain and the line was tied somewhere in its middle. Each end of the chain, therefore, extended 150' from the line, one end with the anchor on it, one without. The chain was a thick 7/16" gage which weighed over 5 pounds per foot. (Do the math: Each end of the chain weighed over 700 pounds!) Brian identified which end had the anchor, and we spent the next two hours trying to bring up the other "bitter" end. We tried using the windlass, the halyards— anything we could think of to try to get the chain aboard. It was so heavy, we could hardly budge it.

After a couple hours, it was Lucille who mentioned that the end of the chain we thought had the anchor was, in fact, the bitter end. She recalled where the boat was positioned when it was at anchor during the storm, and from that she concluded we were pulling on the wrong end.

Brian quickly dismissed Lucille's idea. He was concerned with his own efforts, getting frustrated with the lack of progress, and at one point concluded that we would have to simply leave the anchor where it lay. Fortunately, we convinced him to keep trying.

After trying several ideas, we finally got the chain properly around the windlass and found we could haul it aboard, bit by bit, using the hand crank. As it was getting dark—fully four hours after we had first come out—I was finally able to pull up the chain by hand, getting to the bitter end, just as Lucille had predicted. We reversed the chain on the windlass and now the other end could be winched up under electric power, fast and easy. We returned to the harbor tired but satisfied with a job well done.

Coming back to the marina, we had to go to a different dock than the one we had left. The new dock utilized "Mediterranean Style" dockage. With this method, the stern of the boat is tied to the dock with the bow pointed straight out, secured in place with two permanently positioned anchors with a thick line on each of them. It involves a tricky docking maneuver, for sure, but after a bit of practice it's not too difficult.

Brian didn't do so well when he docked the boat this time. We almost nailed the boat next to us, all three crew using fenders to prevent a collision and damage. (This process is called "fending off," an embarrassing procedure to have to utilize.) Brian got pretty excited, yelling out orders and directing efforts. We really didn't need any instruction: *Our* role was clear; it was *he* who needed to concentrate on the task at hand. It was all a bit disconcerting and, of course, several people came over to "help," which only frustrated Brian further. Eventually we got the boat secured and we all retired below, glad to be in.

It had been a big day and we had accomplished a couple of monumental tasks: fixing the engine and getting the anchor. The day had also identified a couple of weak links: Drew wasn't too useful and Brian was a bit hot headed. We ate some dinner then watched a movie on the boat's entertainment system. Afterward I went to my cabin and crashed into bed. I was beat. What a day!

The next day was pretty lazy. Brian and Lucille worked on odd caulking jobs that needed to be done; Drew and I took a long walk into the real "downtown" of Estepona, enjoying the architecture, the beaches, the bull ring and a nice coffee or two. I made lunch that day; Lucille made it the next. I caught up on e-mail from home and made good friends with Antonio the sail-maker, bugging him constantly regarding the status of the new roller furling system. On Wednesday about noon, I returned to the boat and Brian announced that we were going to Gibraltar. "We leave in an hour," he said. "Go find Drew."

I knew that Drew had gone back to the downtown area, and without too much trouble I found him sun-bathing on the beach. (I'm still having nightmares!) I roused him out of a half-sleep and we walked back to the boat, Drew breathing heavily and unable to keep up, walking ten feet behind me the entire time.

All of Drew's movements were slow and awkward, and by this time the rest of us were all aware of his significant physical inabilities. When going down the companionway steps, for example, he repeatedly lowered one foot then let the other catch up—as a young child might do. He always planned his moves carefully, never acting before he identified the adequate hand-holds he would be depending upon. Watching him get on and off the boat always made me wince! Not much was said on the topic, but I'm sure we were all concerned about Drew's sailing ability. A trip to Gibraltar was probably just what was needed.

Once we were all back at *Allegretta*, it was just a few minutes before we had untied the dock lines and Brian was steering the boat out of the harbor. It was our first sail together, and I was still trying to figure out all of the boat's sailing controls when Lucille took over the helm and pointed the boat "twenty degrees to the wind" so that Brian and I (but *not* Drew) could hoist the main. We then unfurled the small jib (the bigger genoa and its furler were still in disrepair) and set the auto-pilot with the boat pointing toward Gibraltar. The sun shone fully and the wind filled the sails; it was a gorgeous day for sailing.

Less than an hour out, however, Brian radioed the marina in Gibraltar and learned that they didn't have a dock available for us that night. We sailed close to land, and right outside of a harbor called "La Duquesa" we laid anchor. The wind was south at 20 knots—strong enough but not too bad. We were exposed and without protection, but the rather bouncy night passed without incident. We ate dinner, watched another movie, and retired to our beds.

Drew had not done much to help sail the boat that day. He couldn't help with any of the tasks of getting the sails up and trimmed: Those tasks required agility and coordination and Drew was pretty short in those areas. Even with putting out the anchor, attaching a snubber line, or just cleaning up all the lines on deck after the sail—Drew would just sit on his butt and sip on a Coke, totally uninvolved. At one point I asked him to hit a button on the auto-pilot, and he slowly—oh, so very slowly—bent over and eventually pushed the button. Lucille saw this too, and we glanced at each other knowingly. (I'm sure we were both imagining the danger of being dependent on Drew in any sort of emergency.)

That night in my cabin I reflected on the day and what it had illustrated. Drew's abilities, surely, were limited and I wondered what could be done about that. Perhaps his watch could be "sandwiched" between mine and Brian's and the two of us could keep a bit of an eye on the weak watch. Perhaps Drew and I could work as a team, taking a double watch together. I didn't like either of these ideas, but the only other alternative—sending Drew home—seemed cruel. Besides, that would leave only three of us to sail a pretty big boat.

I also saw a red flag in Brian: any time something went a little bit wrong, he would significantly over-react. He did this when his docking maneuvers went wrong, yelling and cursing as the rest of us tried to fend-off from other boats. He showed this tendency again—basically going ballistic on me—when I repeated for a second time my method (which differed from his) of securing a line around a cleat. Also, when retrieving the anchor—and yes, that was a frustrating ordeal—I saw him lose his cool two or three times. Normally Brian was a soft spoken, kind and humble individual. It was surprising to see him lose his temper when small, incidental problems occurred. I didn't know how serious this issue was, at least at the time. It was something I had noticed, something I would certainly keep an eye on. (I wondered if it had played a part in the decision to anchor in the storm. I wondered what role it would play once we were out at sea.)

Throughout this short sail over to Gibraltar and back, I was really focusing on my intention to "let it go." It was Brian's boat. He was the captain; I was one of the crew. He had his responsibilities; there were many things that were *not* my responsibility. My goal was to be as helpful as I possibly could, but to step aside when some issue was not my legitimate problem. Many questions would arise as they always do: Do we have a dock? Where should we anchor? How much rode should we put out? How far off shore should we be? What happens if the weather should turn sour over night? I planned to keep an eye on all of these things, of course, but I also planned to leave the decision making process where it should be: with the captain.

As an extension of this same idea, the next day I was planning on leaving certain sailing tasks where they should be: with Drew! I wasn't trying to be sly, but Drew was *crew* and it was necessary that he start acting like *crew*. If he could *not*, and by that time I fully suspected that he could *not*, this fact needed to be highlighted and addressed. I was interested not only in seeing what Drew could and could *not* do, but also in how the captain and first-mate would react to Drew's limitations. I didn't have to wait long...

The next morning while still at anchor (and Drew still in bed), Brian and Lucille together approached me to discuss the issue of Drew and his sailing abilities. Calmly, we expressed specific weaknesses and inabilities, not so much to criticize the individual, but to identify the effect his physical limitations would have on the total yacht. It was the first of several discussions we were to have about Drew. Even at this early stage, however, Lucille favored removing and replacing Drew while Brian favored keeping him and working with him.

With breakfast and our discussion about the crew complete, Brian, Lucille and I went topside, ready to get *Allegretta* moving again toward Gibraltar. Raising and lowering the anchor is one task with which Lucille and Brian are well practiced, and with Lucille at the helm and Brian at the windlass, the task went smoothly. Soon we were on our way, ready to put up the sails.

I wanted to get very familiar with the raising of the mainsail, hence I took on the hoisting task that morning, asking Brian to guide my actions. As on many large boats, handling the mainsail on *Allegretta* was an awkward job. The halyard, a sun-damaged-stiff and easily knotted piece of crap, was hauled with a (very slow) electric winch, and the winch was too big for the line so the self-tailing feature didn't work so well. Just pulling up the halyard became a full-time job, one that failed often. Somebody else had to steer the boat into the wind (that's two people), and somebody else was required to adjust the sheet, traveler, running back stays and reef lines and make sure nothing fouled during the hoist. It became a three person job just to raise the main-sail.

I was even more concerned about lowering the main. In normal conditions, if the boat was pointed into the wind and the halyard was let go, the sail would lower itself (by gravity) and, in fact, furl itself too. Under storm-like conditions, however, you would likely have to pull the sail down by hand, and since it was quite a height off the deck—about eight feet—this would require that you climb the mast a ways to complete the task. The foot supports and hand-holds for this were less than adequate, I thought, and if one were to fall when attempting the task, one would likely fall right into the sea.

The mainsail on *Allegretta* was a challenge, as it was on *Skyelark of London,* and as it was on *That Darn Cat.* It seemed to be a challenge on all big boats. This is a good argument in favor of, God forbid, a smaller sailboat. I certainly never experienced any problem like this on *C'est si Bon.* (Oh, that was a lovely boat!)

But regardless of these potential problems we might see down the road, within no time we had both the main and jib set, and we were sailing along toward Gibraltar, the engine running the whole time. Drew eventually got out of bed, and once he was fully awake and ready for duty, Brian asked him to do the odd task, purposely sending him up front a couple of times to assess his agility on the foredeck. I also gave him the helm a time or two, and I saw that he *could*, at least, steer the boat. Unfortunately, we all saw that he couldn't do much more.

Well, "let it go," I thought. It wasn't *my* problem. If I were to get involved, I would only screw things up. Better to let those responsible take care of *their* responsibilities. Leadership! I wanted to see leadership, and by this time I started to see that Brian was not the leader I had first thought.

Sailing through the straits and around the Rock of Gibraltar was a sailor's dream, come true. "The Rock" was visible from 20 miles or more (we could always see it from our dock in Estepona) and with deep water right up to it, navigation was a cinch. The sea was choppy and confused—It's always that way in the straits," Brian told me—and we motor-sailed around the south end of Gibraltar with Morocco visible 10 miles off. (It was the first time my eyes

144

had ever seen Africa.) We circled around clockwise, just as I had done on the plane a few days earlier, and on the west side we came up to Queensway Quay Marina. We called in by radio and were assigned a dock where we again tied up "Mediterranean Style," Brian improved over the last time but still missing the first attempt.

We had switched countries, being in the UK territory of Gibraltar, so Brian had to clear Customs for the boat and all of the crew. He took all of our passports and completed the clearance, and upon returning said he could give us each back our passports or he could keep them with the "ship's papers." Since it's a normal procedure for the captain to keep all passports when a boat is in a foreign territory, we all agreed he should keep them. Seemed like a good idea at the time...

Drew and I headed to town, me being the guide since it was my second time to Gibraltar. We walked up and down Main Street, which was very interesting with all its shops and restaurants. Very European! Cars were not permitted on Main Street, so it was a walker's paradise. Eventually we signed up for one of the van supported tours that are a "must do" in Gibraltar. The tour was about 75 minutes in duration and we went to the top of "The Rock," seeing the tailless monkeys, the naturally formed caverns, and the manmade tunnels—all important features of the Rock of Gibraltar. Afterward, Drew and I joined Brian and Lucille at the boat and the four of us had dinner. Stomachs full, we closed up the boat and headed off to Morrison's Supermarket. It was time to complete the major task of provisioning.

"Provisioning," that is, buying all of the groceries required for the voyage, is a huge task. (Imagine planning the meals and buying at one time, all of the groceries required for four hungry sailors for four weeks.) We weren't very well prepared; in fact, we hadn't even discussed the matter beforehand. (Remember: "let it go.") Lucille basically ran the show. Drew and I were asked to

145

direct her as to what foods we might prefer. We all got ourselves some shopping carts and then started picking out potatoes, cereal, milk, bottled water, pop, meat, fish, vegetables and everything else. The job went without too much complication, and after about three hours we headed over to the check-out.

It had never left my mind, the less than clear agreement we had on the payment for food. I never saw it advantageous to bring up the subject with Brian or Lucille, and as the precise time for payment came to pass, I was waiting for somebody else to take the lead.

Again, the organizing e-mails I received stated, "Food and boat expenses with be paid by the captain. The crew might be asked to make some contribution if improved food is desired." Drew and I discussed the matter and we figured a contribution of 75 euros each would be reasonable. I gave my money to Drew and mentioned to Brian and Lucille that Drew and I hoped what we had planned would be acceptable to them. I knew that what we were contributing wasn't a high percentage of the total food cost, but bearing in mind what the understanding was, I thought we were being reasonable. (The total food cost was 1000 Gibraltar pounds, which was about 1400 euros.)

Imagine my surprise when Lucille stated that we were all sharing the food costs equally. I couldn't believe it! Fortunately, Brian came to our rescue, claiming that Lucille hadn't seen the initial e-mails. He stated that a fair amount would be 125 pounds each. Still a bit peculiar, I thought, but I paid up and put it in my mind to get better clarity on this item on future voyages. (So much for "letting it go!") Lucille was still pissed. I tried to console her and explain to her what our original information had said, but she remained largely unconvinced. It was unfortunate that we had the misunderstanding at all, and I blame it on poor leadership. C'mon, man! Get with it!

I had thought that the sail over to Gibraltar was a telling experience, but it was only the start of what was to continue the next day. It began with Brian and Lucille informing me that they had decided they were *not* sending Drew home. (Okay... I thought, with a bit of reservation.) They then told me that he would stay in the cockpit and not go up front. (Probably a good "safety" call, but...) They also outlined the watch schedule for the voyage: each person would take a two-hour watch throughout the night; everybody would sail the boat as a team during the daytime without assigned watches. A bit peculiar—I had never heard of such a thing—but fine.

We untied the dock lines and motored out, Brian once again messing up the undocking procedure and verbalizing his frustrations, just in case anybody on the dock or otherwise couldn't see. Geez!

We got out of the marina and Brian put Drew on the helm. I sat with Drew and watched him steer. He didn't do *that* bad of a job. Once or twice he cut the engine way down by hitting the engine throttle control by mistake but hey, that wasn't so bad. We circled "The Rock" and put up the sails, leaving the engine running once again. It was a great day, sunny and not too chilly, and we were sailing the Mediterranean along the Costa del Sol. What could be better?

Brian went down below and sat at his navigation station while Drew steered along. I was coiling lines, trimming sails, going below and coming back up on deck— all the things a sailor normally does on a boat under way. The navigation station has a tracking device and Brian could easily monitor how Drew was doing. Almost immediately, he started complaining about Drew's steering, directing his complaints not to Drew where they belonged, but to me.

My first inclination was to simply turn the problem right back to Brian. You know, "He's your crew and your problem. Deal with it!" Clearly, Drew was not *my* problem, but the thought occurred to me that Drew was still unaware of all that was being said about him and his performance. He didn't know that his physical limitations were a significant concern of everybody else on board. He didn't know that sending him home was a real consideration at the time. Hell, he didn't even think his steering was that bad! (Well, I didn't think so either.)

Brian and I discussed the matter, again in that quiet, trusting man-to-man manner we had adopted. I offered to have a talk with Drew and discuss all of the concerns we had with him. (He was owed *that*, at least.) I went on deck, put the steering on auto-pilot and stated simply, "Drew, we need to talk."

As I had guessed, Drew was completely surprised when I told him about the concerns. In his mind, he was as agile and capable as anyone else on the boat. I pointed out the several basic sailing tasks he was unable to do. I mentioned the slowness of his motor skills and the fact that he even needed help getting on and off the boat. I asked him how he thought he would be able to tack the boat if the wind changed when he was on watch. I asked what he would do if a squall hit. How was he going to run up front, drop the main, then quickly get back to the cockpit to release the jib sheet and pull in the furling line? How was he going to do these things when he could hardly bend down and push a button on the auto-pilot? I asked him about his prior experience: How was it that he was able to complete those voyages when at this time, he seemed to lack basic elements of strength, mobility and coordination?

He continued to insist that he could do anything anybody else could. "When things get dicey," he said, "I'll call for help—just like everybody else." He was a great arguer, I thought. You could tell he used to be a lawyer. His arguments were clear and conclusive. They simply lacked the essential ingredients of truth and reality.

I felt compassion for Drew. He wanted to sail across the ocean more than anything in the world. He had so little in his life; it would be so good if he could just complete this passage. He was so incapable, however, and I was seeing that he had thoroughly misled the captain when describing his sailing experience and abilities. He deserved to be sent home. He really did! But, that wasn't my business. Time to "let it go," I thought. I told Drew that he needed to concentrate on the steering for the next hour or so. He needed to prove to Brian that steering the boat was something he could do reliably. (This would actually be a significant milestone: If Drew proved he was able to steer the boat, we could probably create something workable.) I wanted Drew to succeed on this. The truth is: I believed that Brian, Lucille and I could likely sail the boat more easily without Drew. But I felt a sense of compassion—pity really—for an "ocean crossing wanna-be," one who had had so much misfortune in his life and in this voyage so far. As Brian and Lucille had informed me, the plan was that Drew was staying on board. He was to be one of a crew of four for this voyage. My intention was to make the best of it. I turned off the auto-pilot and encouraged Drew to do his best. I returned below and met with Brian who was anxiously awaiting my report.

I outlined much of the conversation Drew and I had just finished, omitting one or two key items, simply because I didn't like snitching on my fellow crewman. (I didn't relate that I seriously suspected Drew had lied about his prior experience, for example.) I told Brian that Drew still felt he could honor all his obligations. I told him that at that present time, Drew was demonstrating his ability as a helmsman.

I also told Brian that he and Drew needed to have a man-to-man talk. It was Brian, not I, that needed to assess crew abilities and assign responsibilities. I didn't want to insult him, so I didn't tell Brian that what I really needed was for him to step up to his own role as a leader. In my opinion, neither man—Brian nor Drew—was doing an exemplary job at fulfilling his own responsibilities. Time to get with it! Me, I'm "letting it go."

We got back to the area of Estepona without too much incident, arriving sometime in the early afternoon.

149

Drew did a pretty good job at steering; I was thinking that I probably wouldn't have done any better. Still, like some bitchy little kid, Brian complained repeatedly, showing me on the plotter every error Drew was making. Oh brother!

We approached the town, the time to take in the sails, and I expressed to Brian that I wanted him to walk me through his method of lowering the mainsail so that I would know it thoroughly. I had told him about my concerns with the main and that it was important that I be able to efficiently douse this difficult and complicated sail. He had been doing it for several years, I told him. I needed to know his method.

About a quarter mile from the harbor—sail lowering time with me up at the mast but with Brian still back in the cockpit—Brian yelled up at me to "unlock the main halyard." I unlocked the halyard (opened the jam-cleat) and held the halyard in my hand. I was waiting for Brian to come forward and show me how he normally got the sail down, got it furled, and got all of the other controls tightened up as required. I heard Brian yell again for me to unlock the halyard, this time in a bit of a panic. Already having it unlocked and not knowing what he meant, I looked around the sail so that I could see him, and he began yelling repeatedly, "Unlock the halyard! Unlock the halyard!" He was in full panic now—and there was no emergency—and I finally understood that he wanted me to "let go" halyard, which I did. The sail came down, most of it anyway. The last few feet did *not* come down and only half of the sail fell into the self-furler. Furthermore, the main-sheet, traveler, vang, reefing lines and running back stays all remained as they were—loose and ready to foul—until I went around and secured each of them, one by one. Brian made some smart-ass comment about me not listening, which I basically ignored. I went about my work, wondering seriously if we had sufficient leadership for this voyage. Geez!

We came into the harbor and were assigned the same dock we had been using when we left two days earlier.

Again, this was a "Mediterranean" dock, with a pair of permanent marina-supplied anchors positioned a distance off the dock where the front of the boat would be once moored. Brian steered us in, doing a pretty good job this time. One of the anchors was missing, however, and the other was not out far enough to hold the boat off the dock. We called the marina and negotiated to move to the gas dock, but "only for two hours," they said. Well, Brian did *not* do such a good job moving from one dock the other and major "fending off" was called for. (In this one especially, I was surprised that no damage occurred.) We tied up at the gas dock and Brian and Lucille ran off to a doctor's appointment they had. (Brian had required some X-rays a few days prior and he needed to pick up the results.)

About two hours later the captain and mate returned—packet in hand, hopefully everything okay—and we prepared to move the boat again, this time to another dock, just 20 feet away. We probably *could* have moved the boat by hand, but there *was* a bit of wind, and the boat *did* have to be turned around, so it was probably a better idea to move the boat under engine power.

Well, this became the docking maneuver from hell. We got away from the gas dock and got the boat turned around okay, and really, I thought things were going to go well. Brian steered the boat toward the new dock but came too close to the gas dock, fouling the fenders on the dock and pivoting the boat undesirably. Several people were standing on the dock so they fended-off, allowing Brian to come at the new dock a second time. In he came, not too bad, but then he put the engine in reverse, drawing the stern out to port (to the left, as all sailboats want to do when in reverse), leaving him perpendicular from what he needed. He made repeated attempts, the bystanders each time feeling it necessary to offer conflicting suggestions, and Brian getting as frustrated as could be, going more and more ballistic with each dockage attempt. As the embarrassment continued, Brian seemed to be less and less able to pilot his beloved *Allegretta.* He was getting farther and farther away, and at one point we were several hundred yards from the dock and about to go up on some rocks!

Somehow, we got in. We got two good sterns lines on and two sturdy, well-laid anchors out front. By this time, I knew all of the nuances of Mediterranean docking, so I spent some good time getting all of the lines properly routed and secured. We had a nice secure moorage, sufficiently far away from the dock and/or the boat next to us. It was the only time we had a properly secure mooring. Thank God, too: during that night a storm and a tornado came through.

Yeah, the trip to Gibraltar: What a trip! Usually on a shakedown cruise, you try to find a "weak link" in the chain; I think we found that the whole damn chain was pretty rusty. Drew and I went out to dinner and we talked about the voyage and all that was going wrong. I told him that I kept hoping for a "big turnaround," a moment in time when things started to go right rather than wrong. It didn't seem to be happening. I pictured how things would go if the trend continued after we put out to sea. I had read accounts of several sea-going disasters: Typically they were not caused by one singular factor, but by multiple causes and with plenty of early warnings. Was I presently on such an ill-fated voyage? Perhaps. I wasn't sure. I wasn't ready to jump ship—not just yet—but I was considering the possibility. As I spoke with Drew that night at dinner, I made a plan to do two things: check the internet for flight ticket availability, and get my passport back from Brian. I might have to "escape."

We were all pretty tired that evening after getting back from Gibraltar. Drew and I returned from dinner and went straight to bed: no movie, thank you. I read a bit then drifted off to sleep, once again thankful for that wonderful cabin of mine. It rained quite a bit over night and the wind blew substantially. I had to get up a couple of times to re-tie the main halyard that banged against the mast. One time, about two in the morning, I got up to find Brian sleeping at the navigation desk. Hmmm...

Toward dawn a storm came through. I heard the rain and wind but mostly slept through the whole thing. This storm was one of the "lows" (squalls) that came through the area every other day or so. They're a series of storms that come across the ocean, west to east, along the southern edge of the Westerlies. This was the third or fourth one that had come through since I had been on *Allegretta*, and no doubt, another one was the storm that Brian and Lucille experienced shortly before I arrived. Anyway, this last storm contained a tornado! It didn't hit *Allegretta*, nor did it damage any other boats in the marina, but it *did* hit a couple of restaurants surrounding the marina and it *did* do some damage on land. I was grateful we had a good secure mooring that night, and glad I had taken the time and made sure everything was right.

The next morning, which was Saturday, November 17, I got up and could see the dirty water that remained after the storm. Tony, the captain/manager of the big powerboat next to us, was awakened at home by the storm and came to his charge at 6:00 AM to make sure everything was okay. (Good captain!) Tony saw the twister; he said we were lucky it didn't come our way.

Drew eventually got up, and Brian had his "big talk" with him. I stayed out of the conversation entirely, thankful and impressed that Brian was taking some leadership action. His talk was much like mine: He pointed out the sailing fundamentals that Drew was unable to do. He mentioned the lack of motor skills and the very slow physical movement that Drew typified. He said that he couldn't understand how Drew could have completed the voyages that he had claimed.

Brian had printed the e-mails Drew had sent him and he held them in his hand, asking Drew specific questions such as, "On that passage from Bermuda to New York, what did you do when the jib was out of trim and it needed to be

153

pulled in?" He went over each of the voyages that Drew had said he had been on, asking several questions about each one. The truth came out, bit by bit. It wasn't pretty.

Drew repeatedly proclaimed that everything he had stated in the application for the crewing position was true. He'd would point his finger in the air as he stated his point, then sit back with his arms folded, defying Brian to contradict the relevance of his apparent truism. It was laughable that he would rest on such statements, when it was so clear in each case that he had omitted the real meat of the matter. For example, he stated he had sailed often with (OPO owner) Hank Schmitt, but he didn't mention that on each passage, he was an inactive paying passenger, not a participating crew. He bragged of his "extensive sailing experience off the coast of Croatia," totally omitting he was merely a student on board a boat and that the "sailing school" he attended was more like a wine tasting vacation. His "Tahiti Voyage" extended only a few miles from one island to another, totally sailed by the tour operators. The truth was that Drew had no ability as a sailor and that he had been very misleading in order to get on board *Allegretta.*

What to do? We were pretty short-handed and though Drew was incapable and a bit of a liar, he was a quarter of our manpower. And he could steer, I guess! Brian wanted to think it over, and I overheard the mumblings of the conversations he and Lucille had on the subject throughout the day. Again, Lucille was all for sending the guy home, but Brian, I guess, felt some compassion. Sometime in the afternoon, he announced that Drew would be allowed to stay aboard, but he was to be a "guest," not "crew," and would have no sailing responsibilities. (Brian had made arrangements to have another experienced sailor—a fellow from Italy named "Pierre"—come and take over Drew's responsibilities as "crew.")

It was a good compromise, though it didn't please anybody perfectly: Drew, though happy to still have a spot on board, was a bit slighted that he was to be called a "guest." I considered his issue pretty childish, considering he was almost called "bus passenger," but nevertheless, he eventually negotiated the title "apprentice," which I figured was his way of being a "*legitimate* pain in the ass."

Lucille was still a bit miffed and argued that the extra person aboard increased her work load. In response, Brian stated further than all "guests" pay appropriate food costs, so Drew's share was increased to 25% of the total we had spent in Gibraltar. Also, Drew would have to give up his prized port-side cabin and move to the "milkshake room" up forward.

I was happy, not especially with the solution itself, but for the fact that Brian had finally come to the pump in the leadership category. I was still looking for a "big turnaround." Perhaps this was it.

Brian probably felt some satisfaction, knowing he had come up with a fair and equitable solution to the Drew thing. It was a major problem indeed, complicated by several human egos. I was hoping that solving it would give Brian some degree of happiness. It was only one of many problems that Brian shouldered, however. At the time he was carrying quite an emotional load:

The past few weeks had gone poorly, no doubt. The storm that Brian and Lucille experienced before I arrived had caused extensive and costly damage. It was also the cause of the delay we were now facing. In addition, surely Brian felt a bit of embarrassment with his boat handling performance, both from the repeated docking mishaps, and also being the spectacle of anchoring precariously out in a storm, only to have all the fishermen eyeing his anchor afterward. Then too, he and Lucille seemed to be going through some sort of awkwardness, and Lord knows how that can get a good man down! There was also a potential medical condition—recall the X-rays—and perhaps that was weighing on him as well.

The major repair matter, of course, was that of the roller furling system. Antonio the sail-maker had said it was ordered and shipped (from Sweden), but he was unable to get any tracking confirmation of the shipment. We really didn't know the status. Even when the system arrived, the installation of it would be significant. Who knows how that would go? Also, Antonio's mother-in-law had died—may she rest in peace—and there was a possibility that Antonio would have family obligations and delay us further.

Speaking of delays, at the time we were delayed nine days from our original sailing plan, and the earliest we could see leaving was Wednesday, November 21—a total delay of almost two weeks. *Allegretta* had charter guests scheduled for December 22 and, allowing for clean-up and other preparations, Brian wanted to get to St. Thomas by December 15. The voyage from Estepona to St. Thomas would take at least three weeks, and the delay we were experiencing was taking all wiggle room out of the equation.

I felt bad for our captain with all the pressures he was experiencing. These were supposed to be his "wonderful years of retirement bliss." It certainly didn't seem that way. For him, too, I hoped that the luck of this voyage would turn around.

I made dinner that night for the four of us—curry chicken, a salad, and pasta with oil and garlic. Drew, because of his demoted status, had been pouting all afternoon, but he seemed to come out of it toward dinner time. He helped with dinner, a bit, by chopping up the garlic. Lucille was pouting as well, but she, too, came out for dinner. I made sure I had set a proper table for all four of us. I wanted to re-establish whatever cohesion we still had possible. The dinner went well—all objectives satisfied— and afterward, Lucille retired to her cabin (her standard "isolation") and the men watched a movie—*The Debaters*— which we all enjoyed in apparent harmony. It was just after

156

the movie had finished when Brian verbalized a couple of unsettling changes in the voyage:

He first mentioned that when we stopped again at Gibraltar—we wanted to stop on our way out to get fuel—we would set sail immediately afterward for the open ocean. Since we would be arriving there late in the day, it seemed odd that we wouldn't stay the night and get a good night's sleep. Also, it would be normal to check the weather and wait for a good forecast before leaving. I knew that with the delay we were getting short on time, but the stretch from Gibraltar to the Canaries would be the toughest sailing of the voyage, and it made sense to wait for a promising weather window.

Brian then announced that we would *not* be sailing south to the Canaries, and that we would sail straight across the Atlantic to St. Thomas instead.

Folks, mariners have been sailing from Gibraltar to the Caribbean since the days of Columbus. Sailing straight across would be the first inclination of anybody anticipating a crossing but nobody does it. Why? Because it's a bad idea! Even Columbus knew to sail south to the trade winds and then cut across at that point. I mentioned this to Brian. He said it would be okay. He had done it before, he said. Hmmm...

The next morning, Sunday, I got up early and went and bought a couple of baguettes. So did Brian. We had bread in spades! We put on some coffee and ate a little breakfast and Brian went and read his e-mail on the boat's computer. Drew was still in bed.

After a moment or two, Brian asked me to come and read an e-mail he had received. It was from Hank Schmitt, the owner of Offshore Passage Opportunities (OPO), the company that had sent me and Drew to *Allegretta*. Brian had asked Hank about Drew, and in a return e-mail Hank was saying, "DO NOT TAKE DREW WITH YOU!" The letter went on to describe Drew's inabilities that Hank had witnessed on the various passages Drew had paid to get on.

Hank stated that "he liked Drew, in a masochistic sort of way," but in no way was he qualified for an Atlantic crossing and it was important that he not be kept on board.

Wow! From the man who sent us Drew in the first place! Brian and I stared at each other, wondering about the ramifications of such a letter. Brian asked if he should show it to Drew. "Hell yeah!" I said.

Well, Drew did eventually get up—so did Lucille— and we all had ourselves a nice little talk. Drew was getting sent home and he didn't like it. I stayed out of the conversation for quite some time, but then Brian pulled me in.

It was pretty clear, I reasoned: Not only was Drew unable to sail proficiently, he had misled us in regards to his ability and experience, and now OPO owner Hank was warning us (vehemently) against keeping him on board. "Think of the liabilities if we did otherwise," I reasoned.

Drew remained defiant, first asking to request a clarification from Hank (Denied!) then stating that he couldn't go home anyway because he didn't have a credit card with him or sufficient cash to buy a ticket home.

Here's where I should have "let it go" but where I did *not*: "How can that be true?" I asked. "How were you going to get home from St. Thomas? No one travels without a credit card. You're lying!"

Surprisingly, this got no response from Drew, but Brian motioned for me to settle down, which I did. It really was *not* my business and Brian had only one way to take things anyway. I still regret stepping in. Nevertheless, Drew was demoted once again, this time to "bus passenger." He moped around the boat for a while, closed himself up in his cabin for a couple of hours, and eventually headed off to town on his own. (His gear was still aboard.) I saw him a bit later in the internet café and then later walking back from town, but he pretty much avoided me. Oh well, I thought. Not my problem. I had a new concern. This new route idea of Brian's was quite worrisome.

After our big discussion with Drew, I headed out to the internet café. On the way, I met up with Tony, the captain on the large powerboat next to us. Tony, a licensed captain, didn't own the boat, but he worked full time to "manage" it and operate it whenever the owner wanted to go for a ride. He had spent years gunk-holing all around the Mediterranean and had crossed the Atlantic two or three times. Less than a year younger than me, married with two adult children, bilingual (educated in the UK), he had been an ocean mariner all his life.

Tony and I had developed a bit of a friendship—we shared the same age, the same sailing interest and the same herniated disc problem—and he asked me aboard to help with a repair he was doing. By and by, I asked him about Brian's idea: heading straight across the ocean.

"Why would you do that?" he asked. "If you head south to the trade winds and then head west, it's absolutely gorgeous!"

"To save time," I said. "We need to be in St. Thomas by December 15."

"You won't save any time," he said. "You'll be fighting the wind all the way if you head straight across. You'd go twice as fast if you went with the trades."

We talked about it at length. Tony told me about the series of lows (squalls) that march across the ocean in these latitudes. "That's what all these storms have been," he said, "the ones we've had the last several days. The tornado! The storm that hit *Allegretta* before you got here."

He went on to tell me several stories about people who had tried to sail straight across. One long-time sailor sold his boat and gave up sailing after being battered non-stop all the way across. On another boat, a large powerboat, all 17 members of the crew left ship "en-mass" after a stubborn captain insisted on such a route. "It's a bad idea!" Tony continued. "And why? The trade winds are right there! It's dangerous! If you're on a boat that's planning that route, you need to get off that boat."

159

Quite a set of statements! Of course, I had often read about the recommended route: You head south "until the butter melts," then head west. I recalled the voyage on *That Darn Cat*, where I was the one who wanted to head straight across, and the rest of the crew who insisted on heading south. (And that was from the Canaries—already five hundred miles south of Gibraltar!) Everything I had ever heard or read had told me that you head south first. It was on the pilot charts, in Jim Cornell's *World Cruising Routes*, in every North Atlantic Sailing Guide that had ever been printed. My own experience confirmed it: You head south to get to 20/30 (20 degrees north, 30 degrees west) and then you head west. I had never heard of or seen any discussion on what would happen if you violated this wisdom; now I was hearing from a local captain, a professional mariner with the experience of several ocean crossings: "If you're on such a boat, you need to get off." Upon returning to the boat, I brought the subject up with Brian.

Brian hit the roof. "This is how we're going to sail, and that is that!" he screamed. "End of discussion. I've done it before. I know what I'm talking about!"

I couldn't reason with him. I tried to explain that we wouldn't save time by going straight across. I said that we would run into non-stop storms. "Nonsense!" he said. "We'll simply run into light winds and we'll motor through them. We'll get a couple of 50-gallon barrels of fuel in Gibraltar and tie them to the deck."

Oh, that's a great idea! Four weeks of storms with two big barrels of fuel on deck. What a crazy idea! What a crazy captain! What a nightmare!

I kept my calm. I didn't need to push the point at the time. Really, all I had was Tony's description of the dangers of going straight across. I could research the matter on the internet. Perhaps I could speak to other captains. I sent a note out to Hank entitled "Urgent Suggestion Required." Maybe it wouldn't be so bad. Maybe it would be just a long motor-boat ride across as Brian believed. It would be a shame to not take the pleasant trade wind sail across, especially if such a route was the fastest anyway, but if there was no safety risk it would be negligent to hop ship based on poor information. I needed to make sure of my facts.

The boat was pretty quiet that evening. Drew had been gone all day. We were wondering where he could have been. Lucille cooked up a wonderful Shepard's Pie. (She had been noticeably happier since Drew was asked to leave.) We set the table and served dinner, putting a portion away for Drew in case he came back hungry. It was a subdued dinner. Drew had always been the vocal one and it felt uncomfortably quiet. Afterward, I offered to do the dishes, and as I got started Lucille retired to her cabin. Brian and I were left to ourselves.

Though we had an issue between us, a major one at that, Brian and I were still a good team. We spoke about Drew, about Pierre who would be replacing him, and about all of the repairs that, hopefully, were to begin in earnest the next morning.

Brian mentioned that he was a bit concerned about what reaction Drew would take to being asked to leave. Drew, we agreed, probably felt he was being let go unjustly. We knew he was angry, that the trip would cost him a few grand, and that he was an ex-lawyer. Brian thought there was a chance Drew would sue, and that since they both were legal residents of New York, Drew could call Brian to court. He would have to interrupt his charter business, pay travel expenses, get a lawyer. "Maybe we *should* keep Drew on as a guest," Brian contemplated. "Maybe that would save a lot of trouble down the road." (Funny how we were past doing the *right* thing; decisions were now being made to avoid litigation.)

I agreed. I told him I hated the thought of it, but I agreed that lawyers love to sue and that it would be a no-brainer for Drew. Brian would have to settle out of court, probably at the cost of a few thousand dollars. "Still, if you ask him back, Lucille's going to *kill* you!" I said.

161

I retired to my cabin, read a bit, and then it was "lights out" about 9:30. I was still awake when I heard Drew return.

I heard the two men in discussion. I didn't hear all of what was said, but I think it was a discussion of the *possibility* of Drew coming along as a guest. I heard Drew get into his cabin and then it was quiet, but only for a few minutes.

Yep, within no time at all I heard Lucille and Brian arguing, an argument that was to last all night. I couldn't hear specifics—I was trying *not* to—but the level of hollering reached some spectacular heights at times, with Lucille eventually proclaiming that she was leaving in the morning, and Brian (in full temper) asserting "Fine! That's what you always do anyway!" It was embarrassing, for me as well as for them, I'm sure. The fighting continued for hours, sometimes moving on deck, only to continue again inside. After a while I heard Lucille "move" to the forward cabin, and eventually all was quiet and we got a bit of sleep.

I got up fairly early the next morning. Lucille's bags were packed and waiting by the companionway. Brian was sitting at the navigation desk. I looked in Drew's cabin. He and his gear were gone.

Brian was subdued. He seemed utterly beaten. He had been up most of the night, arguing with the woman he loved, and it looked as if she might be leaving him. The past two weeks, with all the problems they brought, had taken their toll. He didn't even know that Drew had left until he asked me and I told him. He was withdrawn, humbled, hurt. I felt his pain.

He said that things were okay—"Yes, things are fine, now," he said. He had gotten up early to inform Drew of his final decision, giving him back the money he had paid for groceries. Drew was dissatisfied with the decision, and Brian said he even tried one more time to argue against it. With the finality of it accepted, however, he had a plane to catch. (Somehow he had purchased a ticket.) With Brian

162

momentarily in his cabin and not looking, Drew grabbed his bag and left. He never said "goodbye" to anyone.

Those who remained—Brian, Lucille and me—still had the issue of the route, of course. I got out a couple of charts and studied the two routes with Brian looking over my shoulder.

He stated again that his route was okay: the "lows" traced across the Atlantic, north of where we would travel, he told me, and they wouldn't be a bother to us. We would simply have light winds but we would motor through them. It would just save us time.

I told him that I had been advised differently, that the storm he was caught in before I arrived and the several we had seen since were the same "lows" that would hit us repeatedly right across the ocean.

He pointed out that his route was not really that far from the Canaries.

"Yes it is!" I showed him. "It's 500 miles north of the Canaries. And the Canaries would be the absolute minimum; we were supposed to go 400 miles *south* of the Canaries before heading across!"

"Well," he said matter-of-factly, "we're *not* going to head *south* of the Canaries. There's just no way."

I told him I had to research the matter more fully. I told him I had major concerns with sailing straight across. I didn't push my point—he was in a weakened way at the time—but I wanted him to know the extent of my concern.

Monday, November 19, was to be a big day: It was the day the new roller furling system was supposed to arrive from Sweden. Also, Tony, the captain next door, was going to give me a ride into town so that I could get a broken hatch repaired. Pierre, from Italy, was to be on his way, arriving in Estepona a day later. Best of all, I had found a way to call Lisa and I was planning to talk to her.

Lucille got up. (Apparently, she was *not* leaving.) She had a full day planned too, but for the time being she got herself a cup of coffee and sat alone out in the cockpit. A

163

little while later as I was getting off the boat, I noticed that she was still pretty shaken, so I stopped and gave her a bit of a one-armed hug, a gesture I think she much appreciated. Lucille and I had similar opinions on many of the events that had occurred over the last ten days. We appreciated each other's abilities aboard as well as each other's inner strengths. I think she was as happy to have me on board as she was to have Drew *off*. Somehow, it seemed we had bonded. Anyway, she thanked me for the "hug," and I think she was grateful that we could all forget the drama of the previous night.

I went for a walk around the marina, hoping for a cup of coffee and waiting for the rest of the world to get going. I happened by Antonio's sail shop. Daniel, one of the sail-makers, was there and said the roller furling was not in but that it was supposed to be part of the afternoon delivery. No, he didn't have any tracking information to confirm anything. "Should be here this afternoon," he said.

Tony came by and took me into town to get the broken hatch fixed and also pick up a pump that Brian wanted me to get. What a pleasure it was, driving around this beautiful southern Spanish town and acting like a real European. Tony knew his way around, of course, so he drove here and there, stopping to do odd errands and say hello to the many local merchants he knew. I'll tell you, I could really get used to living in Estepona.

While Tony and I were waiting for the hatch repair, we decided to go have a cup of coffee. We went to a small, unpretentious café with wide open doors and seats inside and outside—as all cafés have in southern Spain. As is common among Spaniards, Tony had a *café con leche*; I had a *café Américano*. Both were very good and I paid one euro for the two of them. (I had been paying two euros for a single coffee for almost two weeks.) We talked about all sorts of things, as sailors do. Tony told me about Ceuta, Morocco, Malta and Turkey—all places he sailed to regularly. What an interesting boating playground.

Eventually the discussion centered on *Allegretta* and the planned route straight across to the Caribbean. Tony repeated all of the horrors he had described the previous day and also mentioned a captain named "John," who captained a large boat in the harbor.

"John is coming by my boat this afternoon," Tony said. "He tried that route once, and he can tell you exactly what his experience was. I'm telling you, you don't ever want to try to sail straight across. It's suicide!"

I told Tony that I would love to speak with John, but what I really needed was to have him speak with Brian. I admitted that I didn't think Brian would entertain such a confronting discussion, but it sure would fit the bill. Nevertheless, I made a plan to talk with John. I valued Tony's input, but I was hoping to get a corroborating opinion.

Back at the harbor, I stopped at the internet café before going back to *Allegretta*. I was hoping for an answer from Hank regarding the route issue (It wasn't there.) and I wanted to call Lisa. I was able to get her on the phone, and oh, what a welcome relief it was just to hear her voice! I told her a bit about what was going on, though not too much. At the time, things could have gone either way: I might be home really early or really late. I didn't want her to worry or to have unrealistic expectations, so I kept the conversation as neutral as possible. Still, it was a welcome relief to share some of the load.

I also wanted to check the internet to see airline schedules and flight availability. I saw that I could fly home from Málaga more easily than from Gibraltar. It was a bit costly—one-way tickets generally are—but I had a way home.

I got back to the boat; Lucille was still sitting in the cockpit and we exchanged hello's as I was passing. Thinking it best, I then stopped and sat down and began a discussion about the route issue with her. I figured it was only fair to make her aware of the problem and all of its ramifications. I knew very well that within minutes I would be discussing the matter with Brian. I also knew how strongly I felt on the subject and the fact that Brian would probably *not* concede to my point of view. One thing did *not* happen when I spoke to Lucille in the cockpit: I did *not* ask her to confirm or deny that she and Brian had previously sailed the direct route to the Caribbean. Lucille had sailed with Brian on all of his prior Atlantic crossings, including the three east-to-west passages from Gibraltar to the Caribbean. If Brian had sailed the direct route—as he said he had—Lucille would have been present and could have told me about the experience. For some time I had been searching for somebody to corroborate or refute what Tony had been telling me; here was a perfect witness and I completely blew the opportunity. Damn! Mind you, one way or another Lucille could have said something on her own but this she did not do.

I went down below and gave Brian the hatch I was able to get fixed and the pump he needed. He was pleased— "just what I wanted," he said. We chatted briefly but cheerfully, me knowing full well the discussion we were to have forthwith—as well as its probable conclusion—he, apparently, unaware.

I let him continue with his chores and went to my cabin. I closed the door and packed fully so that, if necessary, I could leave in nary a second. Then, with my "escape" fully planned, I stood in front of the mirror and stared into my own eyes, asking myself if, indeed, I was doing the right thing. I took my time; it was an important decision. And I'd be lying if I said I didn't ask for some special guidance. "Let it go," came the answer, and I knew my path would be made clear.

"Brian," I said as I returned to the main cabin, "we need to talk again about the route. It's very important."

Well, he went ballistic, which was about what I expected. Again came the yelling, now accompanied by the odd insult. I kept calm. There was no reason for *me* to get excited. It ended with me stating that I couldn't sail under these conditions. Thinking it was simply a stand-off he would win, he said "Fine! Go then. Just go!"

I told him that was exactly what I was going to do. "It's not what I want," I said, "but I cannot sail what I think is an unsafe route, especially when a perfectly good one is right there next to it."

"Well, go then," he repeated. "I don't need you. Just go!"

So I got my bag and walked past him, then by Lucille—who was still in the cockpit—and then off the boat. Lucille rushed down and must have said something convincing: I was only about thirty feet away when Brian called me back. His whole demeanor was changed and he pleaded that I return. He needed me, he said, he had no other way. He said that when Pierre got there the next day, we would discuss the matter like gentlemen and come to a consensus.

Big change from a moment prior, I thought. Too big! I asked him if I had his word on this, that we would sail south if that was what the group voted.

"Hey, I'm not a bull-shitter," he said.

That really wasn't an answer to my question, and I took note of it. With his statement I also realized I had lost all trust for the man. I didn't believe he would honor what he had just agreed to, and even if we did have a "gentlemen's agreement" to sail south, I could see Brian changing his mind once we were at sea. In such a circumstance there would be nothing anybody could do. Just as Lucille had experienced in the storm before I arrived, I would be subject to all of Brian's decisions—good and bad. I could see us sailing inescapably into a series of never ending squalls with no way to escape. I could see the barrels of fuel being thrown around the deck and then the slippery mess of spilled diesel fuel afterwards. The voyage had "trouble" written all over it—not one thing had gone right since even before I had arrived.

167

Still, I felt an obligation to stay, at least for the time being. I sure as hell didn't want to. But Brian had agreed to my demand; what could I do? "Okay, I'll stay," I said, and put my bag back in my cabin.

I went for a walk. I needed a break from all of the drama aboard *Allegretta.* I needed to clear my mind. I found myself once again in the internet café, searching the web and finding plenty on what route *should* be taken but nothing on what could be expected if the *wrong* route was attempted. I made a couple of prints and then wandered back to the marina, speaking to Tony once again and eventually finding my way back to *Allegretta.*

Brian was still there (Lucille was not) and when he saw me he announced that, contrary to what he had promised me an hour before, he and he alone would decide the course to be sailed. "I will not be held hostage on my own boat," he stated firmly, pointing his finger into the air. "We will head out and sail whichever way the wind dictates. If that's straight across, that's what we'll sail. It's my boat; we'll do it my way."

I could see his point: It *was* his boat; *he* was the captain. He, not the crew, should, no, *must* make key decisions such as determining the sailing route.

"What about these?" I said, holding out the printed material I held.

"What the hell do you have there?" he asked.

"Uh, sailing recommendations?" I said. I didn't really mean any disrespect, but I knew where this was going, and indeed, I was toying with him.

"Sailing recommendations? Gimmie those," he said, grabbing them from my hands. Struggling at first, he ripped them in half and threw them on the floor. "That's what I think about your sailing recommendations!" he yelled, once again in full temper. "You want sailing recommendations? I will give you all the recommendations you need!"

"I can't sail with you, Brian," I stated.

"Fine!" he yelled.

"I'm sorry, I don't trust you anymore."

It was the truth. It really wasn't about the sailing course any longer, or the temper, the poor performance, the awkward controls for the mainsail, the fuel on deck, the shortage of crew, the time constraint, the excessive delay, the repairs. The truth of the matter was that I no longer trusted Brian's word. And with that, there was no way I could remain as crew.

"Trust? I haven't trusted you since the moment I met you! You don't trust me? I have *never* trusted you!" he yelled.

Well, that wasn't quite true. Brian and I had enjoyed a wonderful trusting relationship right along. I was his confidante, the one he could go to for sound suggestions, the best hand he had on board. Now, he was just throwing verbal stones, trying to do damage. It was time to go.

"Well, I guess I'll go," I said.

"Yes, go!" he agreed.

I grabbed my bag. (It was still packed.)

"Good bye," I said as I walked past.

"Good bye," he said, neither kindly nor unkindly. "Bless you," he added.

"Bless you too," I said. And I meant it. And then I left, and this time he didn't call after me.

Epilogue

Three months later I received an e-mail from Brian. It was pretty tongue-in-cheek. He said he had made it to the Caribbean without incident. I thanked him for re-connecting, wished him well, and apologized for leaving him. Then I let it go.

169

Chapter 5. The Voyage of *Tender II*

This voyage features Lisa. I've mentioned Lisa a few times: that best friend of mine, the one who stole my heart. Born about the same time as I was, but much better looking of course, Lisa inherited from both her minister father and teacher mother a loving and caring manner of being. Retired from her post as an elementary school principal, and the mother of two young adults, Lisa was part of a huge family with her mom and sister living near-by, and half a hundred aunts, uncles and cousins—each with their own offspring—living across the country.

We had gotten into the habit of spending quite a bit of time together, Lisa and me. We enjoyed several activities such as cycling and skiing, cooking for each other and going to shows. We shared core values concerning honesty and integrity, and also in regards to personal health and the careful treatment of others. We both loved to travel, that's for sure, and it was a rare month when at least one of us didn't have to be taken to the airport.

It was with our love of travel in mind, and with the idea that crewing on ocean-going sailboats provided excellent travel opportunities, that I signed Lisa up with Offshore Passage Opportunities (OPO), that crewing organization I belonged to. Ocean sailing is not for everybody, of course, but if Lisa were to catch the passion, I was thinking, she and I could travel to some of the most enviable locations in the world, and at a remarkably affordable cost. Excellent crewing positions for a man/woman team, while never the norm, are not uncommon. Couples often prefer another couple to help sail their boat. I had it in mind that Lisa and I could be that helping couple. It was a stretch, but if Lisa were to like sailing, and if she were to become proficient at it, the possibilities for us were without end.

Now, you must understand that Lisa didn't share with me that blinding "Sailor's Dream." On more than a few occasions, she had made it clear that she would certainly not be up to crossing an ocean. She had said that even doing an offshore passage far from land would not be to her liking. She also had very limited sailing experience, so if she were to participate on any voyage, some sort of learning process would have to be addressed.

My plan was to hook us up on a short and easy delivery. Perhaps somebody wanted to move their boat up the coast, in sight of land, maybe even stopping each night. Passages like these don't come up very often, but I figured one would come along eventually. We only needed one, I thought, and even if Lisa chose not to do it again, completing just the one passage would be an extraordinary experience for her. I talked with OPO owner Hank Schmitt a couple of times, and he said he'd help us get a suitable trip. I watched the OPO e-mails. We waited a year and a half.

On March 20, 2013 I received an e-mail request for crew from a licensed captain named Dale Cheek. Dale was

171

delivering a 44-foot catamaran, a boat from the fleet of a chartering company called "*Moorings*." *Moorings* wanted the boat moved from Tortola in the British Virgin Islands to Great Abaco Island in the Bahamas. Dale estimated that the offshore passage would take six days; he was looking for three or four crew to help him. The voyage was to begin on April 1, just 12 days after I received the initial e-mail.

A six-day offshore passage was more aggressive than what Lisa had said she would be willing to entertain. I didn't think she would go for it. The route would be an easy downwind run in the trade winds, however, and we would be sailing on a comfortable and spacious catamaran. It was a decent opportunity, I figured, one of the easier of passages.

In his note, Dale stated that in regards to crew, an attitude of attentiveness, enthusiasm and compatibility was more important than experience. That caught my attention. I discussed the idea with Lisa, and she both pleased and surprised me when she agreed that I should apply for the position. I wrote a letter to Dale, focusing on Lisa's attitude and highlighting my experience. I added in that we were both good cooks. The next day I received a return e-mail: "Enjoyed your note," Dale wrote. "You and Lisa seem fine. Welcome aboard."

It took a lot of courage for Lisa to accept this deal. Several friends of mine have told me they could never do the ocean sailing I so readily enjoy. "What if something were to happen?" they ask me. "You could get killed out there." Lisa wasn't without these concerns. She could have chosen the safe path. Who could blame her? She had heard my stories. She knew that things *do* happen when out at sea.

Actually, it's not as dangerous as some of my experiences would have you believe. Modern day sailboats are built to take the rigors of the ocean and they carry the water systems, navigational electronics, life-rafts, and satellite telephones to avoid, for the most part, the majority of calamities. Catastrophes are rare, and if the craft involved is seaworthy, and if proper principles of seamanship are followed, I believe ocean sailing is as safe as any adventure can be. That doesn't take away from the courage Lisa displayed: She bravely chose to go hundreds of miles offshore, sailing with strangers, on a conquest with which she had little experience. She also had to have trust in me—in my own sailing ability and in my ability to choose a voyage that reflected *her* needs and *her* level of experience. In the end, she understood the risks, and she assured herself that they were adequately managed. Like me, she calculated that the potential value of completing the voyage outweighed the risks.

We traveled to Tortola on Easter Sunday, March 31—a three-flight trip that is normally split over two days. Not wanting to ruin the whole holiday weekend, we began with a very early flight out of Toledo (rather than Detroit) and scheduled a too-short 35-minute plane-change—all in an effort to save a single day. It made for a hurried and stressful morning, and could have been disastrous had we or our luggage missed the second flight. A little bit of airport running got us on the problematic flight, however, and all of our problems were behind us as we and our luggage waited in the San Juan airport for our final flight to Tortola.

It was not a good day in the American Airlines terminal that afternoon: A flight or two had been cancelled and a couple of gates weren't functioning. Angry customers and frustrated airline attendants were interacting to facilitate the movement of people and the rescheduling of flights. We stood at our gate and observed the chaos. It wasn't *our* problem, and we were tired of worrying anyway. Across the way, I noticed a lean, bearded man with a round gold earring. He looked as if he could be a sailor. I approached the man, and as I suspected he turned out to be our captain Dale Cheek.

Dale smiled easily as he shook my hand first, and then Lisa's as I introduced her. Slim and not tall, he was not a big person, and his mannerisms immediately foretold of a relaxed, unstressed nature. He spoke quietly and friendly, asking a few questions, just enough to demonstrate a genuine interest in his new friends and sailing partners. We watched and waited as the chaos continued around us. Our plane was a full ninety minutes late—I believe I mentioned American Airlines was having a bad day—but I couldn't have cared less: We had our luggage. We were on the plane to Tortola. We had even found our captain.

The small propeller plane bucked and rolled as it flew into the wind on our flight from San Juan to Tortola. Lisa and I had our noses to the window as we flew over El Yunque rain forest, the same one we had hiked a year and a half earlier. Leaving Puerto Rico behind, the plane flew over St. Thomas and St. John, two islands I had visited while on *C'est si Bon*. I could see St. Croix off in the distant south and also several of the British Virgin Islands as we approached the large island of Tortola. As we landed, the captain announced that ours was the last American Airlines flight to Tortola after fifty years of service. The customers all applauded. They too, it seemed, were unconcerned with the lateness of the flight.

Though Dale's flight schedule was less complicated than ours—he had to change planes only once, in San Juan—his singular piece of luggage didn't make it to Tortola. He reported to the baggage control desk where he and a dozen other disappointed customers spent about an hour filling out forms and giving delivery instructions to the less than enthusiastic attendants. I've heard it said that you can learn a lot about a person by the manner in which he reacts when his luggage is lost. The bag Dale was missing contained important equipment for the voyage—valued at about $2500—and though it was critical that he get the bag and get it without delay, he never lost his cool and always spoke in a manner that improved, not reduced, his chances of getting his luggage.

With the baggage recovery forms all completed, but with no idea of where Dale's lost bag might be, we finally left the airport and hopped into a taxi. A half hour later, just as

174

the sun was setting, we arrived at Moorings Marina where the boat was located. We approached the reception desk and Dale stated who we were and what purpose we had. The boat wasn't quite ready, we were told, and there were two people already on it. (We were expecting two more crew but they weren't scheduled to arrive until the next day.) "That's very interesting," Dale said in his constantly positive manner. "Let's go find out who they are."

We started out on a rather lengthy hike across the marina with the attendant leading the way. Dale followed behind him with his small carry-on bag; Lisa and I brought up the rear with our larger duffle bags. Half-way to the boat, we heard a "Hey Dale!" from one of the bars that surrounded the marina. It was Alex Hopkinson and Lewis Turner, the two other crew members, and the two people who had already been on the boat. With the mystery solved, we let the marina attendant go and joined Alex and Lewis at their table to get to know one another and to have a bite to eat.

All OPO voyages have the dialogue that was about to follow, one that involves a group of sailors sitting down and trying to size each other up for the first time. It's never a boring conversation. Typically nobody in the group will know anybody else, and in only a day or two the whole group will be sailing the high seas, fully dependent upon each other. Perhaps you can recall similar gatherings from previous voyages: me having a beer with Ian Glass before the *C'est si Bon* voyage; sitting in the cockpit when I met Dan Bower and the others on *Skyelark*; meeting the crew from *That Darn Cat* at the airport in Madrid. So much is identified in these initial discussions as egos are displayed and personalities are exposed. I determined long ago that it was best to be much more of a listener than a talker. Bragging is a real no-no. Invariably I would be asked to describe myself and my prior sailing experiences; I always endeavored to find the difficult balance between false humility and being too self-serving. Many of the OPO sailors I met over the years had lived colorful lives and traveled the world.

Listening to the tales of these folks could be a tremendous pleasure if the story-teller possessed sufficient style and grace. Some sailors were not so well-equipped, at least socially, and hearing their yarns was never nearly as pleasurable. Still others wouldn't shut up, or so it seemed. It takes all kinds to fill a boat.

Our conversation in Tortola started off pleasant enough as we each took turns saying a thing or two about ourselves. Alex and Lewis, they said, were two real estate agents from Scottsdale, Arizona—fairly successful at it, it seemed to me. They were both married—Alex with younger kids, Lewis with those who are now adults. Both of them were also airplane pilots, passionate Republicans, and gun carriers. Alex, the taller of the two, and at 62 the older, described his somewhat extensive sailing experience and the fact that he had acted as captain on a passage or two. Lewis, one of those enjoyable humble but confident folks, stated that this was *only* his fourth offshore passage, not understanding that he was already in the "above average" category.

Somehow the conversation switched to the topic of gun control, which happened to be a popular but polarizing topic of discussion among Americans at the time. (Several horrific mass shootings of innocents had recently occurred in the US, and the government was considering changing laws regarding the Right to Bear Arms, something very dear to the hearts of our two Arizonans.) It was an odd topic, I thought, given the audience and the circumstances. And though I would not prefer the topic in any event, the conversation exposed several fundamental elements regarding the beliefs and personalities of each person involved:

Alex, who seemed to favor the subject, provided a plethora of statistics, proving, he said, that providing guns to the masses would reduce crime. "No one in my neighborhood would ever harass a stranger," he said, "because they know most people are armed." He continued

176

for quite a while, citing facts, figures—even real-life examples—and though I don't think I could ever agree with his conclusions, I saw that he was clear, logical thinker, armed with adequate, if unverifiable, information. He also revealed a sort of arrogant nature, and a propensity to bully other people with his opinions.

Lewis made points that agreed with Alex, but in a much less abrasive manner. He would listen and respond to counter-points, seeing their truthful aspects, then voice his personal conclusions in a conciliatory manner. It was not so much the value or disvalue of gun control I learned from Lewis—though I did learn much—it was the compliancy in his personality of which I was becoming aware. He exhibited a kindness, a relaxed confidence that was not masked by a nervous ego.

Dale's comments were equally telling. He took no sides, and mostly just listened, but when he spoke, he explained the reasons people felt the way they did. "It's the western culture," he said to explain why people like Alex and Lewis would both carry guns. "It's like chewing tobacco or driving fast cars. You can't say it's right; you can't say is wrong. It's just a part of people's culture and it ain't gonna change." In speaking this way, Dale improved understanding among those with conflicting opinions. It was a way of reducing polarization. As he did in the airport, he improved, not reduced, the chances of success.

Lisa, *not* a republican and *not* a gun toting redneck, couldn't help but state her take on the matter. I happened to agree with Lisa's viewpoint, and I think she went to an appropriate level in stating her opinion, but I felt a sense of despair as I saw Alex become more and more fervent as Lisa stated her views that didn't align with his. She stated her point—as she should have—but she might as well have talked to the wind.

As for me, for what it's worth, I didn't give a rat's ass about gun control but I wanted to solve the problem—not the problem of gun control, but the problem of *discussing* gun control. "Okay," I said when everybody happened to be inhaling at the same time, "One thing we're *not* going to do is have a six day conversation on gun control. For heaven's sake, let's change the subject!"

And this we did. We talked about Lisa's retirement, about her recent trip to India, about the ranch with a hundred horses that Alex's wife managed, about the young daughter of Lewis's girlfriend he had been raising as his own, and about how Dale was living on a boat on St. Thomas in 1989, precisely the same time when I sailed there on *C'est si Bon*. We never did talk about guns again, and after not too many beers, we finished up our discussions and decided to make our way to the boat. Alex and Lewis had already been to it, so they became our guides.

Our new home was a Leopard-44 catamaran called the *Tender II*. Built in South Africa, specifically to *Moorings* specifications, the Leopard-44 was designed with the needs of chartering customers in mind. Central air conditioning, unheard of on real offshore boats, would be a top priority and a "must-have" on all *Moorings* catamarans including the Leopard-44. Customer demand would also necessitate an oversized refrigerator and freezer, a microwave, stereo, movie player, and even an inflatable dinghy with a gasoline engine. Being large and costly to charter, our 44-footer would typically be rented by several people, each demanding the comfort of a private cabin. To meet this need, *Tender II* had four equally sized cabins, each with its own bathroom (head) and shower, windows (ports), closets and storage lockers. The customer oriented design continued with the deck of the craft, which was raised a foot or two more than normal in an effort to provide six feet of interior headroom in as many areas as possible. Furthermore, a shortened mast was mounted, making for smaller sails—easily managed by the typical chartering customer.

These luxuries for the short-distance charterer would often conflict with the desires of an offshore sailor. For example, we all loved the four cabins, but the motion and noise experienced at sea in the two forward ones made sleeping in them difficult. And though we were impressed with the huge horizontally loading refrigerator and freezer, out at sea we could have better used a vertically loading pair instead. The air conditioning, nice in port, was of no use at sea; ditto for the microwave and movie player. The raised deck—so ghastly it gave rise to the term "Tupperware Boat"—increased our resistance to the wind, and the shortened mast and sails lacked sufficient power. The helm pulpit (cramped with all lines leading to it and featuring a super-hard seat) was clearly designed to leave more room for sun-tanning while at anchor rather than sailing at sea. The dinghy was a particular irritant: Not only did it obstruct our movements and vision on the aft deck, its gasoline engine and tank created a significant explosion hazard. Mounted in its davits, it also covered our stern light, making us invisible to other boats at night. The boat had no navigation station, and though one would be more of a convenience than a necessity, I had never seen an ocean-going boat without one. *Tender II* had no water desalination system, a feature on a boat that I had learned to enjoy, and we would have to be very careful with our water consumption. Additionally, the boat had no radar, no weather forecasting system (GRIBS), and no AIS system to alert us of oncoming ships. Of major concern, the boat had no emergency beacon system (EPIRB) and no satellite telephone. Fortunately, Dale had each of these required items—assuming his luggage was delivered.

Tender II (Oh, what an irritating name for a boat!) was designed by a charter company for charter customers. Important to us was that the boat was built structurally strong enough to withstand the rigors of the ocean (It was, Dale assured us.), and that it held sufficient water (200 gallons), fuel (150 gallons), propane (two tanks), and food storage (recall the huge refrigerator and freezer) for five sailors on a six day voyage. The boat *did* have a life-raft, some man-overboard recovery gear, and a GPS with a chart plotter at the helm station. It also had an adequate set of sails, a well-enough equipped kitchen, and sufficient sheets and blankets for all of us. "This'll do," I thought. "Not the most complete boat I've ever seen, but it'll do."

Moorings is a huge boat chartering company with over 20 locations worldwide. Individual investors buy a percentage interest in a yacht and *Moorings* charters out the boats, maintaining them in top condition and managing every aspect about the boat and its chartering business. For their financial trouble, investors get to use the boat a few weeks each year (and they can use any comparable boat worldwide) and after five years the yacht is theirs. Typically, an investor will sell the boat at that time, and judging by the repeat business it's a money-making venture for all concerned.

In several locations the charter fleet is large enough that it becomes feasible for *Moorings* to build their own marina. The Moorings Marina on Tortola was an example of this, and it was the most luxurious and accommodating marina I had ever seen. The reason the marina was so luxurious is simple: *Moorings* would rather have customers hang around the marina, with their boats securely tied up at their reliable docks, spending money at the several bars and restaurants surrounding the marina (all of which are leased out by *Moorings*), than to have these same customers take their boats and their money elsewhere. It works out for the customer as well: They can go out for a day's sail in the beautiful British Virgin Islands and afterwards enjoy free and secure dockage for the night. The kids play in the pool; the parents enjoy the outdoor bar (in view of the kids); everybody is relaxed and happy. *Moorings* understands this business model well. There's no arguing with success.

Lisa's smile said it all when we were shown our cabin, the one forward and on the starboard side. The bed was roomy, even for two people, and the private bath relieved a lot of concerns of unpleasantness she may have had. I opened up all of the windows and we spread out the sheets, blankets and pillows to make up the bed. Lisa was pleased—not only with our wonderful cabin, but also with the boat as a whole and the rest of the crew and captain. She really didn't know what to expect and she had put all her trust in me. We closed the cabin door to give ourselves the privacy we desired, took our showers, brushed our teeth, and went to bed. It had been a long day. We both fell asleep easily. At some time in the wee hours of the morning, Lisa awakened me. Though we were at dock and the motion of the boat was minimal, she felt nauseous. I applied a *Transderm-V* patch behind her ear. I had dispensed these patches many times. They had always done a great job in relieving motion sickness. I had never seen them not work.

We woke up the next morning to the smell of coffee and the sound of Dale talking on his cell phone. He was trying to determine the location of his missing luggage and wasn't having much luck. Again, his attitude and actions wrote volumes as to how Dale would react in a trying situation. He never lost his cool and he always had a specific area of focus. His bag, American Airlines told him, could have been in Miami, San Juan or Tortola; they didn't know which. This type of inadequacy would have driven me nuts, but Dale kept his calm and focused his efforts on identifying next steps and getting a contact telephone number. He had obviously been in this situation before.

I suppose it's unfair to fault American Airlines with this failure: I'm sure other companies perform poorly as well. Still, "you do the crime, you do the time," and it was appalling that, in a day of advanced computer systems, American Airlines couldn't even tell Dale the location of his bag, let alone deliver it. He was on the phone for over an hour, talking to personnel from all three airports. In the end he was no further off than when he started. The bag contained not only Dale's clothes and foul weather gear, but also a fair amount of emergency gear and the charts of our destination in the Bahamas. We couldn't leave until we got that bag, and with their performance thus far, and the fact that American Airlines no longer had flights to Tortola, I found it difficult to believe we wouldn't be delayed.

Other than the coffee Alex had thought to bring, we had no breakfast foods aboard. So, with Dale's telephone efforts completed, at least for the time being, we loaded ourselves in the dinghy and motored over to a restaurant, the same one we had visited the night before. It was still mid-morning but the ample sun and cloudless sky provided splendid conditions. After again sitting down at a cozy outdoor table, we soon forgot our baggage woes, focusing instead on the enjoyment of a wonderful breakfast. A black waiter (every working person we saw on Tortola was black) with a name-tag that said "Popeye," but whose name was really Leo, brought us some coffee, a few expensive bottles of water (there were no free *glasses* of water), and after a while, the breakfasts we had chosen. The meals were good, though not terrific, and about double the price I would expect back home. It was a mark-up we were to experience everywhere we went throughout the voyage and afterwards.

After breakfast Dale announced that we needed to go to town to clear Customs and get provisions. We returned to the boat to drop off the dinghy and pick up our passports, then set off on foot for the business district of the island, located on the far side of the harbor. We stopped at a store called "*Pussers*," a delightful place with all sorts of Caribbean fare: art, jewelry, seashells, clothing an islander might wear, and several different kinds of rum. Lisa had found that the *Transderm-V* gave her a headache, so here at *Pussers* she bought a pair of those wrist-bands that claim to cure sea-sickness by some sort of pressure-point method—said so right on the box. It all seemed pretty fishy to me, but I had never seen them in action. If they worked—even if by a placebo effect—that would be fine enough for me.

We left *Pussers* and went over to the customs building, located in a bustling area next to a system of ferry docks. A hundred people, perhaps more, surrounded the building and I figured we were in for a long wait for sure. Surprisingly, inside the building there was no line at the customs clearance window, and though the customs officer seemed as puffed up and pompous as could be, our passports were quickly stamped and Dale paid the very cheap eight dollar clearance fee. Thinking prematurely that we were lucky enough to avoid any prolonged delay, we were instructed to proceed to the immigration office across the street where, indeed, an exceedingly long line awaited us. Outside of the customs office, however, Dale looked at the boat's clearance papers and said, "Well, I got all that *I* need," and we proceeded to the grocery store, never giving Customs or Immigration any further thought whatsoever.

Whenever accomplished as a group effort, provisioning a boat for a voyage will always be a haphazard, unpredictable process. We all have different food preferences, and few of us will ever know the priority foods that *must* go on a boat to feed half a dozen sailors for half a dozen days. As always, the captain is in charge, but this is certainly one area in which I don't envy such a responsibility. We grabbed a few grocery carts, and the five of us—five personalities, egos and appetites—began picking out the meat, chicken, pasta, rice, bread, apples, oranges, tomatoes, avocados, carrots, broccoli, peanut butter, olive oil, cereal, milk, tea and coffee we thought we might need. Alex and Lewis preferred Perrier water with lemon and they picked up two cases of the stuff and over a dozen lemons. I wanted carrots, so I picked up two bags, not knowing that somebody else had grabbed a couple more. Between all of us, we picked up about ten packages of sandwich meats, thinking we needed plenty for our lunches. Dale watched these excesses continue but said very little. He questioned the odd purchasing decision, but Dale never did spend a whole lot of time on small matters. He had probably been through this process so many times that he knew it would be easiest to just let it roll.

And let it roll he did, but in about an hour we were done. The bill was $550—not bad for five people for six days—and with a swipe of Dale's credit card, "provisioning" was complete. We loaded our wares into a taxi, and by noon we had packed away everything on the boat. Dale's phone rang. His bag was at the Tortola airport.

Lisa and I decided to take a nap, one of the favorite pastimes we retirees like to do. Both of us were pleased with how the adventure was going thus far, and we were excited about the passage that was about to begin. Only a week before, Lisa had returned from a three-week vacation to India, and she was starting to realize how action-packed retirement could be. We held hands and talked about the happy lives we were sharing. As a *Bon Voyage* surprise, I had bought her a Lorimar necklace I saw her eyeing at *Pussers*; she was admiring it as we talked about ourselves and our future. She was very happy. I was too.

After our nap, we got up and had lunch with the gang, again at the same restaurant, again served by "Popeye." Dale's bag was delivered at 3:30. We had a group drink— Lisa and I with our "Arnold Palmers"—and we all gave one another our best wishes for a safe journey. At 4:40 PM, April 1—April Fool's Day—we left Tortola, bound for Great Abaco Island 862 miles away.

The spring trade wind was blowing its normal 20 knots when we took off, and it was coming from just south of east, blowing exactly toward our destination. Out of the harbor, Dale turned *Tender II* into the wind so that the rest of us could put up the mainsail. "Leave one reef in it," he yelled out. It was a wise decision, I thought, considering the 20-knot wind, the approaching darkness of night, and the untested crew. We got the sail up without too much trouble, although in my overzealous efforts I found myself standing on the coach-roof, potentially being swept overboard by the boom. A few firmly spoken words of re-instruction by the captain reminded me to get my priorities in order.

With the main up, and everybody away from the swing of the boom, we turned the boat downwind and headed west. Alex unfurled the genoa and we continued along the south shore of Tortola until we approached the beautiful island of St. John—it being quite close to Tortola—then we jibed over to starboard and headed northwest, just a bit north of our target, Abaco.

"Will we see Puerto Rico?" I asked Dale.

"No, Puerto Rico is probably ninety miles west," he answered. "We might see the glow from its lights, but we won't see land." We stared out at the four-foot waves that *Tender II* was slicing through without effort. The beauty of the sea and its brilliant blue captivated me as it always does. "Should have sweet winds tonight," Dale said after a while. The sun set and soon all we could see were the lights that spotted St. Thomas. It would be our last sight of land for several days.

After a while, Dale announced that he would be taking the first watch. Each person would take a watch by himself or herself, he explained, though I suggested to him that with Lisa's experience, it probably wouldn't be prudent that she take a watch alone. Everybody agreed with this (Thanks guys!) and we set up a schedule of four watches, each of three hours duration. Dale would take the first watch from 4:00 to 7:00, Alex next from 7 to 10, then me from 10 to 1, and finally Lewis from 1:00 to 4:00. This watch schedule gave each person two watches per day—one during the day, one at night—and allowed each of us to have nine hours of rest after three hours of work. It also gave each person the same hours of watch AM and PM, day after day.

Lisa and I made dinner that first night out. Back on shore each of the crew had eaten a large high-protein lunch, so a simple dinner of boiled pasta with tomato sauce accompanied by a salad was approved by all. I set about cooking the pasta while Lisa got busy cutting up vegetables and making the salad. The seas at the time were three or

185

four-footers and though *Tender II* bucked and rolled, the motion didn't seem to bother Lisa. She was wearing her wrist bands but not a *Transderm-V* patch; I wasn't arguing with the success we were experiencing. It was the beginning of her first offshore passage and I was happy to see her enjoying it. Lewis offered to clean up the dishes, and Lisa and I sat down on the aft deck to watch the sunset.

"I don't feel so good," she said after a while. It really wasn't what I was hoping to hear.

I put a patch behind her ear and we spent an hour or so looking at the horizon, looking aft, looking sideways, walking, lying down—all of the things one can do to combat the feelings of seasickness. Her stomach settled down for a while, but then she said, "I might get sick."

"It's okay if you do," I said. "We'll just go over to the side of the boat, and I can hold you to keep you safe."

"I'm not going to the edge of the boat," she said, almost yelling. "There's no way!"

"Don't worry," I assured her. "Everything will be okay. Try to relax."

I had witnessed this situation before. It's not pretty, but it's not the end of the world. I was wishing I had put the patch on earlier, but I wasn't too worried. They had always worked. We just needed to bide our time until it kicked in.

"It might be sooner rather than later," Lisa said, and with that I saw a pained look of disbelief and embarrassment in her face. It surely wasn't her wish to get sick on the first night of her first offshore voyage, but the facial expression came from the realization that getting sick was exactly what she was going to do, and indeed it was to happen sooner, not later.

"Please come to the side of the boat," I pleaded. "Please, please come to the side of the boat," I repeated as if begging a second time would make a difference.

It wasn't bad. She's a small eater. A quick slosh of a bucket of seawater and the mess was gone. She moved to one of the aft deck's seating surfaces and sat silently as her stomach and her mind relaxed. We remained there for an hour or so, gazing out at the sea. The lower limb of the quarter moon peaked over the horizon, its magic creating a distraction for an upset stomach. Lisa and I had often enjoyed watching the moon together; I was especially grateful for its appearance that night.

Shortly before my watch, I thought I would lie down in my bunk for a short rest. Feeling better but not whole, Lisa thought she would retire as well. I told her that going inside normally increased the nausea of seasickness, but she correctly argued that she couldn't stay outside the whole voyage. As a pleasant surprise, we learned that lying down in bed reduced her symptoms.

I was up at ten for my watch, barely on time. Lisa came up on deck with me and lay down on a bench seat in the aft salon. I brought her a blanket and a pillow and sat with her off and on during my watch, the auto-pilot doing its job most adequately. It wasn't the most fun time we had ever experienced but it was a wonderful time of intimacy and sharing. It was our first night at sea. I wouldn't give it back for anything.

Shortly before 1:00, Lewis appeared ready for watch. I handed him the helm and gathered up Lisa as we headed down to our cabin. I tried to warn her to get into bed as quickly as possible but between brushing her teeth, combing her hair, and all of the other routines a woman must do when going to bed, it seemed to take forever before she was ready. All was well however, and though she was a bit queasy, she fell asleep and was comfortable enough for the night.

The morning sun brought a new day, and at about 7:30 I got up, again to the smell of coffee, a routine that was to be repeated each day. We had included in our provisioning several boxes of cereal in numerous varieties, and being my favorite, I chose Raisin Brand and followed it up with a cup or two of coffee. Lisa got up shortly, still feeling queasy, and carrying around with her a small plastic

187

bathroom trash pail "just in case." We sat quietly in the aft salon, she trying to relax her testy stomach, both of us enjoying the gorgeous ocean on what turned out to be a pleasant and sunny spring day. Since the dinner of the previous evening was not the most substantial, and since she had lost it anyway, Lisa was hungry for breakfast. She ate just a couple of saltine crackers with a half of a cup of water, but a minute later her stomach voiced its objection and I was handed a used "just in case" pail, which I quickly refreshed with a couple of rinses of seawater. It was the second time for Lisa—and the last, thank God—and though I changed her *Transderm-V* patch, it would be a couple of days before her stomach settled down and she could enjoy her time without being nauseous.

At 10:00 it was time for my morning watch. I put on some sunscreen and my life harness, and checked the GPS and chart for obstructions that I might see over the next three hours. I then stepped up to the helm station to relieve Alex. "My watch, bud," I said with enthusiasm.

Now, a bit of a dance occurs at the change of watches. Officially, or so I'm led to understand, the person coming off watch is supposed to state the ship's course and the one going on watch is supposed to repeat it. In reality such a formal transfer is rarely completed, but indeed some identification of the course must be made. In addition, if another boat is approaching or if something else of atypical nature is occurring, it would only be prudent for this information to be passed from one watch to the other. Nothing else is required, however, and generally after sailors have become used to one another, very little is communicated as one replaces another at the change of watch.

Often enough, however, and especially when one's ego is in need of inflating, the person coming off watch will take this opportunity to instruct his replacement on basic sailing practices. Although this type of instruction is rarely required (and never appreciated, I would think) it is incredible how often I have had to patiently wait in silence while another sailor took this opportunity to tell me about his *profound* knowledge about some sailing basic, something apparently only said sailor had the ability to understand. On this particular morning, Alex found it necessary to tell me the proper method to keep a lookout.

"You don't just scan the horizon in one continuous movement," he said. "You first look here, then here, then here," he showed me as he pointed out various intervals of a circular sweep. "You won't always pick up ships if you just scan around the boat non-stop."

Hmmmm... He was probably right; I really don't know. Alex was a serious student in all he did. I imagine that somewhere in his airplane piloting studies, or in his efforts to acquire a boating captain's license, or perhaps in his casual reading, he learned of this comprehensive method of keeping a look-out that, indeed, is superior to all other methods. Still, in all my travels I had never heard such a suggestion or anything like it. "Watch for boats!" That's all there is to it. It surprised me that he would think he should instruct me on such a basic responsibility. It wasn't a big deal, this presumptuous practice of his, but I felt as if he were treating me like a child. "Let it pass," I told myself. And it did.

Looking back at our noon-time positions—sailors always record noon-time positions—it can be seen that at about this time we were crossing the north latitude of 20 degrees. Still in the tropics by a couple hundred miles, the 20th parallel is considered the boundary for the trade winds. This doesn't mean that the wind suddenly dies as you cross the imaginary line in the sea, but it does mean that as you continue to travel north of it, the strong and steady easterly winds will decrease in strength and will become variable in direction. The previous night we had seen the winds decrease from 20 to 15 knots, which I was hoping was only a normal decrease often seen at night. The stronger wind failed to return in the morning, however, and as my watch

189

continued, the wind speed fell a bit more. We were entering the Horse Latitudes, that area of light wind that had given me so much trouble on the voyage on *C'est si Bon*. Unlike *C'est si Bon*, however, *Tender II* had a good supply of fuel, paid for by the chartering company. By the end of my watch Dale had started up both of the catamaran's engines and we motor-sailed along at eight knots. I passed the helm over to Lewis at 1:00. "290 degrees," I said, identifying the compass course. I didn't bother giving him any instruction on how to properly watch for boats.

Alex, Lewis and Dale had each brought fishing gear with them on the voyage. Lewis simply brought a lure and a reel with some line, and he used this without a fishing pole. He used a worm-gear clamp to attach the reel to the stern pulpit and had been trolling the lure all day. "You'd better hope for a small fish," I joked at him. "You'd have one hell of a time getting a big fish in." It didn't matter: no fish ever went after his lure.

Dale brought along a large plastic spool called a "Cuban yo-yo." He trolled a lure as well, tying the yo-yo securely to a stanchion and stringing the fishing line across the aft deck. Dale never caught a fish either, but that line caught *me* at least a dozen times. Over time I learned to anticipate the line before walking into it (you couldn't see the clear line), but I never thought that running a fishing line across a walkway was a particularly wise idea.

Alex had a wonderful rig: a top-drawer offshore fishing rod and reel that detached into small sections that could be easily packed for travel. At times I had considered buying fishing gear to take offshore, and this was the type of rig I had always visualized. Alex took the man-overboard flagpole out of its holster and used the holster to hold the fishing rod—which no doubt illustrated we had our priorities mixed up—and he trolled a line along with his other fishing mates.

The lure Alex used was a ferocious looking monster. About twelve inches in length, it had a three-inch cylinder shaped "head," bright lime green in color, with two large, black "eyes" that pivoted in a clear plastic encasement, making it appear as if the lure was always looking directly at you. I don't know if eye-to-eye contact is a factor among fish, but the lure was surely designed with this mental phenomenon in mind. Behind the head trailed several strands of plastic, giving the lure the appearance of a bright green squid. Hidden within these plastic strands was a menacing four-inch hook with a huge barb. It was the nastiest looking lure that I had ever seen. God help the fish that tried to mess with that lure. God help the person who tried to land the fish that did.

Said fish struck that evening as we were finishing dinner. The reel on Alex's rod came to life with its characteristic whirling sound. Dale's yell of "fish on!" had everybody scrambling to the aft deck, leaving the outdoor dinner table with plates, bowls and cutlery waiting to be thrown about by the next jolt of the boat. Alex grabbed the rod, cursed at the man-overboard gear he had left un-stowed, and began the process of fighting the fish and reeling it in to the boat's stern. Everybody worked to support the effort, be that stowing the man-overboard gear, pulling in the other fishing lines, putting the dishes in the sink, or pulling back the engine throttles to reduce the boat's speed. I recalled how on *That Darn Cat* it normally took half an hour to bring in a fish, but it had been only a few minutes when Alex announced that the fish was getting tired. Before long he had the beast closing in on the boat. "A spearfish," Dale called out, recognizing the species. Lewis brought out a sharpened gaff (I would never have guessed we had a gaff aboard) which he pierced into the animal's side. Then, with Alex controlling the head and Lewis heaving on the middle, the two Arizonans brought the fish up on the aft deck.

I had never seen such a mean fish. His pointed snout—the "spear"—was fourteen inches long, and as was his custom all his life, he swiped it back and forth, trying to do damage any way he could. From above, the long narrow fish appeared jet black like ink, the blackness interrupted by two menacing evil eyes and a pointed head that narrowed into the spear. He looked not so much like a fish out of water, gasping his last breath, but like a pissed-off monster who had been woken up in a bad mood. He was certainly not giving up the fight, and as his entire seven-foot length flopped about, his nasal weapon sliced back and forth, threatening to cut our bare ankles to the bone.

Alex knew what to do: "Hand me a winch handle," he yelled out, and when he had one in hand, he landed several thorough blows to the animal's head. The fish thus subdued, Dale used his pocket-knife to stab the fish closely behind the head and cut the spinal cord.

We took a few pictures, of course. Alex held the fish up and the tail dragged on the deck as the spear of the fish reached well above Alex's 6-foot height. A proper fish fileting knife appeared and Alex fileted the fish like an expert. (Where a boy from Arizona developed such a fish fileting skill is something I will never understand.) The choice cutlets we harvested filled two large salad bowls. We probably had twenty or thirty pounds of fish.

So with the fish safely put away and its blood and guts all cleaned up, Alex took the helm for his nighttime watch. Life aboard became peaceful once again and another beautiful night presented itself. Lisa and I sat in the outer salon, gazing at the horizon where the recently set sun still illuminated a few cumulus clouds. The wind and sea had both settled down and we motored along with the sails all stowed.

Our daily routines, enabled by the consistency of our watch schedule and fortified by the stability of sailing in the trades, became unbreakable customs of living. Dinner was served at 6:00 each night, for example, and after the dishes were all put away, Lisa and I would sit on the aft deck, sipping our tea and watching the sun until it was fully replaced by darkness. Tea and sun gone, we would retire to our cabin for an hour's rest, and rise shortly before ten o'clock to replace Alex at the helm. Our course was always northwest, 290 degrees or so, and *Tender II* generally took care of herself, steered adequately by the auto-pilot. Dale always awoke at midnight—so consistently, he must have set an alarm to do so—to check the watch (me) and the conditions, returning to bed only after he was satisfied the boat was humming along in good hands. Lewis, always fifteen minutes early, would be ready to stand watch at 12:45. Then, as the very best routine of them all, I would snuggle up next to Lisa and be rocked to sleep by the lullaby of the sea.

As the days came and went, the passage on *Tender II* became all that I had imagined when I first proposed the idea of the voyage to Lisa. Each morning the sun would light up the sea and she and I would spend hours staring at the ocean, trying to identify the color of blue it had become, be that sapphire, turquoise, light sky-blue or dark royal. Golden strands of Sargasso Weed would often surround us—we were in the Sargasso Sea—and we speculated *ad nauseam* about its origins, its utility in nature, and the numerous crabs and crustaceans that call this floating habitat their home. The wind would come and go—always from the east—and we sailed our luxurious but clumsy Tupperware boat in whatever came our way. At times the wind became strong and the captain would call for a reef in the main-sail. At others it all but left us and he would give the command to start up an engine, sometimes both. It even rained a time or two and this helped settle the sea. Her nausea a thing of the past, Lisa took to helping out in any way she could, taking an hour of Lew's watch from time to time, and doing way more than her share of work in the galley.

The consumption of meals added to the regularity of the passing days. Dale always had coffee perking in the morning and most of us ate cereal for breakfast, served with ultra-pasteurized boxed milk and supplemented with the frozen blueberries and strawberries we had aboard. Lunch was an informal, self-served affair. If you were hungry, several packages of deli meats for sandwiches awaited you in the refrigerator. There was also the reliable peanut butter and jam, several pieces of fruit of varying types, and generally some left-overs from the night before. Dinner was our biggest meal, and we always ate it as a group at the outdoor table in the aft salon.

We consumed fish in some manner or another each day for the rest of the voyage. On Wednesday, the day after we caught the fish, Alex baked up a huge amount for our evening meal. Lisa made up a salad and I cooked up some potatoes, and we all sat around the table, devouring a feast that resembled a family's Thanksgiving Day dinner. There was much mucking about and we joked and laughed, mostly at the expense of the unfortunate fish.

One day Alex made up some ceviche, a wonderful Spanish *tapa* made by submerging half-inch cubes of raw fish in lemon juice for several hours, "cooking" it thusly, and serving it afterward as a cold salad with onions, cilantro and avocado. *¡Que tapa fria!* Alex busied himself all morning with his culinary surprise and it was with childish anticipation that we convened at the aft-deck table in the mid-afternoon to stuff ourselves with delicious ceviche and some cut up fruits and vegetables. What a splendid afternoon "tea!" Not to be out-done, a couple of hours later Lewis extended the feast by pulling out some *filet mignon* steaks—brought all the way from Arizona and kept fresh using dry ice—and cooked them up on the boat's outdoor barbeque. It was a grand celebration indeed and I'll tell you this: there has never been a dinner on an offshore sailboat that would equal the one we had that afternoon on *Tender II.*

It was great to receive the hospitality of these two fellows from Arizona. It had taken a while to see the good side of Alex, but a good side he did have. During the middle days of the voyage, he seemed to be taking leave of his ego and had become pleasantly accepting. Lewis, who had always represented himself as a considerate and compliant

194

person, continued to be a joy to be around. His consistently humble nature, cordially displayed upon admitting that he had over-cooked the steaks, was a trait in his character I will always envy. (By the way, the steaks were done perfectly, and besides, what other volunteer crew has ever shown up for duty bringing *filet mignon* steaks for everybody aboard?) Later that night, as Lisa and I rested for my pre-watch nap, we agreed that we were very lucky to have such good people as Alex and Lewis—and a great captain, of course—along with us on this voyage. As we were talking, we noticed several times the lightning that was beginning to flash around us.

I got up shortly before 10:00 and reported for my watch. Alex was at the helm, it being the end of his. Dale was up as well, looking out at the sea and assessing the weather. "We've got a cold front coming in," he said. "Better be ready."

On *Tender II*, we didn't have the computerized weather forecasting system (GRIBS) that I had seen on *Skyelark* and *That Darn Cat*, nor did we have any communication with land-based weather forecasters, an increasingly popular method on boats with satellite phones. All we had were the lightning around us and the black line of clouds to the north. Indeed, these were sufficient. The wind had gone calm at the time, and with the sails furled we motored along on auto-pilot, running only one engine to conserve fuel. I went below and put on my light-weather rain-suit, strapping on my life-harness for good measure. I felt the cool north wind begin to blow just ten minutes after I had relieved Alex at the helm.

It wasn't a strong wind, at least not at first. Lightning continued to light up the sky, but no turbulence or squalls hit us. It *did* rain thoroughly and one wave came over the bow, though I don't know how: It wasn't that rough out. Even in this relaxed state, however, the large flat surface between the catamaran's hulls (the floor of the cabin) pounded into the waves, shaking the whole boat and

195

slowing its forward motion. As the watch continued, the wind got stronger and I had to turn on the second engine just to keep the boat moving. The seas were still not big but the pounding of the vessel and the noise it made became alarming. I started to wonder if our charter-boat designed for shore-based comfort was up to the punishment of the sea. I went down to check on Lisa and found that the motion and noise was even worse in the forward cabin, making it impossible for her to sleep. I moved her to the main cabin and there, at least, she was able to get some rest. By the end of the watch, the line of black clouds was behind us and the wind had settled down and clocked to the east. I left Lisa sleeping in the salon and found my way to the normal forward cabin. The motion had improved substantially, but occasionally a wave would still hit the underside of the catamaran with an incredible "bang." Finally, at about 8:00 I got up to see that no one had put on the coffee, that we were out of cereal, that the wind had returned to north-west (on the nose), and that threatening rain clouds surrounded us on all sides. Good morning Viet Nam.

What to do? Well, the coffee thing was easily rectified as I put a pot on the stove. Lisa, with her infinite wisdom, addressed the cereal issue with her suggestion, "let's have eggs!" The wind we couldn't do anything about, and the clouds repeatedly threatened us but we never did get a drop of rain all day. Ah, if only all of life's problems were resolved so easily.

Lisa's nausea, though diminishing day by day, never subsided completely. She always felt best in the mornings, and the nausea always came back to some degree in the evening. I imagine the *Transderm-V* patches helped, but the results we experienced with Lisa were the worst I had ever seen. We would never know the effect of the wrist bands, but they certainly didn't relieve the symptoms completely. Lisa's saving grace, contrary to what I had seen in a number of other people, was that she could lie down and this would reduce the symptoms.

196

This pattern continued on Saturday, our last full day at sea on *Tender II*. In the morning, though she had certainly not slept well the night before, Lisa got up feeling fine and in a happy mood. The eggs she had suggested she scrambled up with some ham and veggies, and after adding toast and coffee, she served a wonderful breakfast to us all. She helped me a bit during my day-time watch, helped with Lew's as well, and even did the dishes after dinner. I found it remarkable that she could be so helpful and cheery when the motion was as bad, or worse, than it had been for most of the trip. After she finished the dinner dishes, however, she mentioned that she wasn't feeling so well and she retired to the cabin.

That night, our last at sea, was an exaggeration of the night before. It began with the wind a point or two off the starboard bow, causing us to motor into the same chop, this time with a reefed main-sail up. At about 8:00 the wind veered more northerly, allowing us to turn off the engines and fly the genoa. I thought that reaching off the wind would alleviate the pounding, but the wind strengthened, and with us wanting to sail as high as possible into the wind, the pounding only got worse as the night progressed. As I began my watch at 10:00, I moved Lisa to the main cabin as I had done the previous night. I took the helm, trying my best to reduce the horrible motion. Dale came up to do his check and the two of us put another reef in the main and partially rolled up the genoa. This took some of the punch out of the rig but the pounding was still intense. Lewis came on at 1:00 looking pretty ragged; he had not been able to sleep at all. I went below and changed out of my foul weather gear. I was bushed. The pounding was horrible. Unlike the previous night, this time I elected to join Lisa and sleep in the main salon.

I slept like a rock. In spite of the motion, the noise, and the uncomfortable "couch" of the salon on which I slept, I quickly fell asleep and didn't stir until daylight woke me at 8:30. When I did finally open my eyes, I saw that Lisa, Lewis

197

and I were all sleeping in the main salon as if we were having a pajama party. The motion of the boat was minimal and the pounding had ceased altogether. I went up top and looked around the horizon. Land ho! Great Abaco Island appeared to the west, several miles away. Other islands appeared to the east; these were what had calmed the sea.

Alex was on watch and stood at the helm. He smiled proudly as he showed me our proximity to land. Dale was also up and "on duty," speaking to a Bahamian welcoming service on the radio. There were at least three passages into the protected waters of Abaco Basin and Marsh Harbour, each impeded by shallow reefs. Dale was trying to determine our best way in. "Take Dead Man's Pass in," suggested the announcer, which was all we needed to know. Dale staked out a series of waypoints on the chart-plotter, and he and Alex stood together on the steering platform, joking away like old friends as they guided *Tender II* on the way to her new home.

At 10:30, Sunday April 7, we landed. It had taken us 5 days, 18 hours to sail the 862 miles from Tortola. Two marina attendants helped us tie up the boat and one by one, each of us stepped off the boat to the more solid dock. Lisa mentioned that the world was still rocking as if she were still at sea. It was the first time she had ever experienced "land sickness."

We would have to clear Customs, of course, and though we all had to remain close-by until a customs officer came, Lisa and I set about meeting and speaking to our boating neighbors within ear-shot. We met an older couple from Ohio finishing up their winter-long sojourn to the Caribbean, for example, and also a family of four who had just arrived from Pennsylvania for a week's vacation. (They couldn't believe we had actually sailed "non-stop" from the Virgin Islands.) In the dock right next to us, too, we met Marvin, a Jewish millionaire from New York—he told us all of that in his first words to us—whose beautiful Tartan-40 featured a brand new mast. (The old one lay on the dock—

198

bent in half!) Meeting offshore sailors at an ocean stop-over is always fascinating. I recalled the fine folks I met in Bermuda and St. Thomas, and—my favorite—the Azores. For Lisa, she was meeting my beloved crowd for the first time. It was the end of her first offshore experience and I wanted her to enjoy it all. Part of that was to talk and share with other offshore sailors.

I would have liked to ask Lisa what thoughts she had regarding the voyage, though I held my tongue. If she really liked it, the opportunity of other sailing trips awaited us. If not, I was hoping she at least saw the value in the one-time experience. I knew that the hardships she experienced—the nausea, the pounding—would still be fresh in her mind, but I also knew that these would be forgotten over time. I hoped what remained would be the realization that together we had completed an incredible feat, one that only a few privileged people in this world can claim.

We spent the rest of Sunday on Grand Abaco Island walking as much as possible, Lisa and I eager to exercise our legs and take in new and interesting sights. Our internet research had told us that Marsh Harbour would be a wonderfully quaint town and we planned to stay a few days. It turned out to be dull and uninteresting, however, and the oppressive heat and the "cabin fever" we experienced while staying at the encapsulated Moorings Marina almost had us flying home immediately. Thankfully, Lewis introduced us to Elbow Cay, a seven mile island that *did* feature the gorgeous beaches and the quaint town we desired. Lucky for us too, Lisa and I were able to rent a cottage on Elbow Cay for a few days later in the week.

Back on *Tender II*, the entire crew cleaned up the boat and we all began to pack our gear. Monday night came soon enough and the five of us—the able captain and hard-working crew of *Tender* II—chatted away at the *Curly Cues Bar* as if we had been life-long friends. It had been only nine days prior that we had all met one another and were sizing up each other for the first time, talking about gun control.

199

Since then we had completed a wonderful adventure together—an adventure I will always remember with great favor. Here we were, however, saying our goodbyes, and with a good chance we would never see one another ever again.

Epilogue

Lisa and I enjoyed a most wonderful three-day stay on Elbow Cay. Our cottage, not fancy by any means, was right on the water—so much so that the sea came right under our porch at high tide. We sat on that porch for mindless hours, watching boats enter and exit the harbor. We saw dolphins, barracuda, and some sort of seal we never could identify. "Town" was a wonderfully quaint settlement called Hopetown. It was only a few blocks away and we walked there dozens of times for coffee, a sandwich, a dinner, or sometimes just for the walk itself. The beach was also only a short walk away and on this too, we found ourselves strolling two or three times every day, sometimes in complete privacy. We ran out of money—there were no ATM's on the island—but we didn't care. We meandered aimlessly, not knowing when we might leave and go home. We hitchhiked to the south end of the island and back, getting rides each way on the first golf cart that came by. Everywhere we went, we were greeted by a melodious "helloooo... how are youuuu..."

And when we at last felt like it, we booked a flight and started for home—well rested, overly tanned, and with Lisa's land-sickness almost but not quite gone.

"I didn't *love* it," she finally told me. "It was an incredible experience. I wouldn't give it back for the world. But I didn't *love* it."

I guess I got my answer.

Chapter 6. The Voyage of
Rhapsody in Blue

"She didn't love it." Everyone wanted to know how Lisa liked the voyage, and I always started the answer with: "She didn't love it." It was a joke. Most people were amused. I would then tell the story of the voyage—quick to point out Lisa's courage, careful when admitting to the sea-sickness, anxious to brag that we had caught a seven-foot fish. I would describe the clumsy boat, the gun-loving crew, the sapphire colored sea. Those still interested would hear about gorgeous Elbow Cay and quaint Hopetown that Lisa and I had found. I would tell them about the fantastic beaches we had discovered and about the matured closeness that had come our way. For me, though, what defined the voyage more than all else came in the statement, "I didn't love it." With those words, Lisa confirmed that she didn't share my passion for offshore sailing. Unlike me, she wasn't disillusioned by the Sailor's Dream. "I didn't love it," meant that I would do all future voyages without her. A part of the Sailor's Dream within me died with that statement.

It was the second time my sailor's dream—that fascination I have with sailboats—was significantly diminished. The first came with the purchase of *Wavelength* in 1990, the year after I had sold *C'est si Bon*. *Wavelength* was an old, worn down boat, one in need of a lot of work. I should never have bought it. *Wavelength* took away all desire to ever buy another boat. And boat ownership is a huge part of the Sailor's Dream.

And so, it was with this diminished passion that I returned home from the Bahamas and *Tender II*. Two weeks later, regardless of whatever passion I did or did not have, I was scheduled to begin another voyage, one I had arranged only a week prior to the voyage on *Tender II*.

In late March (2013) I had received via e-mail an OPO Request for Crew: Mark Gerhardt, owner of a 1973, 48-foot Hinckley yawl called *Rhapsody in Blue*, needed two people for crew to help move his boat from St. Maarten to Newport, Rhode Island. (St. *Maarten* is the Dutch portion of the island; St. *Martin* is the French side.) The passage would begin May 4. The e-mail said that the boat was "older but well-maintained and set-up for offshore passage-making." It said that Gerhardt had completed this trip every year since 2006 and that the passage usually took 10 days. Four people would be on board for the voyage, the e-mail continued, and the owner would pay all onboard expenses.

The fact that the yacht *Rhapsody in Blue* was a 48-foot mono-hull sailboat, and a yawl at that, perked my interest. Truth be told, I was getting a bit tired of catamarans. As comfortable as they can be, the motion of a catamaran always felt awkward and clumsy. A catamaran at sea moves with a random bucking motion, rocking and pitching in any and all directions from whatever undulation the sea brings. It's an irritating motion, and as Lisa and I saw on *Tender II*, it can become increasingly so when sailing (or motoring) upwind. In contrast, on a mono-hull boat the side-to-side rocking motion becomes minimized by the force of the wind on the sails and the weight of the keel. Thus held at a particular angle of heel, the boat is left only with the fore and aft pitching motion, a comfortable motion that feels natural as a boat plows forward through the sea.

I was also ready for a smaller boat than the 50-plus-footers I had been on for all of my OPO voyages. Big boats mean big sails: difficult to handle, especially in a squall. I still shivered when I thought of trying to manage the huge mainsail on the 62-foot *Allegretta*, made especially difficult because of the necessity to climb the mast a fair height just to get at the sail. Most captains keep only one sailor on watch at a time—a practice with which I disagree, but one where the risks are substantially reduced if the boat is small enough so that a lone sailor can douse or reef the sails. The shorter length of the Hinkley-48 meant that these tasks would be more manageable on *Rhapsody in Blue*.

The Hinckley-48 was a heavy boat weighing 17 tons, which should make for a reduced motion in a heavy sea. It also had a "full keel"—one that runs the entire length of the boat—and Mark told me, "*Rhapsody* tracks straight as an arrow with that full keel." As with many boats built in the early seventies, the hull of the Hinckley-48 was designed with pronounced overhangs off the bow and the stern. Originally intended as a handicapping rule beater on the race course, I had always thought that prominent overhangs gave a sailboat an attractive nautical appearance. I had heard they were hazardous—though I didn't hear why—and since the overhangs on *Rhapsody in Blue* were not extreme, it didn't occur to me that they would present a problem.

As I mentioned, *Rhapsody in Blue* was also a yawl, an interesting sailing rig and one I had never sailed. A yawl is like a sloop, but with a very small "mizzen" mast and sail, mounted far aft and used to help balance the steering of the boat. *Rhapsody in Blue* wasn't just any yawl, either: She was a Bill Tripp designed Hinckley yawl. A prolific designer, Bill Tripp was famous for the beauty and seaworthiness of the boats he designed. His Sou'wester series of boats defined a new standard for offshore yachts, and the Hinkley-48 yawl was his most produced yacht throughout most of the seventies.

The voyage was to take place in the spring, and as I mentioned earlier, my plans were to focus on the voyages of the spring migration. *Rhapsody in Blue* would be sailing in early May: as late as possible to take advantage of the coming warm weather, but not too late to risk being hit by an early hurricane.

It was a great opportunity, and though I was literally packing my bags for the voyage with Lisa on *Tender II*, I sent Mark Gerhardt an e-mail to apply for a position as crew on *Rhapsody in Blue*. There hadn't been too many OPO opportunities at the time, and I knew that the voyage timing, the quality of the boat, and the experience of the captain would make this one a well-sought after crew position. My attention was occupied anyway, and I kept my expectations in check.

I got a return e-mail from Gerhardt, and in that note he set up a telephone interview. It was an example of excellent management I had not seen before. Mark called at the appointed time and we spoke easily for 10 or 15 minutes. He asked about my knowledge and experience, and, surprisingly, about my cooking ability. (I didn't know it at the time, but Gerhardt had spaced several specific pass/fail questions into our casual conversation; one of them was whether or not I could cook. I also didn't know that after Mark completed interviewing all applicants, he called OPO owner Hank Schmitt for his recommendations. Again: sound management practices, something I was to see several times in Mark Gerhardt.) Somehow I passed the test and was offered the position. "You should fly to St. Maarten on May 3," Mark wrote me. "We sail on May 4."

This trip had "easy voyage" written all over it: It began in St. Maarten and ended in Newport, very similar to the return trip from St. Thomas to New York I had planned on *C'est si Bon.* (Recall that on *C'est si Bon,* Ian and I abandoned the route to New York, diverting to Beaufort, NC instead.) I had always believed that the return leg on *C'est si Bon* would have been wonderfully pleasant had we had sufficient water, a working auto-pilot, and perhaps an awning to shield us from the sun. Sailing a parallel route on the well-founded *Rhapsody in Blue* promised to be a terrific experience, perhaps the most enjoyable voyage I had ever attempted. We would start out in the 20-knot NE trade winds, I was thinking, which would quickly and easily take us several hundred miles north on a beam reach. The super-reliable trades would blow continually from the starboard side, I continued to imagine, and the crew would be left with little or nothing to do. (Ha!) After four or five days, the trade winds would begin to diminish as we approached the Horse Latitudes, but unlike my experience on *C'est si Bon,* this time we would motor through the windless area in a care-free manner until we found the southwest winds—the Westerlies—at about latitude 40. The Westerlies, though not as reliable as the trades, would be sufficiently stable and would take us all the way to Newport on the port tack. It would be much easier this time: On *Rhapsody*, we would have plenty of water and food, a reliable autopilot, sufficient communication and navigation gear, and even a life-raft and safety gear in case we ran into serious trouble. (We had none of these on *C'est si Bon.*) Yep, this was going to be a cinch!

The simple and carefree nature of the trip began with the flight to St. Maarten. (Well, a flat tire on the jet *did* delay my first flight for an hour and a half, and I *did* have to run the full length of the airport in Charlotte, NC to catch my second flight.) But catch it I did, and I was able to get to the boat without incident. (Providing we don't count the three-hour shutdown of the only road between the airport and the marina.) But that too was remedied and I *did* get to Simpson Bay Marina on St Maarten on the planned day. There I met Mark Gerhardt, owner and captain of the sailing vessel *Rhapsody in Blue.*

"Anybody home?" I called out as I walked up to the blue-hulled boat docked in slip B31. There was a fellow on the pier doing a fiber-glass repair job to the bow but he was "just a worker" he had told me in his heavy Caribbean accent. He had a full head of dread-locks that he kept covered in a thick wool tunic. *That's got to be hot*, I thought. My light airy shirt was already soaked with sweat. He, however, appeared unaffected by the oppressive heat and humidity. "Anybody home?" I yelled again, louder this time.

"Yeah," said the head that popped out of the companionway hatch. It was Mark Gerhardt. He had been working in the very hot engine room, as evidenced by the grease smeared on his arms and the sweat covering his face and shirtless upper torso. He came up on deck, wiping his oily hands, utilizing a rag that appeared even worse. He moved deliberately, not appearing to hurry, and he and I both waited while he wiped up most of the grime. Finally pleased with its condition, he extended his right hand to me: "Mark Gerhardt, glad to meet you."

At 59, he was only a year older than I was; at six feet, he was four inches taller. He sported a small goatee of sparse growth and he wore his hair a bit long as an ex-hippy might. I guessed correctly that he was a Viet Nam vet. He invited me aboard and we went below so that he could continue with his task—changing fuel filters it turned out to be. In my e-mails to him I had mentioned that I "almost never drink," but he offered me a beer anyway. As I declined, he handed me the grease covered empty bottle of the beer he had just finished and asked me to reach him another. It was warm in the main cabin where I sat and surely much warmer in the engine room where Mark worked; by the time I could find the refrigerator and get an open beer to him he was good and thirsty. The beer didn't last long. We chatted along while Mark worked, and I began to look at my surroundings, taking notice of the old-boat character and charm of what would be my home for the next several days.

Built in 1973, *Rhapsody in Blue*—named after its dark blue hull, a mainstay of Hinckley yachts—had survived forty years of the same salt water that had threatened to decompose my beloved *C'est si Bon* in only a month. She was an old, well-maintained boat: a near-podium finisher at the Senior Olympics. Her interior, other than appliances, equipment and upholstery, was constructed entirely of wood. It was a light colored wood—I confess to not knowing the type—and a wood whose patina had matured with age. Widespread and abundant, the woodwork was well-crafted: Most visible joints remained closely mitered—even after forty years—and most fasteners were hidden from view. All of it was finished with a clear varnish.

The port and starboard berths, more of a "berth assembly" than simply a bed, each began with a seven-foot upholstered bench seat—called a "side berth"—which pulled out to a double bed if desired. (We never used these beds.) Outboard and above these benches—the backs of the seats—was a series of drawers and lockers, three feet high and the full length of the bench seat. Above this drawer assembly, extending horizontally to the boat's hull, was the actual bed—called a "pilot berth"—seven feet long, three feet wide, with a fan, a light, and a lee board. Again, it was a self-contained "berth assembly," much like a very small apartment, one that housed a singular sailor at sea. I had often visualized such an all-inclusive private berth on a boat; I had heard that navy sailors were afforded similar accommodations on naval ships. I was eventually assigned the starboard berth: I slept there and stored my clothes there. It was my private spot.

The rest of the boat's interior was of a standard design: There was a V-berth up front, but it had so much gear in it that I never saw much of it. A head (bathroom) was aft of the V-berth on the port side. In the stern of the boat under the cockpit seats were two quarter berths separated by the engine. There was also a second head back there, though I never had any cause to see it. Aft of the side berths was the galley on the port side and the navigator's station to starboard—all pretty standard stuff. A unique feature was the fireplace—a stainless steel, solid-fuel burning stove with all the charm one could imagine. We never had any need to use the fireplace, and a leak from where the chimney passed through the deck caused some inconvenience, but I always enjoyed it—a real no-nonsense full-sized heating stove, mounted on real masonry, and with its own charred patina, authenticated by years of use.

After about twenty minutes, Mark finished changing the fuel filters and we continued talking as he cleaned up whatever messes he had created with the chore. Mark lived in Boston with his wife, he told me, and kept their boat on Martha's Vineyard. They had adopted a son and a daughter, twins who had grown to be young adults, aged 24. Mark went on to tell me how his daughter, while in graduate school at Harvard, suffered with a debilitating form of mental illness. This forced her out of school and into an institution; it also forced her to give up her daughter, Mark's granddaughter. Mark and his wife took over the parenting of the child—grateful they were allowed to do so—and this changed any and all of life's plans they thought they had made for themselves. "I thought I was in control," Mark remarked. "Going through this has taught me that none of us is ever in control." Later he continued: "Rita [Mark's wife] and I love that baby more than you could ever know. We would never take back our decision. But the child is three and we're nearly sixty. Do the math..."

With the chores done, at least for a while, and with all the clean-up complete, Mark and I stepped outside to see if we could catch a bit of the breeze and cool off. "Mike, meet Mahmoud," Mark said as we stepped up on deck. Mahmoud, the fellow doing the fiberglass job at the bow, looked up and shook my hand, giving me a "right mon" as he did. Pulling me aside, Mark told me that Mahmoud worked on the boat extensively. He had varnished all of the woodwork—inside and out—and had painted quite a bit too. He could also do fiberglass repair, as I could plainly see. Having a capable person such as Mahmoud at your employ would be handy for a boat owner, I was thinking. "He's a bit slow and sometimes stubborn with how he thinks something should be done," Mark said, "but there doesn't seem to be anything he can't do, and he's available and affordable. In the end, he does a pretty good job. He also has marijuana anytime you want it."

The marijuana remark took me by surprise but I had little time to reflect on it as two middle-aged men—our remaining crew—walked up the dock toward the boat. Bill Woodward, the younger of the two and wearing only a swimsuit, climbed aboard *Rhapsody* as if he owned her. He introduced himself and shook my hand, and I found out that he had already been aboard for several days, which explained his casual dress and manner. Bill looked about my age (58), and his muscular shoulders and the absence of a beer belly told me he had spent time at the gym. He had glossy bright white hair—though well-thinned—and a three-day beginning of a beard that went unshaved for the voyage. He moved in a smooth and relaxed manner and spoke, not loud, with a Kentucky accent. He seemed humble but authentic. Bill and I were both three-year OPO members, each with half a dozen completed voyages. We were also both long-time divorcees, both trying to figure out the God thing, and both handy and capable on a boat.

The other man walking up the dock with Bill was quite a bit older, very tall, and alarmingly thin as evidenced by the pencil-stick legs that protruded from his parachute shorts. His legs, torso, and most visibly his face all seemed to be stretched vertically, with cheek-bones that extended six inches and a face so narrow it threatened to disappear when viewed straight on. "Bertrand McCormick," he announced each time he shook hands with the three of us others in succession. Through his glasses he looked each one of us in the eye, saying his full name and nothing else, and maintaining a serious facial expression without any hint of a smile. He had left his duffel bag on the dock but still carried a clip board with a pad of paper and a pencil, these making him look more like a building inspector than a sailor. But a sailor he was, and a professional sailor at that, one with a USCG captain's license. Mark had hired him to add strength and integrity to the already strong crew, though he had never met Bertrand McCormick until that moment on the dock. Mark welcomed him aboard and offered him a beer. Bertrand—which we shortened to "Bert," though he didn't like it, or "Bertie," which he liked even less—thought the offer through carefully then said, "Half. I'll have half a beer."

Folks, who the hell drinks half a beer? And what the hell did "Bertie" expect his host would do with the unused half? It was comical watching Mark respond to Bertrand's request: He first had to find a clean glass in the galley—not an easy task at the time—then after pouring half the beer he turned one way then the other, trying to figure out what to do with the remainder. Finally, holding up the bottle in the sunlight as if to inspect it, the answer came to him and he swallowed the beer down in a single gulp.

So with thirsts quenched and everybody introduced, we all went below and Mark assigned berths: Bill and I would occupy the two side berths in the main cabin; Bertrand and Mark would sleep in the two quarter berths of the aft cabin. Bertrand and I stowed our bags—Mark and Bill were already well-housed—and after only a slight pause, we closed up the boat and hopped into a rented car to go get "provisions."

Ah, provisioning: critical to be done well, complicated, and always attempted by sailors who barely know each other. I had always loathed the chore of provisioning a boat. I thought of past horrors: the meat Ian

210

and I put in the ice-box on *C'est si Bon* which forced the removal of the labels of all our canned goods, the payment dispute on *Allegretta* the owners left unspoken right until a cashier asked for a credit card, the excessive Perrier water and cereal shortage on *Tender II* that left us without anything to eat for breakfast. It never seemed to work when attempted by a group effort. I was hoping for good success this time, but we were ill equipped, not possessing a shopping list or even a plan. On the other hand, the boat was already "half provisioned," Mark had said, and several dinners were already pre-made, cooked, and stored in the freezer. Perhaps this would go well. We armed ourselves with shopping carts and set out conquer. Two hours and $375 later it was done. We hadn't bought nearly enough, but it seemed like a lot of groceries at the time. Mark paid— that was the agreement—and we transported our wares to the boat. Back aboard *Rhapsody in Blue*, with beers flowing and everybody in good cheer, we packed everything away, labeled the lockers using tape—that was Bill's idea—and got ready for dinner.

I was hoping we could go to the wonderful Arabic restaurant that abutted the marina. Walking by the outdoor tables, I was impressed by the ambiance of the area and the aroma of curry seasoning, typical of mid-eastern food. I hadn't eaten since breakfast and I was good and hungry; sitting down in this convenient location suited me just fine. Mark recommended a popular bar called *"Loonies,"* however, and a quick vote vetoed my preference. The bar was several miles away, but Mark handed me the car keys and I happily accepted the post of Designated Driver.

Not much for bars anymore, I thought a quick dinner at *Loonies* would be okay. A band played popular music with an island influence—it would have been great had it not been deafening. Mark recommended the fish and chips, and if you prefer deep-fried food dripping with grease, I would recommend it as well. Mark and Bill each had a couple of shots of rum with their beers; Bertie managed a full beer this time; I was fine with water. In about ninety minutes we had finished dinner and I was more than ready to go. It was not to happen: More beers were ordered, these accompanied by shots of rum, these followed by still more. The night wore on.

Dale Cheek, the same Dale Cheek that captained *Tender II*, showed up and I invited him to join us. It was great to see an "old friend," and if the band had been reasonable with the volume, I'm sure we would have had a great conversation. We *did* get in a word or two: He was doing another delivery, one from St. Maarten all the way to Denmark. It would be a long, cold and stormy trip. "Challenging sailing," he called it. He said he wished I was on board with him. I was flattered but glad I was *not*. Later in the evening I saw Dale and Bertrand swapping sailing stories as sailing captains at a barroom table will do. I couldn't hear much of the conversation, but I did hear Bertie bragging about his own sailing exploits and belittling Dale for his. Dale didn't waste too much energy defending himself, but I was embarrassed that he was subjected to Bert's insults at all. I knew that Dale's expertise made him deserving of much better treatment. With Bertie, I wasn't sure.

I awoke early the next morning, and after grabbing a marina shower I made up a bowl of the Muesli we had purchased the day before. By this time Mark and Bertrand were up and busy discussing weather tactics and route decisions. Mark's inclination was to utilize various weather forecasts and alter our sailing route to obtain the best winds. At his disposal, he had GRIBS, the weather forecasting system that had become the standard on ocean going boats. In addition, he had phone and e-mail contact with a weather advisory service offered by a Ken McKinley, the same service I saw Dan Bower use on *Skyelark of London*. Bert, who in my estimation was over-stepping his authority, repeatedly advised that we should simply follow the rhumb line—not "chase ghosts," to use his term.

The scene reminded me of a similar occurrence on *That Darn Cat*: On that yacht, owner Mike Stafford and crew member Julian Cohen were also discussing tactics. In time Julian announced, "We're not ready; we can't go," thus beginning a most amazing reversal of power, one that ended with Julian replacing Mike as "captain" on his own boat. I recalled my naïveté on *That Darn Cat* and how I got involved in the discussion, oblivious to what I was getting myself into. I wouldn't make the same mistake on *Rhapsody*. I didn't think for a moment that Bert would try to overpower Mark—Mark would cut his nuts off, I was sure—but by this time I had begun to distrust ol' Bertie and I knew he would weasel his way in somehow.

Two factors complicated the weather situation: First, a huge storm had formed off Newfoundland and it would move south, right into our path. Second, instead of the trade winds blowing from the east as they always do, they were blowing from the southwest—and very light at that—an almost unheard-of condition.

The storm we would have to avoid: Its winds were northeast and they would be contrary to the fast and powerful current of the Gulf Stream. Entering the storm in such conditions would be suicide. Fortunately, it would be a week before we and the storm would be in the same vicinity, and by that time the storm would probably subside.

The lack of the normal trade winds presented an immediate problem but one with only a single solution: motor through. This required more fuel than *Rhapsody's* tanks would hold, but Mark had eight 5-gallon fuel jugs aboard which we planned to use. If necessary, we could also stop at Bermuda to refuel. In the final analysis, Bert's suggestion to follow the rhumb line and not "chase ghosts" became the obvious sailing tactic, at least for the first several days of the voyage.

To get out of Simpson Bay Harbor we had to catch the 11:00 drawbridge opening, which firmly set our departure time and removed all casual time we might have had. Mark made a quick trip to the customs office to get our official clearance, and while we waited for our 9:45 appointment at the fuel dock, he gave us an hour-long presentation on *Rhapsody in Blue*, her features, procedures and rules:

> Fuel: *Rhapsody* had tanks for 90 gallons of fuel, plus 40 gallons in jugs. The boat burned a gallon an hour under power at five knots, making a range under engine alone of 650 miles.
>
> Water: The vessel's tanks held 200 gallons of water, plus we carried 30 gallons in plastic bottles. *Rhapsody* had no water makers, so we would have to be careful with our water consumption. (No one ever took a full shower throughout the entire voyage.)
>
> Watches: Each man would take a solo 3-hour watch twice per day—Bill (12-3); Mark (3-6); Mike (6-9); Bert (9-12). If someone on watch needed help, he would call the person next on watch.
>
> Rules: 1. No booze. 2. Always go behind a ship when crossing its path. 3. Life-harnesses must be worn when on deck at night. 4. No going up front alone at night.
>
> MOB Procedure: If a man falls overboard, the person discovering this will keep visual contact with the MOB while yelling for help and will maintain visual contact at the exclusion of all else until help arrives.

We were also shown the life-raft, the rig-cutting tools, and a chart of all the boat's thru-hull fittings. Mark demonstrated how to work the stove, the head, the engine, the bilge pump, the auto-pilot, the navigational instruments and the anchor gear. Some tasks, such as lowering the dagger-board or switching fuel tanks, were explained to us but Mark would always do these tasks as required. *Rhapsody* wasn't a complicated boat and we were all experienced sailors. Mark had to explain things to us only once.

We fueled up at our appointed time, then motored out to the swing-bridge and waited for the scheduled opening. Several other boats were waiting as well, all within shouting distance. One salt-worn boat from Brazil had stopped at St. Maarten on her way to Europe, a fact I was able to establish by speaking Spanish to the Portuguese-speaking crew. Another group—Canadians they told us—after determining our destination asked us where we planned to sleep at night. "Out at sea," I told them, confused at their question. It was an illustration of the different categories of sailors one meets at ocean ports: seasoned salties next to chartering day-sailors.

Through the bridge, we put up the mainsail and motored around the west side of St. Maarten. The wind was light and southwest—I would have never believed it—and the air became still and hot right away. Each of us lathered up with sunscreen and put on our "summer" clothes. Bill went on watch at noon. The voyage had begun.

It was like going to a grand celebration, but when you finally arrive at the long-anticipated event you're the only one there. I had pictured a vivacious beam reach with *Rhapsody in Blue* skipping from one wave to another, yawing back and forth between the rollers, you know, "acting like a puppy dog finally let out to play." Instead we sat looking at each other, smothered in the heat and humidity that hung in the dead air. Similar conditions were predicted for days; what were we going to do with our time? I looked out to starboard and saw the island of St. Maarten/St. Martin beside us. Several fishing boats drifted about. It would be hot for them too, I thought. The seascape of grey pastels reminded me of an artist's canvas with everything still and quiet except for one moving object—us—that passed from one side of the painting to the other. We passed St. Martin then Anguilla both to starboard, then Dog Island and the Sombrero light well to port. I recalled going through the Sombrero Passage on *C'est si Bon*, unsure of my celestial determined position and racing along through the night

215

triple reefed. Did *Rhapsody* even have a third reef? I guessed it might never matter.

"I don't like to cook," Mark announced, not quite so abruptly but with a marked finality in his statement. "I do all the cooking at home, so when I'm aboard I prefer that someone else do it." I recalled his interest in my cooking ability during my telephone interview with him. "Mike," he said, "you said you're a pretty good cook, right?"

"Yeah, I do okay," I said. "I seem to find myself in the galley quite often." I was repeating my lines from our discussion on the phone, mindful that if I wasn't careful I was about to make myself a full-time cook. "I don't cook up anything all that special, pretty simple stuff really, but people seem to like whatever I come up with."

That was all it took: I was asked to make up some dinner for that evening, and everybody assumed I was to do the same every night. It really wasn't such a bad deal: I had always preferred my own cooking and with me having this well-acknowledged responsibility, other chores (i.e.: the dishes) were left for someone else. Bill stepped up to the dishes that first evening, and again, everybody assumed the permanence of his designation as "chief dish washer." It was the beginning of a partnership—a brotherhood—that Bill and I formed. We were the two non-professionals on board, the two OPO members, the two non-USCG certified sailors that slept "in steerage" in the main cabin. From the very start we worked well as a team and quickly developed a friendship and respect for each other.

Not nearly deserving of respect, Bertie approached me shortly after I was asked to cook dinner that day. "Since you're going to be the one of us closest to the galley, can you keep an eye on the freezer and refrigerator settings?" he asked me. "We need to make sure that all foods stay cold, but only those in the freezer actually freeze. Can you do that?"

It was simply one sailor aboard a vessel asking another to do something. It happens all the time: "Can you hand me that wrench, Mack?" "Don't forget to turn off the engine, Joe." These are not "orders." They're simply communications. Being asked to monitor the refrigeration controls was more than "hand me a wrench, Mack," but I didn't think too much of it. (And this was evidenced the next day when I let the lettuce freeze.)

Dinner that night: Cold pre-cooked Cornish hen, heated-up baked beans, store-bought potato salad. What a gourmet feast! I started prep at five and dinnertime became 5:30 for that night and all others. We ate in the cockpit, the preferred location as I had learned on *Skyelark*. Bill would do the dishes and I would go on watch at 6:00 after dinner. It was a schedule that allowed me to cook and perform a watch, and though my 6-9 watch was the best of the bunch (Bill had the worst from 12 to 3), the responsibility of preparing dinner relieved me from any guilt feelings.

So, with dinner finished and six o'clock approaching, I checked the navigational instruments and the radar and confirmed the course from Mark who was finishing his watch. I grabbed my life-harness—though it wasn't dark and the sea was still flat—and sat in the aft corner of the cockpit, in reach of the steering wheel and in sight of the compass. After a while the others went to their bunks for some rest and I was left alone, accompanied only by *Rhapsody* and the sea. We motored along in the light breeze that came from astern. With the boat's forward motion, I couldn't feel the wind at all.

Bertrand couldn't sleep. He came up on deck, checked the engine's tachometer, the compass, and then the radar. He eyed the main from foot to head and pulled in the sheet a foot or two. He made a quick nod that told me he was pleased with this adjustment, though with no wind it made no difference at all. Not saying a word, I watched as he walked up to the foredeck and gazed around the horizon. "We'd better turn on the running lights," he said.

He was right. I hadn't thought of the lights, though it wasn't yet dark. Had I remembered, however, I would have

217

turned them on right about the time he suggested it. Together we searched the controls for the proper switches. Switches on, we checked the various lights to make sure they all functioned properly.

"Nice night," Bert said, sitting down.

"Yeah, a quiet one," I agreed. "Might be quiet for a while. Hope it cools down."

"So, you married, Mike?"

"Me? No, divorced. Been divorced for almost thirty years. All her fault." It was a joke, a true joke, and one I had been telling for all thirty years. I glanced at the compass; the auto-pilot was doing a perfect job. The wind came up just a bit, and I let out the main to where it had been before Bert had pulled it in.

"Got a woman in your life?" Bertrand continued.

"Yeah, I've got a great girlfriend. Lisa. We've been together more than three years, which is a long relationship for me. She's a great..."

"Yeah, I was married," Bertie said, cutting off my answer. "For 25 years. Divorced now. I've dated a lot of women, and a few real honeys, but nothing now. The best gal I had was an alcoholic. She was a hot red-head and we had a ball, but I couldn't take the drinking."

"Do you think you'll ever get married again, Bert?"

"No, probably not. I'm too set in my ways. I enjoy being alone. I like to get up in the morning and do what I want."

It's a decision many of us bachelors (and bachelorettes) must face: We can live our lives as part of a partnership, creating a complete life of love and companionship, but one that requires "work." Or, we can be alone—perhaps lonely, perhaps not—living an easy but incomplete and unfulfilling life, "getting up in the morning and doing what we want."

"Sure would like to get laid though," Bert continued.

"How old are you, Bert?"

"69."

218

Bertrand told me about his home in Maine, how he liked the cool weather there, about his Motobecane bicycle that he liked to ride to town, and about his adult son that his ex-wife planned but he did *not*. ("She seduced me in order to conceive him," he said.) He told me of a Nauticat-39 he delivered from Granada to Tortola—without a working engine—and how he was still employed managing its repairs. The two of us were getting to know each other. Though my first impressions of Bertrand were not flattering, his life-long experience as a sailboat captain and his obvious sailing knowledge impressed me. I remembered my mantra: *We don't have to resolve any deep, underlying differences, but we must get along for the duration of the voyage.* I didn't like Bert. I didn't like his pretentiousness, and I saw that he believed himself to be somehow superior to the rest of us. Like Alex on *Tender II,* he was self-promoting and gave instructions as if he had authority. But I needed to get along with him—not forever, but at least until we got to Newport. So, as he told me about himself and his life that first night at sea, I let him talk. By 9:00, though, I had had enough. I let him know it was his watch and went to bed.

The continuing sound of the engine woke me early the next morning, as did the wet sheet and pillow, both soaked from my own sweat. The heat of the day hadn't even begun, but as I scooped a bowl of Muesli down my throat prior to my 6AM watch, I noticed the beads of perspiration already forming on my brow. I made a cup of instant coffee—"instant" is the way to go on a boat, believe me—and joined Mark in the cockpit. He held the wheel to manually steer *Rhapsody* behind a ship whose path we had been crossing. "Didn't even show up on the AIS," Mark said, referring to the *Automatic Identification System*, the system that was supposed to alert us of oncoming traffic. The big vessel crossed our bow, and with it safely behind us, Mark re-set the auto-pilot.

"We'll be motoring for quite a while," he said. "Maybe several days. Hopefully, we'll get some wind and not use up

219

all our fuel. It would be good to make it to Newport in one shot, but if we run short of fuel we'll have to go into Bermuda. I was there on a trip a couple of years ago, and the crew got so drunk I couldn't get them out of there. Then, the next day they told me they had fueled the boat, but they had left one tank empty. We had no fuel once we left Bermuda— the only reason we went there in the first place. I like Bermuda. It's one of my favorite places. But it's a black hole: once you get to Bermuda, you can't get out."

One of the reasons Mark chose his 3-6 watch assignment was so he could be free at 6:00 each morning to communicate with Ken McKinley about weather expectations. Ken is an ocean weather expert and operates an advisory service called *Locus Weather*. For about a hundred dollars Ken will provide a one-time analysis of the weather expectations for a planned voyage. (I could have used his service when I was dealing with Brian Matroka on *Allegretta*.) Ken also offers a more expensive service that includes a daily update of the analysis as a voyage progresses. Mark had purchased this service; he estimated Ken was monitoring and communicating with 40 boats at the time. (One of them was probably *Skyelark of London*, the yacht on which I had sailed two years prior.) Mark had also purchased Ken's premium service where he interfaces with Jennifer Clark and puts her Gulf Stream analysis into the picture. Some might call it quite a racket—all Ken does is look at information readily available on the internet—but I was amazed at the accuracy and utility of the analysis. Indeed, shortly after the voyage I contacted Ken and arranged how I could purchase his service on future voyages.

Finished with the story about his drunk crew at Bermuda, Mark fired up his computer and looked for Ken's update. Each morning we were supposed to get an e-mail from Ken, sent to us through the satellite telephone. Mark had received an initial analysis from a Wi-Fi hot spot at St. Maarten; it pleased him to see that he had received another one, this one using the satellite phone while out at sea. "We'll be getting light southwest winds today and tomorrow, but they're going to switch around to the east on Tuesday," Mark yelled out from the cabin. "It'll be pretty hot until they change."

It wasn't the best news but it would have to do. I figured we would be out of the trade wind belt after three or four days, and if the east winds didn't come along until Tuesday (our fourth day) we might miss them altogether. We had only five days of fuel. It looked like a Bermuda stop to me, even at this early stage of the voyage. It didn't matter to me one way or another, but since Mark had a significant desire to avoid the stop, I kept my thoughts to myself.

Hearing Mark reading aloud the updated forecast, the others arose, each commenting on the elevated cabin temperature as eyes were rubbed, muscles were stretched, and heads were stuck out through the companionway to greet the sunny day and proclaim "good morning" to all the others. We had passed our first night sleeping around our watches: I had slept from nine to six, a perfect uninterrupted all-night rest; the others had all slept for shorter periods during the somewhat cooler darkness of night. Each would require additional sleep each day, and in the day-time heat of the cabin, that would be a challenge. For the time being, however, Mark set about showing Bill how to use the espresso coffee maker while I settled into my watch routine and Bert joined me in the cockpit, looking around for something to do.

"What would you do if I fell overboard right now?" Bert asked me. The question took me by surprise and I had to stifle my initial inclination to state something sarcastic. (What would *you* do if someone you disliked fell overboard?)

"I would visually spot you in the water, yelling 'man-overboard' and maintaining visual contact until the others arrived to help," I said, proud that I had remembered the procedure Mark had so vehemently identified to us all.

221

"No!" Bert corrected. "I would want you to pull back the throttle to stop the boat, throw the MOB gear into the water, then yell for the others as you turn the boat around to come and get me."

It was a good quiz. It brought to mind a procedure that any sailor should always be ready to implement. We discussed the topic, agreeing later that pushing the MOB button on the cockpit tracker, something nobody had thought of, should be the first step. Bert asked me the same question two or three times throughout the voyage, bringing into the discussion the problems experienced trying to get a fallen sailor—perhaps unconscious—back aboard in a rough sea. (Coincidentally, a sailor on an America's Cup boat had recently drowned after he had fallen overboard, clipped to the boat with his life-harness, but with the crew unable to stop the boat and pull him aboard.) The fact that Bert thought to quiz me on the critical and complicated MOB procedure—and revisit the topic numerous times— demonstrated his sailing prowess, seasoned by life-long experience. It increased my mastery and awareness, and that's what a good coach and mentor will do. The fact that he was counseling only one crew member, and devising an important procedure that disagreed with the instructions of the captain, however, said that he had a way to go in the leadership category. I asked him about this issue and he nodded in agreement, but he never did circle back and discuss the matter with Mark.

We fought the sun and the heat for the next several days. *Rhapsody* had no Bimini cover or awning to shield us from the sun, and finding shade proved difficult. All of us used sun-screen, especially in the mid-day sun. Mark demonstrated the disadvantages of buying the cheap stuff: His failed to soak into his skin and made him appear like a slimy white ghost. I never had anyone apply any on my back—probably due to some homo-phobic paranoia—and it became sunburned, making it difficult to sleep. I had purchased a light, airy hat that I had hoped would shield my head and shoulders. It only made me feel hot and smothered, however, so after a couple of trials it remained in the cabin. We ran through our first of five 40-gallon water tanks, pleased with our conservative usage. We also transferred some fuel from the jugs to the vessel's tanks, less than pleased with our fuel consumption. In the galley we agreed to save those meals that required the oven for the cooler days we would experience later, so my chef responsibilities were minimal. Each day I fixed up some sort of evening meal; each day Bill did the dishes. All of us would try to keep things in order during the day, and Bill became the police officer, remarking when anybody left a dirty cup or fork in the sink. Bill also saved me from what could have been a severe injury: The cockpit floor on *Rhapsody* was deeper than I had been accustomed to, and stepping down into it, I fell—not once, not twice, but three times. As chance would have it, Bill was seated where I was going to fall on each occasion and caught me each time. It was embarrassing and I apologized profusely, but Bill only smiled, saying nothing as he put up with my clumsy behavior.

On our fourth day out, though it was the hottest of all the days of the voyage, a bit of a southeast wind came up on my watch and I turned off the engine and sailed—for all of thirty minutes. By that time we had run the engine for 58 hours, using almost half of our fuel capacity. Ken's updated forecast said that the SE winds would increase over the next six days, and then we would cross a front that would bring rain, thunderstorms, and a 35-knot north wind. We had GRIBS aboard and we could see the significant storm not far south of Nova Scotia. We had known about the storm since before the voyage began. We hoped it would subside, but that didn't seem to be the case. It was a race to Newport: us against the storm. We couldn't power through the storm with the horrendous conditions it would create as it passed the Gulf Stream. We needed to get in before the storm arrived.

The four of us got along, by and large. Bill and I were becoming best buddies, and Mark proved to be an ample leader and captain. Even Bert behaved himself respectably, though not always: He made constant attempts to demonstrate his superiority, be that in trimming a sail, steering the boat, or even in his sailing acumen. Once I saw him trying to assert power over the captain, saying we should steer more easterly—toward Bermuda—but Mark had a way of listening to differing opinions and making the right decision. One day Bertie made it a point to brag to Bill and me that he was a paid hand. On another day he told us he was brought on as "mate," and just in case we didn't understand what that entailed, he continued to outline that he was responsible for everything that happened on deck. "The captain should never have to be involved with any of the activities on deck if the mate does his job adequately," he told us.

One night, after I had whooped Bert in chess for the sixth time—which precluded all future games—he stayed up with me on my after-dinner watch as he had before. He turned off the auto-pilot and hand steered for a while. "You should really consider doing this yourself," he said. "Hand steering will always out-perform an auto-pilot." I didn't agree with him regarding the superiority of hand-steering, and though I found his statement insulting, I said nothing. He put the auto-pilot back on and began re-trimming the sails, it being one of the rare times we were sailing instead of motoring. He spent quite a bit of time at it, and by the time he was done he must have re-adjusted every sailing control on the boat. It was an irritating side of him—telling me what I should do and showing me how best to perform basic sailing duties. He had me steaming. I recalled how Alex had instructed me on how to look for other boats: "Look here, then here, then here," he had said as he looked around the horizon at intervals. Bert was exhibiting the same behavior: self-assuming a position of authority and giving instruction to others on obvious well-understood matters. Bertie's method was especially irritating: He didn't *tell* me how to trim the main, he *showed* me. I felt insulted, belittled. I didn't know how to react. Verbally lashing out with an F-bomb occurred to me, but that wouldn't be "getting along for the duration of the voyage." I let it go and let him finish. Finally he went below. Boy, was I mad.

The weather update from Ken McKinley of *Locus Weather* kicked off each morning. The majority of the information detailed the southwest, southeast or south wind, which had little bearing on our sailing decisions. Jennifer Clark's analysis of currents was also included, however, and we used this to adjust our course, chasing the various beneficial currents in our vicinity and avoiding the contrary ones. We would often get a knot and a half of favorable current, a good boost to our five or six-knot average speed.

The navigational instruments mounted in *Rhapsody's* cockpit were superior to any I had ever seen. We had dual knot meters, for example—one that measured the boat's speed "through the water" utilizing a paddle wheel, and another that worked off of GPS and measured "speed over ground." Comparing the two knot-meters identified any fore and aft currents affecting the vessel. The second knot-meter also provided "course made good," and comparing this with the compass would identify sideways currents or leeway affecting the boat. A wind indicator was also mounted in the cockpit. This instrument showed wind speed and direction, and could be toggled between true to apparent wind with the flip of a switch. The Raymarine Plotter completed the instruments. One mode of the plotter showed a chart (map), which provided a zoom-able picture of the vessel progressing through the waterway. It also had a radar mode which displayed ships, land, navigational beacons and storm activity in the vicinity of the boat. The Raymarine Plotter also had a feature that pleased me to no end: a Velocity Made Good (VMG) display, and one that was properly dampened to provide a stable, unvarying reading. (Perhaps you can recall the VMG issue we experienced on *That Darn Cat*.) The superior instruments on *Rhapsody* took a lot of the guess-work out of sailing and we often switched from one tack to the other based on currents they identified. Likewise, when an interfering Bertie would claim that I had set the rig incorrectly, I could say, "No, Bert, the true wind is to port, the boom is correctly set to starboard." And I especially enjoyed sailing the most efficient wind angle using the VMG display. Finally we had it, folks: a properly dampened VMG indicator, mounted within convenient view of the helm.

As we approached latitude 25N, we started to get a stronger and more consistent wind—exactly the opposite of normal experience. With the wind always behind us, we tried putting up the asymmetrical spinnaker a time or two. This powerful and beautiful sail gave our forward speed a boost but it was always ungainly. Putting it up or taking it down required a group effort, and if the wind exceeded 15-knots the sail would start the boat rocking back and forth out of control and threatening a broach. We used it when we could, and it did help, but using the spinnaker was always troublesome.

A more secure method of sailing downwind is to fly the mainsail to one side with the genoa held in place to the other using the spinnaker pole: the "wing-on-wing" rig we used extensively on *Skyelark of London*. Securing the heavy pole in place was quite a bear, and stringing out the genoa in a rolling sea can be a lot of dangerous foredeck work, but especially if the following wind is expected to continue, the result is generally worth the effort. One morning at the 6:00 change of watches, Mark and I set the rig and Mark almost lost a toe as the pole crashed on deck. (Tip: Wear shoes when working on deck.) With the rig set, however, and all sails drawing and all toes accounted for, we sat in the cockpit sipping our morning coffees, admiring the stable rig and the fine speed it produced. With the others still in bed, the serene morning sea was ours alone to enjoy. In the peacefulness, Mark told me the story of his knockdown a year and a half earlier:

"I was bringing *Rhapsody* south in the fall of 2011," Mark began. "We were registered as part of the NARC Rally [North American Rally to the Caribbean]. Hank Schmitt [of OPO] runs that rally, you know, and he had hired some gal— Dorothy was her name, I think. Anyway, Dorothy was a weather advisor and she was clearly out of her league. A nor'easter called *Sean* was off the Carolinas moving east, and she first advised to go west of it. Then she changed her advice, saying to go east of it. Then she changed it again and said to go toward Bermuda and go hove-to when the storm approached. Horribly inept advice," Mark said, "and you wouldn't believe how pissed she was when she learned that Hank had ignored her suggestions.

"This was before I had heard about Ken [McKinley] and *Locus Weather*. I suspected that Dorothy was pretty useless so I used GRIBS. It looked as if we could get through in front of the storm. Well, we didn't: we were west of Bermuda when it hit. I had two crew members I had never used before; my regular crew had cancelled on me. I was up front taking in the jib. One of the crew was back here reefing the main. He secured the clew but not the tack [the two bottom corners of the sail] and when he pulled the halyard, it pulled the boom up in the air, which ballooned the sail and the wind tore it to bits.

"We went along with the storm, sailing under bare poles [with no sails up.] I didn't have a drogue [a sea anchor that would keep the boat pointed downwind] and with the storm blowing, I couldn't get up to the anchor locker to get the chain. [He would have liked to drag the anchor chain off the stern in a loop to control the boat.] The winds were fifty knots and the waves were—I don't know, but they were huge. Anyway, *Rhapsody* rounded up into the wind and broached. She went right over but came up the same way, so technically that's a knockdown, not a capsize. I was clipped on with my life-harness but I was several feet underwater wondering if we were going down. She came up—I was still overboard but clipped on—and even with the hatch-boards latched in place, the boat was at least half-full of water."

Getting the boat back in order was no small task, Mark told me. The electrical power in the boat was disabled so the water had to be pumped out manually. (It is said that the best bilge pump is a scared sailor with a bucket.) This was done while the storm continued, and as Mark describe it to me I tried to imagine how difficult the ordeal would have been. In the middle of it all one of the new crew members went hysterical.

"He went nuts," Mark continued. "You know, 'We're going to die! We're going to die!' I had to shake him out of it and scream, 'we're *not* going to die; we're *not* going to die!' Then he locked himself in the john for like, a whole day."

The affected crew member never helped at all, but Mark and the other crew spent the next two days putting the boat back in order before they could get underway. Once mobile they proceeded to Beaufort (where I went with *C'est si Bon*) where the two crew left the boat and Mark stayed to finish repairs.

"I met some good friends at Beaufort," Mark said, "and they helped get everything back together—both the boat and my nerves. I was pretty devastated. I didn't want to sail ever again, but those guys convinced me to take a month off, then come back and continue down to St. Maarten. I was a wreck. I think I had a bit of a nervous breakdown myself. I felt so guilty, thinking I almost left my wife and the kid [his granddaughter] alone."

"What about the two crew?" I asked.

"I don't really know," Mark said. "The one wouldn't even shake my hand. That hurt."

His accounting of the near disaster finished, Mark gulped down the last of his coffee and retired to his bunk. In the continuing peace of the early morning, I sat alone in the cockpit, contemplating the extraordinary story just revealed to me. The knockdown had occurred in November of 2011: a month before I had sailed on *That Darn Cat*. It was during the fall migration, that dangerous small opportunity of sailing when both hurricanes and nor'easter storms are frequent. George Tripler, the other OPO member with me on *That Darn Cat*, was sailing in the same storm—*Sean*—in the same area. (I recalled he had told me that his delivery was in a gale the entire distance. "But it was a tail-wind, so it was no problem," he had said. I wondered why *Rhapsody in Blue* rounded up into the wind under bare poles; sailboats normally don't do that.) I recalled also that someone else sailing in the NARC Rally was lost overboard during that same storm. (It was on the yacht *Triple Stars*, an Island Packet-38—a good boat—sailed by husband and wife team Rob and Jan Anderson. Jan was lost overboard and Rob, totally distressed, took a ship rescue and left his boat adrift in the open sea.)

It was my last 6:00 watch, that wonderful watch that allowed me nine hours of continuous night-time sleep. I had offered to switch with Bill after five days—the expected half-way point of the voyage—and five days had expired. I didn't mind: I felt guilty hogging the best watch, and Bill was having a real problem trying to sleep around the midnight watch. Besides, I was bored and wanted a change. It was time. I was only too happy to help out my friend. We agreed to share the first noon watch, which meant only that we would *both* sit and stare at the sea while the auto-pilot steered the boat. Anyway, my watch was changed to 12-3, day and night.

We were a hundred miles southwest of Bermuda, and we had to decide whether to continue northwest to Newport or veer northeast to Bermuda. Mark calculated that we would have to average over six knots all the way to Newport to beat the storm. He thought we could do it with little trouble. Bert was upset. He had always favored going to Bermuda and was not happy taking on the risk of getting hit by a significant storm.

"We need to go into Bermuda," he told Mark.

"Well, not yet," Mark said. "We can continue motor-sailing for a few more days and get six and a half knots, and after that we should get some good southerlies that'll get us in on time."

"What happens if we don't make it in time?" Bert challenged. "You can't just take a crew into that kind of danger."

"I would never subject anybody into that kind of risk. I just wouldn't do it."

"What would you do? I mean, what are you going to do when we're in the Gulf Stream and the storm comes in?"

"I'd either go hove-to or run with it. There's any number of things you can do. That's what we do: we view the situation and take action."

"You'd be low on fuel and we'd be pushed north by the Gulf Stream, right into the teeth of a nor'easter!" Bert said. "You don't have that right. Just because you pay me to come aboard doesn't mean you have the right to put me in undue risk."

He had made a point—quite the ultimatum, really—but Mark wasn't convinced. He went below to recheck his navigation. Bert, who was on watch at the time, went about on deck trimming sails, coiling lines—anything to keep himself from boiling over. Bill had the good sense to retire below, but I stayed in the cockpit, there being not much else to do.

"We gotta go to Bermuda," Bertie told me. "Don't you agree?"

"Oh, it's not up to me, Bert," I said. "Not up to me at all." I was impressed I had finally learned to keep my mouth shut.

"Well, I'm about to make a statement," Bert said, staring into the cabin toward the navigation table where Mark worked. I saw the muscles at the side of his jaw clench and his lower lip shake. He was pissed. His hands were fists and he looked like a boxer ready to fight. (Though a very skinny boxer you must understand.) I wondered what sort of a *statement* he was thinking of making. "Pull in that main, dammit!" he yelled at me. I looked back at him, thinking he might launch himself at me. "Oh never mind, I'll get it myself," he said as he choked on his words. I thought he was going to cry.

Mark was on the satellite phone: "Ken, we're nearing Bermuda and we need to make a decision whether to continue to Newport or go into Bermuda." (I noted that we were now past e-mails and into verbal conversation with the weather expert.) I was grateful that Bert had gotten us to this point. Between Mark, Ken McKinley and Bert, I knew the correct decision would be made. Mark spoke for several minutes with Ken, then came up on deck. "Okay," he said. "We go to Bermuda."

I saw Bert relax in an instant. "Okay," he said. "Bermuda it is. What's the course?"

This changed everything. We altered course to starboard, which gave us a better point of sail and as well as quite a bit of boat speed. We turned off the engine, finally enjoying the music of the ocean instead of the noise of a muffler. The hot air temperature continued, but the increase of apparent wind brought some cooling relief, if only a bit. All in all, it was a pleasant change of conditions, at least for those not in a hurry.

A stop at Bermuda would delay our progress, and it did nothing to get rid of the storm coming our way. We would have to wait for it to pass and that would be several days. Also, there was a secondary low behind the storm and it looked as if we would have to wait for that as well. Ken's words said it all: "I don't know when I can get you out of Bermuda." I remembered what Mark had said regarding this favorite place of his: "Bermuda is like a black hole; once you get there, you can't get out."

Mark had lost all hope in continuing the voyage and getting his boat home: "You guys can stay on the boat all you want," he told Bill and me. "I'll fly home and get some work

231

things done. I'll have to come back in a few weeks and take the boat home."

Bert, on the other hand, was elated by the change, though I think he was trying to hide the fact. An unmistakable liveliness returned to his actions and I thought I heard him whistling as he finished the whipping of a line he had started. The line done, he went below to his bunk and quickly fell into a deep sleep. He had forgotten he was still on watch.

Rhapsody in Blue sailed to Bermuda *with a bone in her teeth*, the southeast wind just aft of her starboard beam. The sun brought the familiar turquoise blue to the sea, and for the first time of the voyage we saw "frequent white caps," one of the descriptors of Force 4 on the Beaufort Scale. It was a grand afternoon of sailing indeed, although at one point we saw a waterspout (a tornado on the water) off to port. Mark instructed us of what to do if one hit the boat: "go inside and close the hatch; they'll suck you right off the boat."

Mark and Bert rarely visited the galley. Neither of them had cooked even a single meal, and this left the menu selections along with all preparation to Bill and me. He and I alone were aware that we were almost out of food; without a stop in Bermuda we would have been in big trouble. We still had one or two of the pre-cooked dinners in the freezer, but we had no fresh vegetables or fruit, and we were all but out of milk and juice. That morning we emptied our last box of cereal—a real breakfast staple—and we had also discovered that mold had invaded our last two loaves of bread. For our last dinner before Bermuda, I reached into the freezer and brought out one of the two frozen pizzas I had been eyeing in distain all the time I had been aboard. I cooked up some rice and added to it a can of black beans and a can of corn and served this with the pizza. I was a bit embarrassed to serve such a meager meal, but the guys didn't seem to mind and I even heard a couple of compliments. During the entire voyage I never received a complaint from the diners aboard, and that made the job of chef much easier.

The night passed without incident, something of a luxury on a sailboat out at sea. In the hours before my first midnight watch I tried to get some sleep but could not. At the stroke of twelve, sleepless and drowsy but armed with a cup of strong coffee, I headed up to the cockpit to relieve Bert from his watch—the first time I had done so. He said he needed to show me something:

"Our course is 25 degrees," Bertie told me, "but you need to keep a good eye in case we come up on the islands." (We were still 60 miles away.)

"Okay," I said. It was my first night up at midnight, and although I hadn't been able to sleep, I wasn't quite awake yet either.

"And keep an eye on the genoa: the wind has been clocking back and forth."

"Okay."

"You've got your life-vest on, right?"

"Yeah, of course." This was starting to get tiring. I didn't need all this mindless instruction. "What was the course again?" I asked.

"25 degrees—magnetic, not true." (We had been using magnetic references since the voyage had started.)

"Okay 25 degrees. Got it."

"And keep an eye for boats; there's bound to be a lot of traffic around here."

"Okay, Bert, I got it. Go to bed! I'm fine."

Gee, what a pain! Finally he went below and I had some peace. I fought to stay alert, helped by two more cups of coffee. The wind did clock back and forth a couple times—no big deal—and three boats passed to starboard, all going south. Twenty minutes before three, I saw the light in Mark's cabin and a moment later he was up in the galley, fussing with his espresso coffee maker. *Three hour watches sure are better than four hour ones*, I thought. My first midnight watch hadn't gone too badly. I had enjoyed it, actually. But I was bushed. Mark came up and I went down to bed.

I awoke at 7:30 hearing Mark talking to Ken on the satellite telephone. I could hear just enough of the conversation to know that the men were devising a plan to go to Beaufort—the same place I had diverted to on *C'est si Bon*, the same place Mark had gone to for repairs after his knockdown. I got up and fixed a bowl of Muesli—Bill had miraculously found an unopened box, and also a box of milk. As I ate my cereal, Mark told me the plan: We would go into Bermuda for a day or two for fuel and groceries and then head to Beaufort. "There's a place there I can leave the boat, and I've got a few repairs I could have done there too. Also, once we get near the US coast, we'll have a better slant on the Gulf Stream and the southwest winds. If the storm abates, and that's unlikely, we'd be able to head north to Newport."

"How many days is it to Beaufort?" I asked.

"About four," Mark said.

So the voyage was still "on," and it included a stop in Bermuda and a detour to Beaufort. One of the personal objectives I had for the voyage was to compare it with the one on *C'est si Bon*. A stop at both Bermuda and Beaufort pleased me to no end. I was also happy for Mark: He was going to get his boat out of the black hole of Bermuda and to the more acceptable Beaufort. It was a good spot, not only because of the accommodations there, but also because it would be an easy trip to Newport from there for him later.

On we sailed for Bermuda, making good speed, though momentarily delayed by a particularly bad squall that forced us off course by a few miles. We found the inlet to St. Georges Harbour, made obvious by a substantial cement light-house at the beginning of the approach. We didn't even consider using Sugarloaf Hill to find our way in, though the piloting instructions continued to suggest it, just as they had 24 years prior when Ian and I came this way on *C'est si Bon*. In accordance with those same instructions, however, we came in from the southeast this time, not from the north as I had before. Also, instead of heading straight for the bar as Ian and I had done, on *Rhapsody* we immediately reported to Customs, tying up at Liberty Dock Friday at noon—six days out of St. Maarten.

I knew that Officer Lee, the proud Ethiop with the perfectly pressed Bermudian outfit, would not greet us as he had when *C'est si Bon* tied up at Liberty Dock. Still, I hoped for a similar display of the formality and dignity I thought was typical of this former British outpost. As it was, nobody came out to welcome *Rhapsody in Blue*, and after waiting five or ten minutes, the four of us went into the customs office to see about completing the clearance procedure there. Inside the office, three men and a woman sat in various chairs, two of them reading their newspapers, one fixing her hair, and with not a pair of the traditional black Bermuda shorts among the whole group. No one looked up as we entered, and after we had waited a moment or two, it was the woman who finally found the energy to put down her hair brush, raise her considerable self out of the ancient wooden swivel chair in which she sat, and waddle over to the counter to attend to us.

"Can I hep you?" she asked, her shortened form of the word *help* not at all indicative of the islands. In her fifties or sixties and not well-aged, she walked with a substantial limp, her entire body moving with each step as if her hips had lost most of their mobility. She wore "coke-bottle" glasses and sported a toothpick which protruded from her mouth. I noticed that one of her shirttails hung outside of her pants and that a middle button of her blouse was missing, exposing her underwear. She wore a black plastic nameplate. Her name was "Ms. Walker."

"Yes," replied Mark. "We're on the sailing vessel *Rhapsody in Blue* docked outside. We've just landed and we'd like immigration clearance."

Ms. Walker knew exactly who we were: We had been talking to the port authority via radio for the last hour, and we had been directed into the harbor. Also, unlike *C'est si Bon, Rhapsody in Blue* had been closely monitored on the Bermudian radar. By the time we walked into the office at Liberty Dock, all Customs and Immigration personnel on Bermuda understood who we were and what business we had. Ms. Walker, with her offer to "hep" us, was playing the Customs game. We had all played it before. We could do it again.

"You got your clearance form?" Ms. Walker continued.

"No, I don't have any form," Mark answered. "We just got here."

"Well, you got to have a form," Ms. Walker demanded. "How you 'spect to clear, you got no form?" She leaned the full weight of her upper body into the counter, an unattractive posture that exposed a plumber's butt and also tugged precariously at the unbuttoned opening in her shirt. She maintained a stare back at Mark through her coke-bottle glasses, switching the tooth-pick from one side of her mouth to the other, thinking, perhaps, that her theatrical pause was creating some sort of crescendo of guilt. "How you 'spect to clear, you got no form?" she repeated as if she enjoyed the obvious inspiration of her question. "You got to have a form to clear, don't cha?"

"Well, I don't have a form," Mark said. "You must have a form here, don't you?"

"Yeah, I gotta form right here," relented Ms. Walker as she reached into the drawer beside her. She had several dozen forms, all of them similar, and she handed one to Mark along with a pen as if the drama of the previous few minutes had never occurred.

Mark filled out the form as Ms. Walker remained beside him and watched every stroke of the pen. Finally completed, Mark handed the form to Ms. Walker who inspected and stamped it and asked if we had a flare gun. Satisfied we did *not*, she informed Mark of the $189 landing fee—an increase from the $25 I paid on *C'est si Bon*—and

236

accepted his credit card for payment. We were never welcomed to Bermuda, nor asked to surrender our passports, but we were free to go. We untied *Rhapsody in Blue* from Liberty Dock and headed over to the fuel dock.

It didn't take long to charge up almost a thousand dollars of fuel cost. (That's why I no longer bother with boat ownership.) While we filled the boat's tanks and the eight 5-gallon fuel jugs we had, Mark dispatched Bert to see if we could get a dock for the night. Several sailboats from the ARC—the Atlantic Rally for Cruisers—were already at Bermuda, and with all the good docks taken, we had to settle to tie-up along a wall with huge black tires (fenders) that eventually covered *Rhapsody in Blue* with a horrible black sooty filth. Still, we were grateful: Without the dock, we would have had to anchor. And without a dinghy, we would have had to beg a ride to shore.

Immediately after tying up at our "tire dock," Mark broke out some cold beers along with shots of rum for himself and the other two drinkers. "Cheers!" they all said as one drink after another was consumed. They drank with gusto, anxious for that first taste of alcohol after several days of abstinence.

"Nothing for you, Mike?" Mark asked.

"No, you guys go ahead," I said. "I'm fine." It had been several years since I had felt the desire to drink alcohol, though I recognized the enjoyment the men were having at the time. One drink sets up the desire to have another, I know, so I turned my attention elsewhere. It's the desire to drink—plus the drinking itself, of course—that I'm happy to avoid. It felt good to not feel the need.

While the drinks flowed, I left the boat and walked to town to check on *Chicks Bar and Grill*, the bar Ian and I had rowed over to in our dinghy when we first landed at Bermuda. I couldn't recognize what might have been the bar, but I asked around and several Bermudians pointed to the *Limelite Café*, remembering that it used to be called *Chick's Bar*. The building had been expanded and the

237

exterior was refurbished, so it looked nothing like my memory imagined. It was also closed in the mid-afternoon, so I couldn't even go inside. I had hoped for more. I would have loved to sit at the bar and recreate the time when I *sat with a nice, cool drink in my hand, electrified by the smell of a woman's perfume as she walked behind me, listening to the Reggae music that made normal a world that continued to rock after six days at sea.* And though I could not, the nostalgia I experienced resuscitated my soul as I relived the particulars of my very special 34th birthday, one that seemingly had passed a lifetime or two prior.

Later in the day, we stopped at the only grocery store in town and filled two carts with enough food-stuffs to feed four hungry sailors for the four days it would take us to get to Beaufort. We even picked up a little extra for the unlikely extension in case we veered north for Newport. The four of us, along with the other shoppers, squeezed through the narrow aisles of the small store. Those ahead of us were lucky because we cleared the shelves everywhere we stopped. Bill had created a grocery list, which made our selection efforts more efficient than our prior ones in St. Maarten. I made sure we got a lot of Muesli, a real carbohydrate necessity. Mark liked his salads, so we got plenty of lettuce and picked up all the fresh fruits and vegetables we could find. Boxed milk was in short supply but Mark challenged me why we didn't use regular milk; that's what we got and it worked fine. The bill set Mark back half a "boat unit"—b.o.a.t.: break out another thousand—and for a small tip, the manager's nephew delivered the groceries to the boat.

We ate dinner that night at the *Wahoo Restaurant*, a rather elegant affair a short walk from the boat. It was a busy place that evening with a dozen or more patrons sitting at patio tables outside the front door, each armed with a cocktail. At one table sat four or five sailors, made obvious from the raggedy clothing they all wore, as well as the deck shoes, beards and dark tans well-sported in the group.

Their table was littered with several empty glasses of past drinks and a couple of ash trays overfilled with cigarette butts and well-chewed cigar ends. They were a boisterous bunch, quite drunk it seemed, and they stood as a sharp contrast with the occupants of the table next to them: three couples of well behaved, well dressed, seemingly affluent senior citizens. A third table contained several younger women, all dressed up for the evening and carrying on in an animated conversation at a volume that superseded all others. Behind these women, hidden by a table and some chairs, sat a teenaged girl on the concrete ground, her back up against the wall of the restaurant. The girl's white blouse was smeared with dirt and her short, lime-green skirt was hiked up inappropriately. She stared off into space with drugged eyes, oblivious to the activities around her. She had to have been alone, I thought. No friend would let another friend be abandoned in such a manner.

We were escorted through the long and narrow three dining room establishment, and I saw that most tables were filled, some by patrons wearing tie or gown, and others by boaters casually dressed in foul weather jackets. (I was disappointed that I still didn't see the black Bermuda shorts with the white shirt, dress shoes, and long gartered stockings that are traditional—and normally ubiquitous—in Bermuda.) Eventually we came to an outdoor portion of the restaurant, a large patio with a nautical motif which made the room appear like the aft salon on a catamaran. A large corner table was presented to us and we were still trying to figure our seating arrangements when a black woman carrying a water pitcher appeared and introduced herself as Yolanda, our server.

"Hiya darlings," she said with a large smile of beautiful white teeth. "Oh, I see we have a table of good looking gentlemen here tonight," she continued, her mischievous eyes suggestively scanning Bill's backside as if he were a possible escort for later. "How you fellows feelin' this evening?" she asked, her island accent and diction becoming obvious by this time.

We could all see that Yolanda enjoyed having fun and joking around with customers. She had a carefree nature and she carried her voluptuous body unapologetically and with the pride of a liberated woman. As she filled our water glasses, the curves of her body—both up top and in her hips—were obvious to us all. I was certain that all of us found the sight of her cleavage rather distracting, but nobody said a word, at least at first. It was a crowded room, however, and Yolanda was not a small woman, so after she bounced her hips off one or two of our chairs, Bill made a few jovial and flirting comments and the ice was broken. From then on, discussions of various body parts, as well as their related functions and non-functions, became the norm. We had a lot of fun that night—good food too—and as the evening progressed, and one alcoholic drink was replaced with another, tongues really began to loosen up.

Bert and Mark, two veterans from the war in Viet Nam, began talking about their prior use of drugs. The conversation began harmless enough: Each man told about smoking marijuana during the war—"everybody did it," they said. They also spoke (bragged, really) about the use of pot, hashish, mescaline, and "acid" in high school and in college. As the drinks were replenished, the conversation continued with each man talking about his extensive drug use and the several close-calls he had experienced.

"Yeah, Nam wasn't like you see in the movies," Mark told us. His words were now slurred and I noticed that his eyes were almost closed. It was getting late.

"How so?" Bert asked, one drunk sailor encouraging another.

"Most of the time we sat around with nothing to do," Mark went on. "Hell, we'd go three or four days, sometimes a week, without doing a thing. Someone always had pot—it was everywhere—so what the hell: We smoked."

I was wondering how we could end this "drunk log" that had been going on for a couple of hours. I was bored. It was past midnight and I wanted to go to bed. I didn't want to be rude, but I knew I would be leaving soon.

Mark continued: "Sometimes we'd be allowed to go to town and that was always a relief. A lot of the guys would go see Mama-san [the head mistress at a brothel] but I was never into that. I used to go to the opium dens. Yeah, they were fun. Real mellow! They're really like a bar, but they serve both booze and opium. I liked opium okay, but it makes you real tired. And the withdrawals are pretty bad."

The conversation was deteriorating, I could see. Both Mark and Bert had been revealing a lot of history that, without the lubricating effects of alcohol, they never would have shared. I had heard enough. It was time to go. Too bad I didn't...

"Then I tried heroin, and man..., *that* I could really get to like.

"Get out!" I said in disbelief. "You did heroin?" I had never met anyone who had used heroin. I found it incredible that Mark, the captain of the boat I was sailing, was now telling us that he had once been a user.

"Oh yeah! I was a junkie. A lot of us were. And with heroin, if you stop you get sick. I mean *throwing up* sick. You can't just stop; you have to go to a medical detox. I was a junkie for three months. Then my time was up and I came home and went into detox. It's scary shit, man, but it wasn't too bad, and I'm fine now."

"You haven't used since?"

"Oh, hell no! You can't go back. That's how it works. You go back, you die!"

The next morning I awoke to somebody pounding on the boat. It was the dock-master. He had somebody else reserved for the dock and we had to move. It was 7:00! I grabbed a quick shower at the marina and came back to the boat to see Bill untying the dock lines. I gave him a hand and we jumped aboard, the horribly sooty deck made even

241

worse by the awful dock lines. Mark headed for the channel and we were on our way again. We had been on Bermuda only 20 hours. It was the shortest duration anyone could recall.

We sailed around the north end of Bermuda and headed west, tracing in reverse the course Ian and I had made on *C'est si Bon*. I saw St. David's Head sector light, the same one that had guided Ian and me as we defied the piloting instructions on our way in. On *Rhapsody in Blue* we traversed the route during daylight hours, and I was surprised at how far offshore we had to remain to avoid the reefs, infamous for their treachery. Indeed, those reefs have taken so many vessels that the Bermudian government set up a free radio-based service that guides all boats in. They found it cheaper to do so, rather than rescuing all of the distressed sailors.

The wind, though light, remained more or less southerly, similar to what we had experienced since the beginning of the voyage. The grey sky looked like a huge, featureless wool blanket, its opacity denying the sun all presence. A few showers came our way as the already hot and humid tropical air passed over the islands where it picked up even more moisture and dumped it on us after clearing land. The rain felt neither cool nor pleasant, and immediately after each shower a wave of heat would overcome us as if someone had opened the door of a blast furnace. After a few repeats the wind died completely, abandoning us when we could have used it most. Resembling drowned rats, we struggled to remain positive. We had both the main and genoa up, but the two sails hung uselessly, looking like a couple of bed sheets that someone had hung out to dry in the rain. We turned on the engine, hoping to move along as best as possible.

The *unendurable agony* lasted but a few hours. We sailed on, motored actually, and sometime in the afternoon we escaped the island interference. It was as if someone had flipped a switch: The southwest wind rose to a

242

respectable 12 knots, and the heat, humidity and cloud cover all cleared away, bringing a sunny but cooler afternoon, accentuated by two rainbows and a blue sky that contained nary a single cloud. The "Westerlies" had arrived! We were finally free from the heat of the tropics, that which had been with us since before the voyage began. We all changed out of our wet clothes, the pronounced change in demeanor of everyone evidenced by the laughing and yukking about going on. I noticed a couple of long sleeved shirts coming out, a reflection of the new temperatures. For the first time on the voyage we hoisted the mizzen sail—the "jigger" Bert called it—proving at last that *Rhapsody in Blue* indeed was a yawl, not just a sloop with a small mast and an always furled sail near her stern. It was the beginning of a wonderful beam reach, one that would continue for several days.

As we were hanging up our wet clothes, Bert offered to cook dinner, another "first" for the voyage. "Beef stew," he said. "I'll cook up my famous beef stew, made in red wine sauce."

"Sorry, no booze while underway," I reminded him.

"Oh, it's okay," he said. "All the alcohol cooks off."

"No booze while underway," I repeated, making a point and not about to budge. I had seen this half-beer drinker in action, and I wasn't about to give him or either of the two others any opportunity to bend the rule on alcohol. Fortunately, Mark came to my aid.

"The rule is no booze, Bert. If even one of us insists, it's no booze."

"But..."

I had seen Mark diffuse opposing opinions before: he would let everybody have their say, then announce his decision—and hold to it. I was grateful that he stood up for me this time. Indeed, it was Bert himself who had previously taken me aside, sharing with me his *expert* knowledge on the change that overcomes a person after even a single drink. I agreed on that point—though not on

243

his expertise—and I was surprised at his current leaning. Regardless, with the captain's orders given, Bertie changed the menu from beef stew to re-heated meat-loaf, which avoided the issue altogether.

Each morning we all read Ken McKinley's weather analysis, matching it up with the GRIBS weather chart. Ken's report always discussed the then familiar storm, the one that had lingered in our path for over a week. The same storm also monopolized the GRIBS chart, an obvious counter-clockwise formation half way between Newport and Bermuda, 300 miles from our present location. We had expected it to subside over the several days—most storms will—but instead, the gale had worsened with winds up to 50-knots.

The *Beaufort Scale*, an ancient but still used mariner's scale of worsening weather conditions, places a 50-knot wind at "Force 10," a designation made infamous by a storm that sunk several sailboats and took several lives during a race off the UK coast several years prior. Wave heights nearing 30 feet can be expected in Force 10 conditions. The sea would appear like a white sheet and all other visibility would be severely restricted. (You wouldn't be able to look into the wind.) On shore, trees would be uprooted and poorly secured buildings would be blown away.

I couldn't see any way that we could sail to Newport. None of us could. Indeed, even if the storm somehow disappeared, a secondary storm—a "low"—followed it, and with the additional complication of a Gulf Stream crossing, it looked like a Beaufort landing for sure. In spite of it all, however, each morning Ken's analysis identified a "possibility" of getting through. "A possibility of a Newport attempt exists but depends on the storms moving easterly," Ken's report said in its normal ultra-formal language. "Until that happens, I advise maintaining the current plan and sailing toward Beaufort."

I had told myself that I would never wish away any of this voyage. Bert's irritations aside, it had all of the ingredients of the best voyage of my life. With the uncertainty created by Ken's alternate sail plans, however, I recognized that all too familiar marked decrease in enthusiasm. It was the same change of attitude I had experienced and tried to defy on so many prior voyages. On only one voyage—the one with Lisa on *Tender II*—did I *not* at one point wish for an early end. I tried to force my attitude: *Stay positive*, I told myself. *Enjoy the moment. Accept all alternatives.* My attempts were successful, but only partially so.

It didn't surprise me when the others voiced similar feelings over the next day or two: Bill mentioned that the fun of the voyage was over and he felt like he wanted to be in. Bert said that he had "channel fever," meaning the same thing. In a philosophical conversation, Mark and Bert questioned why either of them went to sea at all. "It's not comfortable, not really fun, it's costly, and it takes up a whole lot of time," Mark said. "I really don't know why I continue to go to sea."

"I don't really enjoy it at all," Bert agreed. "I do it for pay."

All of these were over-reactions to a little bit of bad news—and it was actually good news: we *might* be able to make it home. It was that period of disillusionment that comes along during every significantly long adventure. I had experienced it many times, and had discussed it with several groups of friends and adventurers. I had come to believe it as unavoidable but temporary. On this voyage I tried forcing my attitude, not knowing if such is even possible. The others came out of their disillusionments as well, using whatever mental tools they possessed. We had a long way to go. We might as well be happy.

One aspect of the voyage that had become increasingly difficult for me to endure was the briefing I would receive from ol' Bertie each night at midnight as I went on watch. Bert had a real need to be recognized for his sailing prowess and his best opportunity to get his "fix" was at midnight. One night he burned my ear off, bragging how he had maintained a particular course, one that was impossible to sail. The chart plotter clearly showed the actual course, and I found it incredible that he took so much trouble trying to convince me of a mistruth that had so little bearing anyway. On another evening he told me I should sail east of a rhumb line when the captain had told me otherwise. He put up quite an argument then secretly checked on me, returning later with, "You're right, Mike, Mark says to go west." What an ass, I thought. And I had to take his shit every night. Why? *To get along for the duration of the voyage.* Indeed, I had to take a lot of shit from ol' Bertie. We all did.

Repeatedly I asked myself what the proper reaction to Bert's comments and behavior should be. Should I lash out at him verbally? No, that certainly wouldn't be appropriate. Should I sit him down and calmly tell him my concerns with his behavior? Possibly. Should I discuss the problem with the captain? I thought not: One fear I had was that Bert might back Mark in a corner where Mark would be forced to announce his legitimate authority as "mate." Then we'd have an *authorized* pain-in-the-ass to deal with.

So west we sailed, toward Beaufort, and for some of the most beautiful sailing days I had ever experienced. The southwest wind blew strong and steady and we took it on the port beam. It's a very normal summer wind in the latitudes we were sailing, the same common wind found all summer in the Great Lakes. Born in America's west, the southwest wind gets its strength from the heat of the Sonoran Desert and its direction from the earth's rotation— two very reliable phenomena. It's a formidable force in the atmosphere, and many a storm has been pushed off its course by our old friend, the southwest wind. Day by day, Ken could see its influence on the storm that was obstructing our way to Newport. As his twice daily forecasts appeared, I could see that he was more optimistic of a Newport landing. By late Monday he was advising us to sail north.

Well, not just yet. The storm still lingered and the normally friendly southwest wind in the area between Hatteras and New York was too strong for safe sailing. "Continue west for now," Ken's analysis read, "and remain south to avoid some serious eddies coming off the Gulf Stream." He mentioned that the winds north of Hatteras would remain very strong and unsafe for at least a few more days, and that we would probably go through a corner of the storm on Tuesday. We set a waypoint where we would eventually turn north. It was two days away, and not in the direction of Newport.

I wrote Lisa an e-mail, explaining the situation. She had gotten her hopes up for an early landing in Beaufort; now it would be a late landing in Newport—probably a difference of five days. I appreciated that Lisa missed me and would have loved to have me home early, but when she wrote back and said she was *disappointed*—twice—well, *that* I didn't really appreciate. I sent another note, saying I missed her too and encouraging her to stay positive. Inside, however, I was bummed. I didn't need to be told twice that she was disappointed. I know she didn't say she was disappointed *in me*, but that's how I took it. As luck would have it, shortly after my last e-mail Mark's satellite telephone ran out of minutes and we were unable to get it reset. We would have no communication—no e-mail, no GRIBS, no Ken McKinley forecasts—for the rest of the voyage. Lisa wanted to write and say that she had over-stated her point. She wanted to apologize. She was unable to do so. It was a lesson that sometimes you don't get a second chance.

Lisa wasn't the only one learning a lesson that day: Shortly after dinner Mark smelled propane in the cabin. Propane, the fuel for the stove, is heavier than air, and if it leaks from the stove it can fill a boat and explode. It is very dangerous and there are several safe-guards on a boat to prevent a disaster. One of these safeguards is an electrical shut-off at the propane tank. Another is the stove valve at each burner, very much like the ones you see at home. Both should be closed when turning off the stove.

At a seamanship safety course, Bill was shown to turn off the tank switch first, then the burner valve. This lets the propane out of the line leading to the burner and seems like a good idea, at least at first. Bill forgot to close the burner valve, however, and later when somebody else used the stove, they used a different burner and the valve Bill had left open allowed propane to flow freely and fill the cabin. Bill had no idea that his switch sequence allowed the problem to occur. I told him about it in private a while later, but after a couple of days I saw that he was still following the procedure he was taught—and he again made the error of leaving the burner valve open. Some habits die hard.

On Tuesday, what was left of the huge storm that prevented us from going to Newport finally reached us. By this time it had lost most of its fury and we would receive it simply as a cold front. A cold front generally involves a wind switch from warm southerly winds to cooler northerly ones. Squalls often accompany the front, and rain usually follows it as well. Without outside communication, we were unclear what the front would bring. More importantly, we didn't know when it would hit—sometime in the afternoon or evening we figured. In preparation, Mark had us work together to put two reefs in the main and put the staysail up—all well in advance of the front. We were set for the worst.

At 10:00 PM—two hours before my watch—Bert had Bill wake me to help the two of them tack the boat. Tacking is normally a one man job, two under trying conditions. Calling for a third man was unnecessary. This was just ol' Bertie once again trying to establish his authority. I was next on watch, however, and if a call for help was made, it was my responsibility to provide it. I put on full foul weather gear and reported to the cockpit.

The wind was still south but cool, so the front was on its way. A half an hour later the wind switched from south to north, suddenly and strong. Maintained by the auto-pilot, *Rhapsody* held her westerly course while the three of us let go the sail on one side and pulled it in on the other. Ten minutes later the wind died and we turned on the engine. Bertie said he wanted me "on stand-by," and with that being his call, I sat with him for the full two hours until his watch ended. I wouldn't have minded losing sleep or providing help had it been required, but this had nothing to do with required assistance. I was very happy to see ol' Bertie go below at the end of his watch. His last words to me were, "whatever you do, don't turn off the engine." My last gesture to him was my middle finger behind his back.

I wasn't long into my watch when the north wind began to blow once again. An hour later it was a near-gale of 30 knots. I had quickly disregarded Bert's instruction about the engine, but the switch wasn't working and I couldn't turn it off. I was on my knees looking at the switch with my flashlight when Mark and Bert got up, giving me the obvious instruction to turn the engine off. (Leadership was not at its best that evening, folks.) I told them of the problem and Mark informed me about a second switch that Bill must have hit when he turned on the running lights at dusk. (I had never before seen two ignition switches for the same engine.) Turning this switch finally got the engine off and I put the transmission in reverse—an important step to stop the propeller from spinning and prevent damage to the engine. Convinced the boat was in safe hands—oh, I flatter myself—the captain and his self-promoted *mate* returned to their bunks and I was left alone in the heavy sea and 30-knots of wind. A squall came by, increasing the wind and waves further, but the boat was well-reefed and indeed, in capable hands. We were both in our element, the boat and I, and together we sailed the high sea as the others slept. By the time Mark came on watch, the squall was long gone and the winds had settled as well. I had been on deck for five

249

hours and robbed of important sleep before midnight. I crashed in my bunk, exhausted but thankful for the glorious sailing just afforded to me.

As I slept the northwest wind from the long-watched storm continued to subside and by the time I went on watch at noon, it had reversed itself again to the southwest. Still a light wind of 10 knots, it did little to reduce the seven foot seas which continued from the north, contrary to the wind. The auto-pilot had always worked perfectly, but with the confused sea and weak wind *Rhapsody* drunkenly snaked along her way. I tried resetting the auto-pilot and re-trimming the sails but the wayward steering continued. Something was wrong. While I hand steered, the others checked all the switches and circuit breakers they could. When Mark determined that the drive motor of the auto-pilot had blown, I thought for sure we'd be forced to hand-steer for the remainder of the trip. When he produced a spare, I was impressed and delighted to no end. We went hove-to and began the repair.

(A note on going hove-to: to go "hove-to" is to turn the boat beam to the wind, with a well-reefed mainsail set normally and a staysail or well-reefed genoa pulled hard to windward, seemingly from the wrong side of the boat. The rudder is then locked in place as if to turn the boat into the wind. With the boat set as such it will remain abeam to the seas, calming bobbing like a duck in water, and moving with only a slight drift to leeward, that is, downwind. It's a safe way to leave a boat unattended, and can be used in all but the most extreme of conditions. We went "hove-to" to do a repair, but it can also be used if a lone sailor requires sleep, or even if a tired crew wants to sit out a storm.)

The repair was extensive, requiring a partial disassembly of the steering mechanism and movement of quite a bit of gear. All the while we didn't know whether or not the spare motor actually worked, and quite a cheer went out when its functionability was proven. We had been hove-to for three hours by the time the repair was completed.

While we had worked, the wind had freshened to 25 knots. In the hove-to position, *Rhapsody* was already pointing north toward home. We had been heading west— not the direction we wanted to go—for over four days and we saw *Rhapsody's* orientation as a sign. Mark looked out at the sea, first west and into the wind, then north. Finally he made the call we all wanted to hear: "Let's go home," he said. Before he could change his mind, Bill and I re-set the sails and rudder and kicked *Rhapsody* in the butt, sending her on her way. We had almost 500 miles to go, but the southwest wind was howling and the currents in and around the Gulf Stream would push us along for much of the way. With any luck we would be reach Newport in about three days. First, however, we had quite a seaway to deal with, and that evening we would be crossing the dreaded Gulf Stream.

"It's going to be a tough night," Mark said to us all as we furled the mainsail. He instructed us to avoid using the auto-pilot that night, stating that the heavy sea might blow our last motor. He had some plugs specially made for the cubby-holes around the cockpit and he began putting them in place. He was obviously expecting severe conditions. "Bill," he continued, "I'm going to double up with you on watch. We can switch on and off at the wheel." Yep, I thought, it was going to be a rough night.

With just an hour to go before his watch, Bill fired up the stove and cooked up the last of the frozen pizzas we had aboard. I'm normally not one for a pre-made dinner purchased in a box, but I was hungry that evening. The pizza tasted pretty good and I gulped down my share. Bill appeared sluggish, not eating even half of his meal. I wondered what was wrong. He left his unfinished plate on the gimbaled stove and sat quietly in his berth.

"Not hungry?" I asked him.

"No."

251

"Are you seasick?" I asked. The wind and the seas were up and we had been cooped up in the engine room for several hours. It would be no surprise to see a bit of seasickness aboard.

"No," he said. "Just got a few apprehensions."

Apprehensions. It had never crossed my mind to be apprehensive. Yes, the sea was up. Yes, we were about to cross the Gulf Stream. Yes, it was going to be a rough night. But I had never felt any reserve, any fear, any *apprehensions*—not at this time, nor at any other time on any other voyage I had been on. Boredom? Yes. Anger? Of course. The desire to murder a certain lanky arrogant know-it-all? Let's not even go there. But *apprehensions?* No, I had never felt apprehensive on a boat. Well, maybe once during my first storm experience on *C'est si Bon,* but never since. Not even one time.

But apprehensive or not, at 6:00 Bill donned his foul weather gear and life-harness and reported to the helm for his watch.

"It's blowing quite a stink," Mark yelled into the wind. "Here take the wheel. You gotta make sure it doesn't round up on you."

And so, a very rough night at sea began. Mark and Bill took tricks at the wheel for the first three hours while Bert and I tried to get some rest. The wind screamed in the rigging and *Rhapsody in Blue* was tossed around like a toy. At one point I heard a great rushing of water, and I learned later that a huge wave had come from behind and pooped the boat, completely filling the cockpit with water. (Those cubby-hole plugs had come in handy.) Shortly before nine, I suggested to Bert that we double-up as well. He didn't seem to like the idea, but with a shrug and a grunt he accepted my suggestion. We dressed up in full foul weather gear, put on our life-harnesses and tethers, and at 9:00 we relieved the two tired sailors at the helm. Bert took the helm first. I sat in the cockpit protected by the dodger. The southwest wind came over our port quarter and was up over 35 knots. The seas, though we couldn't see them, were ten or twelve feet.

Throughout the voyage Bert had practiced hand-steering much more than I. He was good at it. (He was good at most aspects of sailing.) He took the wheel, and though only the genoa was up—and it partially furled—*Rhapsody* repeatedly tried to round up into the wind. Each time it did Bert would have to fight to keep her pointed downwind. Most of the time he kept her sailing along pretty straight, but every now and then *Rhapsody* would round up out of control and Bert would have to put all of his weight into the wheel to bring the bow back down. I didn't look forward to my turn at the wheel but soon enough I heard Bert's, "Okay, your turn," and I moved back to take over.

"Now, if you keep an eye on Cassiopeia, then you..." Bert said as he pointed up at the constellation. The boat turned sharply to starboard and Bert had to fight with all his might to stop the boat from broaching. "Anyway, keep Cassiopeia just off to port and..." *Rhapsody* threatened to broach again, this time to port. "Or you can steer by the compass..." Another near broach. Then another. Then another.

"Bertie, why don't you just let me steer the boat, God dammit?" I yelled at him. "I know how to steer!"

And with that he handed me the wheel and went and sulked under the dodger. I steered the boat; it was unbelievably difficult to keep her pointed downwind. If I allowed it to round up even a little bit, the huge waves coming from behind would take hold of the stern, swinging it around and threatening a full broach. It was a design fault of the hull, I would learn later. The rule beating overhangs I thought were so dainty and nautical were two giant levers that the sea used to turn the boat around as if it were a wing-nut. One moment of inattention and the boat would round up square to the wind in a full broach, the momentum rolling the boat over into a knockdown, perhaps flooding the boat with sea water. I could see now how *Rhapsody* had suffered the knockdown in the fall nor'easter *Sean*. I knew now why overhangs were so dangerous.

Steering by the compass was difficult and fatiguing. I tried Bert's idea of using the stars. "Hey, you're right! It *is* easier to steer by Cassiopeia." Bertie gave me a smirk. He was still sulking and not speaking. That suited me just fine.

Bert went back on and fought the weather for his next hour. I recommended that we furl the genoa a bit more but he refused. Finally, out of breath and physically exhausted at the end of his second turn at steering, he agreed that we should reef. "Go get Mark to help us," Bert commanded.

"We can do it ourselves, don't you think?" I asked. Reefing (partially furling) the genoa is a relatively easy affair and Mark needed his sleep. I thought we ought to give it a try.

"No, get Mark," he said.

I didn't want to argue. By this time, I had had it with Bertie and his pompous ways. I had used every social skill at my disposal to get on the right side of him but I found him an impossible ego-maniac. My goal with him was to get along as well as possible until the voyage ended. I had no plans of "letting him have it" at the end, but I looked forward to never seeing the scrawny old goat again. I went down and woke up Mark.

"Bert wants you to help as we reef the genoa," I told him. I didn't want to blame it on Bert, but I was embarrassed at the request.

"Why don't you two just do it?" he asked.

"Bert says the three of us should do it."

"No," Mark said. "One of you can steer while the other lets off the sheet and pulls in the furler. Do it two feet at a time. It'll work."

I was embarrassed. I felt inadequate. Mark was walking me through a very simple job as if I had never been on a boat before.

"Okay, we'll do it," I said and went back up on deck. "Mark says we should do it ourselves," I told Bert.

"What?" he exclaimed in disbelief.

"Mark says we should do it ourselves," I repeated as I picked up a winch handle. I put the handle in a winch—not even the correct one for the job—and Bertie went ballistic.

"You little son-of-a-bitch," he yelled. "You'll do what you're told and that's all there is to it. Your problem is that you don't know how to follow orders. You never listen to what I tell you, only Mark. Now God dammit you will do..."

All right, you get the picture. With his finger in my face, and nearly broaching the boat several times, he went on and on with all the energy he could muster. Mark eventually got up, scolded us both, and helped us reef the genoa to a more manageable size. He went back to bed and Bertie and I were left with ourselves and our red faces, both consumed with all the anger and humiliation we possessed. We exchanged a couple of insults, a couple of acknowledgements of fault, and in time, even a couple of compliments. As I had done on *That Darn Cat,* I sat down next to Bert and tried to gain his confidence by bolstering his ego. I told him that I thought he was a good, knowledgeable sailor. I told him that we needed to get along while aboard and that I was going to do everything I could to respect his opinions and do what he asked. My speech was not as unrehearsed as it had been on *That Darn Cat.* I didn't shake Bert's hand as I had done with Julian, and the results I achieved were not as good either. It worked well enough, however, and by the end of the watch we had reconciled enough that we probably wouldn't kill each other. He knew he had gone too far, however. *He* was the professional sailor on board, not I, and *he* had demonstrated to the captain how unprofessional he could be under pressure. He had screwed up and he knew it. And though we were congenial with each other and he treated me with kid gloves for the rest of the voyage, Bertrand

McCormick—ol' Bertie—will always be a man I hope to never see again.

After a short sleep, I awoke at 7:00 to a gorgeous sunny day with the winds down to a manageable 25 knots. From the cabin I could see that the sea was still pretty wild, and every so often a wave would hit the side of the boat and send a shower of seawater into the cockpit. Under auto-pilot *Rhapsody in Blue* sailed true, oblivious to the stormy seas and hot emotions she was asked to endure the previous night. I spotted Bill who was on watch, standing on the aft deck and holding on to the mizzen mast for support.

"Good morning," I called to him. "I'm putting the kettle on. You up for some coffee?"

"Hey, good morning dude," he yelled back, a smile quickly coming to his face. Bill and I had become as thick as mud over the course of the voyage. While Mark and especially Bert could be supercilious at times, Bill and I were the ones who performed most of the sailing maneuvers and did all of the cooking. We were proud of the way we handled not only the boat, but also the trying personalities of the others on board. We had developed a great camaraderie, and as with the divisions between union and management, or between officer and enlisted, we saw ourselves as the "grunts in steerage" who did the real work. Bill had previously voiced an admiration of my sailing ability—though I thought his was at least equal—and I was grateful for his unending eagerness to help in any and all situations. On a personal level, he impressed me with his ability to share personal feelings (like his apprehensions) and his ability to act calmly when some of those feelings (i.e.: anger at Bertie) were really eating at him.

He came down into the cabin. "You making coffee?" he asked. "Sure I'll have one." We chatted a while, acknowledging the rough night, of course. All of us had had a tough time, but Bill had to conquer his personal fears in addition to the challenging sea. We were all glad we had finished the Gulf Stream crossing, but I think Bill was especially relieved.

Bert got up. "Good morning," he said to each of us, nodding as we returned the greeting. He turned on the stove and started heating up a pot of water. "Anybody for oatmeal?" he asked.

I was still angry with Bertie but I had to admit he had his favorable attributes. When not trying to prove his superiority or establish authority, he really wasn't an unpleasant individual. One thing he did exceptionally well was making oatmeal: "Sure, I'll have a bowl," I said.

The coffee was ready so I poured each of us a cup and we began a meandering three-way conversation. We talked about the rough night, the present conditions, the short 300 miles to Newport, and the beauty of not having to chase Ken McKinley's "ghosts" across the ocean. One would have thought we were brothers. At one point I mentioned the conflict between Bert and me:

"Yeah, Bert and I really got into it for a bit," I admitted. I didn't need to discuss the matter, but the topic needed to be tabled, just so that Bill knew where we all stood.

"Yeah, I heard ya," said Bill.

"Hey, it's over," Bert said with finality.

"Yeah, you're right, Bert. It's over."

It required no more. All four of us on board were now aware of what had occurred and where the outcome stood. Nobody cared about details, and the matter was best put out of our minds. Our conversation wandered to other topics, and soon we each had a bowl of warm oatmeal in our hands. As I've mentioned, Bert did a good job at making oatmeal, and this time he out-did himself, adding raisins, pecans, brown sugar and cream. The cereal warmed our bones and took the chill out of our hearts. Soon we were carrying on like boys at a tent party, but in hushed tones so as to not wake the captain who had slept very little all night.

By mid-day, the sea had settled down leaving moderate five and seven foot waves. The wind remained from the southwest, and at 20 knots it made for a pleasant broad reach. It was a glorious sailing day—another one in a voyage that had seen its share. We were all getting along again, in fact better than we had the entire voyage. It was as if the previous night had exhausted all the anger and hostilities we possessed. I took to reading, something I had not been able to do with the duties at hand. *Great Expectations* and the adventures of Pip captivated my attention and before long Charles Dickens' epic of description had come and gone. Bill spent much of his time in the galley making us up a special penultimate dinner of roast beef. Mark was able to acquire a telephone signal and spent much of his time conducting business. (You can take a boy out of the country, but...) Bert became obsessed with the Raymarine Chart Plotter, and spent hours going through the manual and testing out the various functions as he learned them.

All of us had taken on changed modes of behavior, enjoying a content and tranquil existence. None of us— including Bert—seemed inclined to do the sorts of things that caused irritation. We gave each other space and spoke kindly and respectfully to each other. We had finally found our groove. We ate the fabulous dinner of roast beef, potatoes, carrots and broccoli that Bill had worked all afternoon to create. Terrific dinner. Terrific company. It truly had been a terrific voyage.

Ten days prior you couldn't have convinced me that I would need a second blanket at night on this voyage. It seemed like a long time past, but I could recall the searing heat we endured day and night. As we reached the New England coast, however, a cold northwest wind came at us and the night-time temperature fell to 40 degrees. In the two hours of darkness before my watch, I covered up and stole a bit of sleep. Shortly before midnight, dressed in long pants, a sweater, and my foul weather jacket, I reported to the helm to relieve Bert.

Old habits die hard and Bert wasn't about to let me off with only the required identification of the ship's course or even a short monologue of instructions. He had been reading the plotter manual all day, and he couldn't help but show me all he had learned. He showed me the dimmer to provide a night-time screen. He demonstrated how he could toggle between the radar and chart modes. He showed me the zoom, the audio enhancement, the horn. Okay, he didn't show me a horn, but he went on for over a half an hour, showing me everything I could ever know about a Raymarine Chart Plotter.

I let him go on. In fact, I encouraged him by asking questions and having him re-demonstrate some of the more complicated routines. It wasn't as if I needed the information—I had never been one to get too excited about electronics—and it wasn't as if I was really interested. I simply chose to see this man in a new light: he enjoyed improving his already vast sailing acumen, and he was eager to share his new-found knowledge.

I realized I needed to change the way I react to difficult people. Bert's imperious and arrogant behavior was tough to endure, but if I had developed a better relationship with him—in spite of his behaviors—I probably would have made things easier for myself. I tried—believe me, I tried—but I never succeeded. I had seen arrogance numerous times—not only with Bert on *Rhapsody in Blue*, but also with Julian on *That Darn Cat,* Brian on *Allegretta*, and Alex on *Tender II.* I suppose it's unavoidable in today's world of strong egos. What I required was a better strategy to deal with these people: Lord knows it's not as if they're going to go away!

Likewise, I realized I needed a better method to deal with self-appointed authority or authority that a captain assigns to a second individual, sometimes well after the voyage has started. On *Rhapsody* when Bert claimed that he was "mate," for example, I probably should have asked the captain for clarification right away. On *That Darn Cat,* where the owner casually announced that Julian was captain half-way into the voyage, probably my solution of acceptance was the only alternative.

There are other sources of problems with authority: If on board, the wife of a captain will always have some degree of authority, whether or not it is announced or even acknowledged by the captain. Any professional sailors— and Bert was one of them—simply because they are paid hands, will have a voice typically heard before that of unpaid help. And as I saw with Brian on *Allegretta,* even owner/captains with vast experience and legitimate authority can be lacking in leadership ability or emotional stability to a dangerous degree.

But I would solve none of these problems that night on *Rhapsody* as Bertie rambled on about the workings of the chart plotter. It was half past midnight when he finally finished. I thanked him for the demonstration, and he went down the companionway to the main cabin. "Call me if you need any help," was the last thing he said. After he was in bed, I realized he hadn't told me what course I was supposed to be sailing. I looked at the chart plotter. (I had to figure out how to switch it out of the automatic radar mode of which Bert was so proud.) Switched to the correct mode, I realized we had been sailing 20 degrees west of the rhumb line. I didn't know if there was a reason for this or if Bert had ignored the obvious responsibility while studying the plotter manual so intensely. I thought to awaken him and ask but did not. I split the difference and let *Rhapsody* sail on. It was cold. I went below and made a cup of tea.

Friday, our last full day at sea, dawned exceedingly cold and with little or no wind. I slept as late as possible but by 8:00 I was up with the others. Our food stores were running low, but we still had plenty of oatmeal and Bert honored us with his prize meal once again. Fluky winds— "light and variable" they're called—would rule the day, and we motored along in an arc toward Newport. Being in the waters near his home, Mark knew the area well and hardly needed a chart to find our way along. Aware that we would be landing soon, the mood was changed from the previous day: then it had been one of accomplishment; now it was one of anticipation and looking forward to getting in. I began packing my bag and started cleaning the galley and main cabin. We had pre-made lasagna for dinner and afterwards I joined Bill on deck to see one of the glorious sunsets he had been telling me for days that I should not miss. It was a wonderful sunset, indeed, and as the sun fell I noticed Bill was looking not at the sun but aft off the stern. He had his head bowed as if in prayer. I think he was probably grateful for a fabulous voyage. I was too.

During Bert's 9-12 night-time watch we would cross the busy shipping lanes that allow ships in and out of New York City Harbor. There are two lanes—one in, one out—separated by a half-mile neutral zone. The ships move at about 20 knots—three times our speed—and are sometimes lined up one after another as if on a freeway. This was one time I was glad for Bert's experience.

"Do you need a hand getting through the channels?" I asked him, looking up from the book I was reading. Bill was still on watch and Bert was about to relieve him.

"No," he said. "I've been doing this all my life."

It was the type of comment I had learned to expect out of Bert, but I was happy to let him have this one. In spite of his confident words, I could see that he was anxious and it occurred to me that his cockiness was brought on by the stress of the situation. He went up on deck, and he and Bill worked to line up *Rhapsody* perpendicular to the first shipping lane, ready to charge through between ships when they could see an opening. We had the VHF radio on and I could hear the ships talking about us. I heard our engine slowed to idle, and then revved to full speed as we passed through the first of the two lanes. A half an hour later Bill came down, obviously distressed:

"That damn know-it-all Bert," he said as he threw down his foul weather jacket. "Do you know what he did? He... Oh, never mind!"

This was Bill's strength. Bertie had said or done something to offend him. Bill was belittled and frustrated—I knew the feeling. But in just a few seconds he let it go, thinking it wasn't worth his energy to concern himself with Bert and his unendurable mannerisms. I chuckled to myself and returned to my book.

I never heard any indication of the second shipping lane, but when I reported on deck at midnight Bert informed me that both lanes were behind us. He gave me his now very familiar send-off presentation—again mostly about his newly discovered secrets of the chart plotter—and then he went below. I breathed a sigh of relief, knowing that I had endured his last change-of-watch speech. It occurred to me that these repeated harassments were of my own doing: Had I not changed watches with Bill, I would have never even been aware of them.

The wind was fluky the last night out. I constantly altered the trim of the sails and the direction of the boat as we motor-sailed approximately fifty miles off of Long Island. I was proud of myself for the fine sailing job I was doing. Mark would be pleased, I thought: His crew was doing a diligent job at the helm.

Shortly before the end of the watch, with Mark already awake and making his coffee, the wind strengthened, allowing me to turn off the engine. I turned off the ignition switch but I could still hear what I thought was the engine running. I feared maybe Bill had turned on the second ignition switch and I didn't want to put the transmission in reverse with the engine running. I got on my knees and was using my flashlight to inspect the bank of switches in the back of the cockpit when Mark yelled out from the cabin, "Put it in reverse. It's spinning."

I couldn't quite explain the potential problem I saw with the switch, and much more impatiently this time, Mark scolded, "Put it in reverse, you're going to ruin the engine."

Still not convinced that the engine was off, I put the transmission in reverse and all was quiet. Mark went on explaining the problem of the propeller shaft left spinning— which was obvious—and never fully accepted my explanation that I was trying to prevent a major breakage by ensuring that the engine was off. Later, and a bit more apologetic, he stated to me, "it's not personal," which meant that it was *not personal to him*. It was an unfortunate way to end my last watch, especially when I thought I was doing such a good, diligent job.

I got up four hours later and saw we were an hour from landing. I got myself a cup of coffee and the four of us all stood in the cockpit, gazing at the geography of Rhode Island Sound and the Newport area. Thinking each of us would have at least a day before our flights home, we talked about the several activities we might do once ashore. Mark and Bert both suggested a tour of the mansions around town, and enthusiastically Mark blurted out, "Hey Mike, if you're looking for an expert to give you a tour, Bert would be the one. You could rent a car and you guys could drive around."

"That would be a good idea," I said, knowing I would never entertain such an option.

We landed at 8:30, and as soon as the dock-lines were tied the rum was out and we all toasted the fine voyage, me using water in my glass, of course. We fueled up the boat and a short, fat customs officer came aboard and cleared us into the US. At a restaurant on the pier I was able to get an internet connection and I booked a flight for 1:30 PM—just five hours after we landed.

I pleaded non-culpa at not being able to help clean the boat: I had to catch a shuttle to the airport right away. (I was glad I had cleaned up the galley and cabin the night before.) I said goodbye to Mark, and he shook my hand warmly and told me I was welcome to come and sail with him any time. Bert and Bill were on the pier ready to go to breakfast, and I said my good-byes to them as well. We all shook hands with each of us providing that one-armed man-hug that seems popular these days. As I continued on, Bert called out, "If you ever need somebody to yell at you in a gale, give me a call." We all laughed. A couple of hours later I was in the airport waiting in line to check in. The world was still rocking. I had not yet recovered from the motion of the sea.

Chapter 8. The Second Voyage of *Allegretta*

With the completion of each successive voyage described thus far, all of them fun and learning experiences but each one also a challenge of endurance and patience, I observed an undeniable whittling away of any novelty I used to feel with the sea, the wind, and even of the various sailing crafts I had previously loved so much. Certainly the recent passage on *Rhapsody in Blue*, with that most exhausting experience with Bertie McCormick, had pushed me in this direction, but that was only one man and one voyage. The others had had their cumulating effect as well. The truth is, it had been some time since I had felt the all-encompassing thrill that sailing used to instill upon me so readily. That great passion of mine, that Sailor's Dream, had all but run its course. I started to see potential future voyages as simple repetitions of those passed. Little remained to induce me to continue sailing endless miles across innumerable seas. No more did I long for the sea; no more did I stare at sailboats with awe. I saw the ocean not so much as an avenue for adventure, but rather as an endless watery expanse, the transit of which required subjecting one's self to days and weeks of heat and cold, rain and storms. By the time the delivery of *Rhapsody in Blue* came to an end, I was thinking my sailing days were over. I had felt this way before; hell, I had felt this way after virtually every voyage. This time, however, I was rather certain. One doesn't have to do anything forever, I told myself. It was time for a change.

But then a most extraordinary event occurred, an event which would change everything: Lisa and I broke up!

It happened very quickly, unpredicted by either of us. We had gone to a counselor, which, as I was told by a friend later, is something couples do only when they are about to break up anyway. Our argument was something about long term commitments or long term goals—I don't know—but before I could say "wait!" I had lost a most wonderful woman, and by far, the very best part of my life. I was stunned, numb. I felt as if I had been hit by a truck. I spent the summer in a state of semi-consciousness, unable to believe what had occurred. I was about as lost as a man could be.

"You'll be all right," a few friends said. "There'll be another." I didn't think so.

"I'm so sorry about your loss," most said. "You were such a great couple." Yeah, I know.

"It'll get better," I was told. "Time heals all wounds."

It didn't. The pain only became worse as the weeks apart became months and I came to comprehend better the loss I had incurred. The sore in my heart festered. I felt a sense of despair I didn't think possible.

I held your love on the tips of my fingers.
Then I let you fall right through my hands.
Steve Wariner

I had lost the love of a most remarkable woman, the most loving and forgiving I had ever met. If I couldn't succeed with Lisa, there was no one in the entire world who could make it easier. I had always known this. I had been saying it for years. I began to plan that I might be alone forever. I didn't know if I could do it.

Life goes on. Time will pass regardless of any pain or loss we endure, and in spite of our best efforts to slow its passage. Each night I would fall asleep, almost forgetting how damaged my soul had become. Each morning the sun would rise, and I would have but one choice and that was to stand erect and put one foot in front of the other. Life goes on.

I filled my days with my favorite hobbies: riding my bicycle, playing chess, reading—anything to convince myself and others that everything was okay. Summer expired and I started looking for activities to distract me further: I rented a condo in the mountains for ski season. I signed up for a cross-country bicycle ride the following summer. In the same regard, I convinced myself of a continued sailing ambition, renewing my OPO sailing membership, even signing up in a second (worldwide) crewing network. I spoke to a friend or two about the possibility of doing a world circumnavigation. It was a complete reversal of the conclusions I had come to just a month or two earlier. Was it escapism? You bet! But again: Life goes on.

I received information regarding numerous sailing opportunities for the fall migration: I saw that Mark Gerhardt was taking *Rhapsody in Blue* back to St. Maarten and he was again looking for crew. He had Bertrand McCormick on board again, this time officially referred to as "First Mate." (No thank you, I thought.) I also saw that Bert was doing a second trip, this one in stormy December and on an old wooden gaff-rigged schooner. (What a nightmare that would be!) An unusual number of boats were signed up for the two fall-migration rallies: the Salty Dawg and the

North American Rally for Cruisers. Rarely a day went by when I didn't receive an e-mail requesting crew.

I wasn't interested in any of these: Every year I had read about the problematic weather experienced in the fall-migration trips south and I wanted no part of them. (Later I read that a record number of rescues were required by the Coast Guard during the fall-migration of 2013. One boat sank, two others required a tow in, many gear failures, lots of problems. There was also a heart attack on one boat and a broken arm on another. Even pros like OPO owner Hank Schmitt weren't above the law of the sea: he tried to sneak in a late season delivery and ended up abandoning ship and taking a helicopter rescue to safety.) Fall migrations: No thank you!

I also received a request for crew from well-known adventurer, Eric Forsyth, and his 42-foot sloop *Fiona*. Eric had been around the world a few times, had stopped once or twice in Antarctica, and was best known for a circumnavigation of North America utilizing the previously un-transited Northwest Passage. Eric was looking for crew for another epic voyage, this one down the length of the Atlantic and back with a stop in Antarctica. Though scary, it seemed like an extraordinary adventure. I applied for a crew position for the Antarctica leg, careful to mention that my application was contingent upon the entire plan. Eric and I e-mailed a few times, and it appeared I was to be selected. The "stop" in Antarctica, however, turned out to be a circumnavigation of the icy continent, most of it along the Antarctic Circle and heading east-to-west, opposing the "screeching sixties." That seemed reckless to me, maybe even a death-wish for the elderly widowed adventurer. I sent Eric my regrets. (Reading the ship's log later, I saw that after only three days into the Antarctic leg, *Fiona* was sinking and the captain and crew had abandoned the idea of going to Antarctica, and instead were heading to South Africa to save their collective asses.)

There was one other voyage I had been considering for some time: a second attempt of an east-to-west Atlantic crossing with Brian Matroka on *Allegretta,* the same yacht and captain I had abandoned exactly one year earlier. Though it was a prudent decision I had made the prior year—the *right* decision—I had never been entirely happy with the fact that I had left Brian without crew, knowing he still had to sail across the Atlantic. I owed him nothing, and of this I was certain, but I felt a sense of unfinished business, of amends that still had to be made, of closure that was still required.

"Why would you even *consider* it?" Mark Gerhardt on *Rhapsody* had asked. "After what you've seen? You'd be crazy!" (Mark was never unclear.)

"Oh, I'd be careful with that one," my chess buddy John told me. "He might throw you overboard one night. He might come after you with a knife! I'd find another boat if I were you."

"He's an asshole!" my skiing buddy Tony proclaimed. "You *so* made the right move getting off that boat. Tell me: What has changed between then and now?"

Indeed: What had changed? Brian and I had e-mailed a few times over the summer. After his first *tongue-in-cheek* note relating that the crossing I abandoned had gone just fine, and after my *above-and-beyond* note thanking him for reconnecting and apologizing for leaving him, we had communicated several times, all of our notes friendly. Perhaps his behavior the previous year was because of abnormal circumstances, I thought. He had been under a lot of stress: Repairs were going slow; he had a timetable to make; he had medical problems; his lover was threatening to leave him. His letters seemed to portray a different person than the temper-fueled, incapable sailor with horrible leadership skills I had encountered in 2012. Maybe I had misjudged him. Maybe he really was that quiet, thoughtful, able leader with loads of sailing experience, the one I perceived last year before all our troubles began.

I sent him an e-mail: "I'm in the process of choosing a fall voyage," I wrote. "Do you have a need for crew aboard *Allegretta?*"

"Yes," he said. "I have just begun putting together a crew for the fall-2013 crossing. We would love if you could join us. We will leave from 'Gib' [Gibraltar] on October 25, stopping at the Canaries and the Cape Verdes before crossing over to St. Thomas."

"I'm a bit concerned with your planned timing," I wrote back. "Hurricane season extends through November. When do you plan to cross?"

"No problem," he stated. "The passages and stops at the Canaries and Cape Verde will take some time. We won't start the crossing until at least November 10."

If we left November 10, we would still encroach on hurricane season. I recalled the simple rule: "Don't go into hurricane territory during hurricane season." Leaving the 10th, however, we wouldn't be in the Caribbean until at least the 20th—the very end of hurricane season. With modern day weather forecasting, I figured, we would be able to avoid trouble. Once again I accepted that Brian and Lucille had already crossed the ocean nine times and would likely succeed this time. I asked Brian when and where I should meet him and made plans to go.

The voyage for 2013 contained every bit of promise I had seen for the one in 2012. Armchair sailors and active ones alike spend their whole lives dreaming to do this voyage. I had been most fortunate to receive a second chance to complete it. To sail it on such a fine and luxurious vessel as *Allegretta* was simply icing on the cake.

Though most of the entire voyage would probably be rather easy, downwind sailing, I was thinking the first leg might have some challenging conditions. "Expect strong southwest winds between Gibraltar and the Canaries starting in October," says Jim Cornell in *World Cruising Routes.* This could make for a tough 700-mile beat to windward, I knew. I looked at some pilot charts I had at home, however, and they gave no indication of the difficult and contrary winds Cornell described.

The "lows" might be a problem, and I knew this as well. The "lows" are those storms that march across the ocean every couple of days, the ones that worried me so much in 2012. I was hoping that with standard weather forecasts we could slip between the storms, however. Also, by heading south instead of straight west from Gibraltar, which was Brian's surprise variation the year before, most of the risk of those storms would be alleviated.

Once south of the Canaries we could expect heavenly sailing for the rest of the voyage with fair weather, warm temperatures, and steady following winds. My goal for the voyage was to "live in the moment," totally content to be sailing downwind in the trades, never concerned with however many days the voyage might require. I would enjoy the island stops, especially the one at the island nation called Cape Verde. I had heard about the African charm of these islands and I looked forward to this unique experience.

The voyage was to end in St. Thomas, that very special destination of my first voyage on *C'est si Bon*. I wondered if my impressions of the island this time would include the poverty, the clutter, and the racial bigotry I had seen in 1989. St. Thomas had been damaged severely by two hurricanes since I had been there. I wondered if I would recognize it at all. Would the *New York Bar* still be there? Would it still be a popular hangout for the "have-nots?" Would I meet any newly-arrived sailors, chasing their dream to follow the sun? A stop at St. Thomas: What a great way to "come full circle."

The idea of *"coming full circle"* became a defining theme of the voyage: I was *coming full circle* returning to the destination of my first voyage; I was *coming full circle* putting my life back together after the broken relationship with Lisa; I was *coming full circle* agreeing again to crew for Brian after refusing to sail with him the year before.

Crewing for Brian would satisfy the sailor's obligation I had imposed upon myself, an obligation that when you agree to a crew position, you honor that agreement. I knew it wasn't quite a legitimate obligation: Brian fully deserved to be left by himself and I was fully in my rights to leave him. But now I could finish up unfinished business. I could make things right. No longer would I think of *Allegretta* as the boat I had abandoned. No longer would my last recollections be of Brian saying "bless you" as I walked away. It could turn out to be a magnificent passage. If all went well, I thought, I could crew for this fine boat and captain again and again.

That is not to say I didn't see several issues with this trip, issues I would not normally accept. Brian had proven to be pretty hot-headed, to such an extreme that his temper was my number one concern. His habit of hurling verbal insults was not only demeaning and horrible for morale, but could escalate to something serious—perhaps a physical fight—if, say, another crew member was prone to react in such a manner. And I couldn't forget how Brian's boat handling ability and judgment had become affected by his emotional escapades. It was a big problem. For the time being I was willing to excuse the inexcusable behavior I had witnessed, but nevertheless, Brian's inability to control his temper remained a principal concern.

I also thought about Lucille, Brian's girlfriend and first mate. Lucille might be less accepting of me than Brian, and the last thing I wanted on a voyage was to have a quarrel going with the captain's girlfriend. (Although that sounds like fun, doesn't it?) Lucille and I had begun a good bonding friendship the year before, but in abandoning Brian I had also abandoned Lucille, leaving her alone with her crazy boyfriend/captain. I didn't think I deserved her wrath, but Lucille could well have thought me culpable for jumping ship.

I was also concerned about the abrupt change to an unsafe route Brian had made the prior year, and even more

272

so about the manner in which he dictated that change. "I am the captain, and I will not be held hostage on my boat," he said at the time. "We will sail the route I decide and that's all there is to it." It was a situation that simply *could not* be accepted—not just because of the dangerous route, but because I couldn't trust he wouldn't *dictate* another unsafe decision once we were out at sea. I didn't think he would try a stunt like that again—he'd be looking at a mutiny if he did—but I had no way of knowing for sure.

There were still other issues: Brian was *not* a good leader, and though this was no longer any surprise, I had never sailed with such a poor leader and I wondered about the effects of this leadership void. He had also made hasty and poor crewing decisions in the past. (Remember Drew Dickerson, the inept and physically challenged guy from New York who had lied about his ability and experience?) I figured there was no way in hell Brian could repeat such a poor choice, but you never know! Brian also had a few peculiar ideas such as strapping barrels of fuel on deck and an unsafe practice of keeping watches only during nighttime hours. These, I was sure, would remain unchanged, but I chose to simply accept them for the time being and deal with them as they arose.

In the nights leading up to the voyage, I often lay awake in bed with these issues going through my mind. I was accepting a whole lot more than I ever had before. I worried that I was putting myself in an overly risky situation. *Apprehensions*: it was a word Bill on *Rhapsody in Blue* had used, a word that described the worry and fear one felt when a risky event was about to occur and when things might go very wrong. It was a word that could well be used to describe my state of mind at the time. I had apprehensions—lots of them. And as the voyage approached, I went from a passive acceptance of the issues I had identified to a real fear that the voyage might very well end in disaster. I thought of cancelling, but that struck me as a cowardly thing to do: I had accepted the voyage

273

knowing the hazards; it seemed wrong and selfish to cancel with the voyage so near at hand.

I thought of Lisa often. We talked every week or so. (We had yet to have even a single unkind word between us.) I missed her horribly, and I'd be lying if I said the worries I had about the voyage didn't rekindle the pain I felt from our break-up. We had not made our decision hastily, however. We had discussed our differences thoroughly and had been advised with the tough questions we were asking ourselves. We had been congratulated for our strength, our honesty. We were doing the *right thing,* we were assured. Now, with my resolve weakened by the unrelated worries of the voyage, I thought it immature and unfair if I were to voice my real feelings: that I loved Lisa deeply and that I had never wanted to lose her. I occurred to me that she might never know how much I still loved her, how much I regretted our break-up.

I called Lisa a few days before I was to leave for the voyage. I had no purpose other than to tell her I was leaving and to say good bye. It was just a courtesy call, I figured, but my voice choked when I realized the finality of what I was doing. It was the end of a 4-year trail for me and Lisa, and with the many issues I saw with this second try at *Allegretta* and her crazy captain, it occurred to me that I was leaving a comfortable and loving environment for one that might be unpleasant, dangerous or even catastrophic. Lisa must have sensed the significance too: She said that if I ever changed my mind, even a year or two down the road, I should let her know. Her words opened a door, just a crack, but enough that I could see a bit of daylight. We started talking. It was the start of a second voyage, one that would occur simultaneously with the one on *Allegretta.*

Coming full circle? You bet!

I left home for the voyage on October 22, arriving at Queensway Quay Marina in Gibraltar the next day. I could have flown right to Gibraltar for about $1600, but a flight to Málaga—only 50 miles away—went for half-price. I took the cheaper flight. It was a long 20 hours of travel—three flights to Málaga, then three bus rides to downtown Gibraltar—but I prided myself at having become an experienced European traveler. I found bus depots and asked directions in Spanish. I walked across the international border to Gibraltar. It was a long trip over, no doubt, but the novelty of being such a nomad still had its lure.

I stepped off the last bus in the downtown area of Gibraltar in the late afternoon, about 5:00 Gibraltar time. I slung my sea-bag over my shoulder—all sixty pounds of it—and walked a mile or two in a heat and humidity that left me tired and sweaty by the time I reached the security gate of the marina. Blinded on one side by the sea-bag, I walked through the gate, almost colliding with a man and a woman walking out. It was my captain, Brian Matroka, accompanied by a young woman.

"Brian! Hello!" I stated, surprised that he was leaving, but more so because he was with a woman other than Lucille. The woman was rather busty, a fact well identified by the revealing low-neck sweater she wore.

"Mike! How good to see you. Here, let me help you with your bag. *Allegretta* is at the far end of the marina. Oh, this is Claudia. Claudia has been on board two weeks. She'll be crewing on the passage."

"Hello Claudia, glad to meet you," I said, shaking her hand.

"Oh, *Michelle*, I so glad to meet him," Claudia said in a very thick French accent, the change of my name and her errors in English grammar immediately apparent. "I hear so many good things about you. Lucille, he tell me I like you," she continued.

Normally I enjoy a French accent, but Claudia spoke with an irritating whine and had a way of reciting a portion of each sentence in an equally irritating high pitch as if she had learned the art of conversation from a book. I was to learn that she was originally from Tunisia, immigrating to

France ten years prior, which would explain the awkward accent that wasn't quite French. The boobs were nice though, and for the moment I excused the accent, the whine and the bad grammar.

The boat was, indeed, a distance away on the far side of the marina. Refusing Brian's help, I carried my sea-bag past the inviting patios of several outdoor restaurants and bars until we reached the locked gate at "Dock B." Punching in a combination, Brian held open gate and pointed out the *Allegretta.* "Well, there she is," he stated proudly.

Allegretta had seen better days. The grey hull, with a color that doesn't fare well in the sun anyway, was badly in need of a rub-down and wax-job. The sail cover, also grey, was equally sun bleached and raggedy, as was the canvas awning and cover for the cockpit table. The teak decks, left in their natural, unfinished state, and subjected to years of damaging sun, added to the gloomy picture. I recalled the fine impression the boat had given me a year earlier. How could a boat deteriorate so much in just one year?

I was welcomed aboard with the usual formalities. Once below and in the main cabin, I noticed that the boat's disheartening appearance continued with the functional but ugly slip covers that had been added to save the upholstery. Similarly, an industrial matting had been installed to protect the floor, hiding the magnificent mahogany and oak carpenter's dream I had seen before. Even the large dining table, the real show-piece of the interior, was covered with a huge and obnoxious grey piece of protective cloth. The main cabin, hell the entire boat, was depleted of the opulent luxury I had previously observed. "We added the slip covers to protect the furniture for charters," Brian mentioned. I think he was as embarrassed as I was.

I was shown my cabin, the same starboard cabin that was mine before. I had very much enjoyed this cabin the previous year, and I was flattered that Brian had thought to assign it to me again. In time I would assess the other cabins, and it was clear that mine was better than all others, including the captain's quarters. During the voyage, I would appreciate this cabin as much as I did the prior year. It was a most comfortable place to read or write, and it became an important place of refuge.

When I arrived, Brian and Claudia had been on their way to pick up a few groceries; they started out anew, leaving me to unpack and settle in. Thinking correctly that I might be hungry, Claudia returned after only a minute or two and fixed me a delicious, if a bit excessive, lunch of ratatouille with chick peas and legumes, some baguette bread, several cheeses and sausages—even a glass of chilled wine. I thanked her for the meal, trying to look her in the eyes rather than the neckline. Like most men, I enjoy a good shot of cleavage, but I saw the very obvious display as inappropriate. In casual conversation I verbalized that we would be like "brother and sister" for the voyage. This did much to establish a friendly basis between Claudia and me, but it was also my way of making our relationship clear. Again: nice boobs, but just having a woman on board was complicated enough; we didn't need to complicate things further. Regardless, the ratatouille was outstanding—and indeed I *was* starved—and I was sufficiently nourished and unpacked by the time Brian and Claudia returned about an hour later.

"I received an e-mail from Lucille," Brian told me as we settled into a conversation. "She said to say hello." I was wondering about Lucille: Where was she? Were they still together? What was busty Claudia's relation here?

"Oh? She's not here?" I asked.

"No, she had some family business she had to take care of, and she has a couple of new granddaughters she wanted to be with for the first time. She's in North Bay [Ontario]. She left a few weeks ago."

"You had a charter a couple of weeks ago...," I continued, prying for information. He had told me about this charter and I knew he didn't do charters alone. I was still wondering how Claudia fit in.

277

"Yeah, we had a couple aboard in St. Tropez. Claudia lives there and she came on board to help with the charter. Her French came in handy and she was able to take the clients around St. Tropez and show them all the sights. It's not what we normally do, but it worked out fine."

"And you're a sailor, Claudia?" I asked.

"Oui, Oui!" she said. "I make regattas [crew on sailboat races] in St Tropez. It is amazing, I make tactique...?"

"Tactician?" I guessed, trying to help her with the language.

"Oui, I make tactician with the...?"

"Winches?"

"Oui, winches all circling, and I...?"

"Grind?"

"Oui, I work them one by one, it is very, very amazing, and it is very complicated and I make them all around me, and it is amazing..."

Wow! Forgetting for the moment the whiny voice, the irritating accent, and that horrible tone thing as was her habit, Claudia with the boobs seemed like a bull-shitting bimbo with boobs. She was describing a crew responsibility called "working the pit" found on some high-tech racing boats. Normally reserved for your more experienced sailors, working the pit involves standing in a sunken pulpit surrounded by six or eight winches, operating one after another in quick succession. Perhaps it was the language that made Claudia sound like a fake, but I didn't think so. Could this be another Drew Dickerson in a female form? Surely Brian couldn't make such a horrible choice in crew two years in a row. Or could he?

"We are expecting two more crew," Brian interjected, somehow aware of my concern with the crew at hand. "They were supposed to be here yesterday. I'm sure they'll be here soon. They're coming from France as well."

And so the night progressed, Brian and me catching up on small talk, each trying to repair our relationship that

278

had ended so horribly the year before. Claudia entered the conversation from time to time, and I started to pick up on her misuse of verbs so that I could understand her. I pushed myself to reserve judgment on her sailing abilities, knowing there would be plenty of time for that. The three of us talked into the night and enjoyed a nice chicken and risotto dinner that Claudia prepared. I was tired after a sleepless night on the plane, so I retired about midnight, hoping to erase the effects of flying all night across five time-zones. I slept well, not rising until 11:00 the next morning.

When I got up, Claudia was not aboard—visiting "The Rock," I was told. Brian and I shared a pot or two of coffee; I also had some toast and jam for breakfast. We had been scheduled to leave shortly after I arrived, but we needed to wait for the rest of the crew. Several minor repairs had to be done as well:

1. The drinking water had developed a foul taste and Lucille had poured quite a bit of bleach into the tanks to kill whatever bug was growing. Nobody had thought to finish the job by changing the water, so I elected to take on that job.

2. The solenoid on the engine starter motor was blown. Brian had a spare starter and we made a plan to install it.

3. A battery or two had gone bad. (There were a total of 18 batteries on the boat; we eventually replaced five of them.)

4. Brian announced he wanted to mount two 55-gallon barrels on the deck to carry spare fuel. I hated the very idea of it, of course, but Brian had assured me that he had done it successfully on several crossings. Each full barrel would weigh about 500 pounds, and I couldn't imagine that at least one of them wouldn't come loose in a heavy sea. If one did, I figured, I'd just push it overboard. Nevertheless, we mounted them, and they never did give us any trouble.

279

All of these tasks took time, which was in our favor: Looking up the weather forecast on Passage Weather (passageweather.com), I saw that a storm was battering Spain and Portugal outside of the straits, with another one a few days away. A small window of fair weather existed between the storms and was expected to come our way Sunday. I didn't want to be delayed further, but leaving early wasn't a good idea either. Fortunately, the need for repairs and Brian's own desires aligned with the weather.

The ability to use Passage Weather shows both the technological progress of the time and the willingness on my part to utilize it: Just two years prior I was unaware of the weather forecasting system called GRIBS. When it was introduced to me, I was skeptical of its reliability and reluctant to rely on it in a salty ocean environment. "Use of Pilot Charts is the way to go," I would say. "They can't fail like some electronic gizmo and they've been used forever." By the time of this voyage, however, I was not only convinced of the utility of GRIBS electronic charts, I had purchased a portable e-book computer and had discovered Passage Weather. With this I could get free GRIBS charts for any location, anytime I had access to the internet. This doesn't mean that paper charts are not required for any area to be sailed—anything electronic on a sailboat is still susceptible to failure—but I had surely been sold on the utility of electronics, and Passage Weather was one of the best tools out there.

On Thursday afternoon the last two members of our crew showed up. Brian had said that they were expected on Tuesday; the crew stated that they were always expecting to report on Thursday. (See Leadership and Communication: lack there-of.) Guillaume (31, from France) and Malina (26, from Poland but living with Guillaume in France), each with an accent thicker than butter, had hitch-hiked across France and Spain to arrive in Gibraltar. They both carried back packs; he wore a beard, she a single dread-lock that extended halfway down her back. Vegetarians, both of

280

them, non-drinkers with clear eyes, he a bit skinny, she not, they were a couple of old hippies, except they weren't old. Neither had much more than a working knowledge of English, and as I found out, neither had ever been on a boat of any kind ever before! Indeed, as I watched Brian and the couple greet one another, it became apparent that they were meeting for the very first time. (See, again, Leadership and Communication: lack there-of.)

Clearly we had a personnel issue aboard *Allegretta*: a leader who couldn't lead, and two, perhaps three sailors who couldn't sail. Brian's crew selection, of course, had been a problem the year before. In preparing for the voyage this year, I had intentionally *not* asked Brian about the crew selection—or about any of the other issues that presented themselves the year before—as a way of reducing the divide between us. (The planned route, the biggest issue last year, was the exception.) Issues regarding crew selection, fuel barrels on deck, poor boat handling skills, inept leadership ability, or anything else—I chose to leave ignored. Each had been addressed the year prior with failed results; this year, in an effort to allow the voyage to continue, I let each go unaddressed. I figured we'd survive one way or another and we would deal with each issue as it came along. Regarding the crew selection problem at hand, Brian and I could well sail the boat ourselves; whatever help the inexperienced crew could give us would be a blessing. As it turned out, Guillaume and Malina were wonderful people, and though inexperienced sailors, I found them to be helpful and very much a joy to have on board *Allegretta.*

On Friday I handled the water tank problem. *Allegretta* had three stainless steel water tanks with a total capacity of 300 gallons; my job was to empty the tanks and flush out any dirt, algae or anything else of unhealthy nature, and then refill the tanks with good, clean water. It took the boat's water system pumps several hours to empty the tanks, and the simple job of removing the inspection plates proved not so simple. Also, flushing the tanks and the water system clogged the boat's water filters, and this required a trip or two into town for replacement parts. It wasn't until the next evening that I was able to fill the tanks, but at least we had an ample supply of healthy water. We also had a super high capacity (35 gal/hr.) water desalinator aboard and an emergency supply of water in plastic bottles. Water was never going to be a problem on the voyage.

Brian had never mentioned the topic of sharing costs for the voyage. (See Leadership and Communication: lack there-of.) The cost of food for five people for five weeks—half purchased in Europe, half on one island or another—would be substantial. Fuel at these locations is double that found in America, and then there are dockage and clearance costs as well as the replacement of items broken or lost during the voyage. All of these are in addition to normal maintenance of a boat and all of its accessories. The cost of operating a boat runs high. Don't ever think otherwise.

Though many owners take on the responsibility to pay all costs—Mike Stafford did on *That Darn Cat;* Mark Gerhardt did on *Rhapsody in Blue*—it is not abnormal for the captain and crew to share the cost of food (provisions) equally. The arrangement should be agreed upon in advance—it is normally identified in the introductory request for crew—and I had never experienced any confusion except with Brian on *Allegretta.* Leadership was not Brian's strength, and asking for money to help with expenses was surely his weakness. I recalled our experience the previous year when Lucille wanted a contribution much higher than what had been expected, but waited until we were at the check-out counter and the cashier was asking for payment before she announced it. Wishing to avoid the embarrassing experience, I raised the subject with Brian one evening:

"What are your thoughts regarding payment for provisions, Brian? I'm thinking we should pay equal shares. What do you think?" I asked and answered all at once.

"Yes, that sounds fair," he said.

"What do you think that share might be?" I asked.

"Oh, I don't know, a few hundred euros each should cover groceries."

"Well, here: here's a check for a thousand dollars," I said, handing him the check. "I know it's more than a few hundred euros, but I've got the money [the others, I figured, were all pretty short of cash] and I don't mind paying extra."

"Thanks," he said, taking the check.

"Is that enough?" I asked.

"Oh, yeah, that's more than enough," he said. "Yeah, that's plenty."

A few hundred euros wouldn't cover a person's food for five weeks, and I predicted future requests to replenish the bank. With me paying a cool grand—not an unreasonable amount—I lined myself up to be excused from any and all of those discussions.

"No, you're fine," Brian continued. "I'll get what I can from the others, and simply use my credit card each time we go to the grocery store."

It was a good move on my part. Brian mentioned to the others at dinner that he was expecting *some* monetary help from each of them, but he left it up to them to decide how much. "None of them has paid me anything yet," he complained to me later on several occasions. I was glad it wasn't my problem and I intended to keep it that way. It wasn't until we were at the gas-dock leaving Cape Verde— half way through the voyage—that Guillaume and Malina finally settled their bill. And I have my suspicions that Claudia never paid at all.

On Saturday, the day before our departure, Brian, Guillaume and Claudia walked to Morrison's Grocery store (the very same that we had gone to the previous year) to buy provisions. I was a bit concerned as to what decisions they might make, but my relief at not having to participate in that awful chore out-weighed my concerns. They came back with well in excess of what we would need for the 6-day passage to the Canaries, and the five of us packed everything away in the boat's refrigerator, freezer, and the many storage lockers in the main cabin. Afterward, Guillaume cooked up a wonderful lasagna dinner, with a delicious pate appetizer, a salad with copious vegetables, and chocolate cake for desert. It was a great meal, but I was wondering if there was a good understanding that the groceries had to last some time. I said nothing—it wasn't my problem. By this time I had realized that I needed to be involved with some problems but with others I should steer clear. With regards to the buying and consumption of provisions, I needed to "let it go," the same concept I had used the year before. And "let it go" is exactly what I did.

On Sunday morning Brian and I mounted the fuel barrels on the deck. This was the fourth time Brian had used this method, he said. The first time he had used metal barrels, which rusted through and had to be thrown overboard. (Imagine the pollution!) He switched to plastic barrels after that and had been modifying the method to strap them down, settling on an acceptable method a year prior. He had photographs to show how it was done and I strapped the barrels down exactly as directed. They seemed very secure but I still couldn't imagine that at least one wouldn't become dislodged, resulting in an oily mess all over the deck. "Are you sure we need to do this?" I asked three or four times. "We'll be downwind in the trades. The last time I went, we ran the engine for only a single hour," I said, recalling my experience on *That Darn Cat.*

"They'll be fine," Brian assured me. They worried me to death.

In mid-afternoon (10/27) we left Queensway Quay Marina and motored a few miles north to a fuel dock by the Spanish border. *Allegretta* had two fuel tanks with a combined capacity of 250 gallons, so with the barrels we mounted on deck we could carry 350 gallons of fuel. At the fuel dock we filled the barrels and topped off the tanks, taking on 250 gallons, which cost about $1200. The engine on *Allegretta,* motoring at six knots, burned two and a half gallons per hour, so we had a range under power of about five days or 750 miles—less whatever we used while running the generator. All fueled up, we left Gibraltar at 4:30 PM, bound for the Canary Islands 700 miles distant, south by southwest.

We had rarely felt any wind at all in the four days *Allegretta* sat at Queensway Quay Marina. Almost immediately out of the gas dock, however, we picked up an abundant wind of 30 knots, thankful it was coming from the southeast. We would be spending the night on a westerly course through the Straits of Gibraltar, which put the wind on the port quarter, only 20 degrees from dead aft. For the entire voyage the wind would remain behind us in one way or another: sometimes from the port quarter, sometimes from starboard, but always almost dead aft.

Perhaps you will recall how we experienced the same dead-aft wind, a difficult point of sail for a sailboat, during my previous east-to-west Atlantic crossing on the catamaran *That Darn Cat.* Perhaps, too, you will recall the differing opinions the crew had regarding VMG and the proper method to sail downwind: Julian Cohen, an experienced multi-hull sailor, argued to sail quite high into the wind. Julian's tactic would produce incredible boat speed—we reached 26 knots on *That Darn Cat*—but most of that speed wasn't to where we wanted to go. George Tripler and I, a couple of mono-hullers, held the contrary opinion: "Keep the boat down," we argued. "Yes, you'll go slower but you'll be going in the correct direction."

On *Allegretta*, we would use a third tactic: sail straight for your destination, rigging double head sails—one to leeward (as usual) and the other to windward, held in place by a spinnaker pole. We never used the mainsail with this method, eliminating the problem of a sail that is clumsy to raise and lower and which chafes easily, two problems exaggerated when sailing downwind. The double-headsail method of sailing downwind is a bit slow, but it's a rig that can be set and left alone, sometimes not requiring any

285

adjustment at all for a week or more. It's a rig often used by trade wind sailors, those accustomed to facing thousands of miles and multiple weeks of sailing downwind with the wind dead-aft.

On our first night out from Gibraltar, we made things even easier for ourselves: We left the spinnaker pole stowed and flew a single headsail by itself—the set-up I had suggested to Julian two years prior on *That Darn Cat.* With just the one sail this rig risked being under-powered, but since we had plenty of wind, we were able to surf away at over eight knots as we paralleled the Spanish coast.

Brian and I each established our "posts" that first afternoon and evening out. Brian's was the navigator's desk, and after we got the sail up and the auto-pilot set, he went to his post and started up all of the instruments so that he could monitor most boat functions from the comfort of his desk. He would spend most of his awakened hours at the navigator's desk, going outside only in mornings when he and I did sail changes, and other than that, leaving his desk only to eat or sleep.

My post was simply any spot in the cockpit that happened to be free, and though I didn't restrict myself to my post as Brian did, I spent the majority of my time awake sitting in the cockpit where, with book in hand, I could adjust the sails, alter our course, and keep a look-out for anything out of ordinary.

The others—not Brian—would often join me in the cockpit as they did on our first evening out. Claudia had cooked up a pasta dinner and we all sat in the cockpit, eating our meal and gazing at the two mountainous landscapes: the green one of Spain near-by, and the brown one of Morocco in the distance, south and across the water. As nighttime fell, the magic of a million shore-lights on both sides mesmerized us.

We set up two-hour watches for the night with Brian's and mine both interspaced between those of the less experienced crew. Traffic was busy with ships all around, and I cautioned everybody to keep a good look-out. I was up often "just checking" throughout the night, but it passed without incident as we traversed and crossed the straits, moving away from Spain but never getting any closer than ten miles to Morocco.

Daylight woke me the next morning. Brian was up; the wind was down. I climbed the companionway stairs and from the cockpit I looked all around us, seeing only the sea on all sides. Once again, I found myself in a favorite spot: the center of a six-mile disc of sea, defined by a 360-degree horizon that is only three miles away. We would not see land again for several days, and the six-mile disc I was viewing would be our entire world for all but a few days of the remaining voyage.

"Good morning, Brian," I said with a smile.

"Good morning," he replied. "Did you sleep okay?"

This was Brian's good side, the side of him that was kind and caring. His question wasn't to make conversation; it was one of compassionate interest: He wanted to know if my bed and cabin were comfortable, if I had been able to relax with all of the close-by ships the past night, and if I was sufficiently rested to take on a full day at sea. I loved this side of Brian. It was the side of him that used to be a ballet dancer, the side that meditated, that loved opera, that treated crew and guests aboard with kindness and tenderness.

"Yeah, I slept fine!" I said. "You?"

"Yes, I slept well too," he said. "I think I need to change up the watch schedule—I should go on at 10PM, not midnight—but we can do that easily enough. Here, I made some toast, and we have some nice jam. Do you want coffee? Have some breakfast."

Well, this was top drawer! I couldn't believe my good fortune, a wonderful circumstance I had brought upon myself. Here was the captain who just a year ago I had abandoned after judging him to be a reckless lunatic, the one with the horrible temper, the one I said I couldn't trust.

He was the same man to whom I had given the benefit of the doubt, a second chance, when all others said it was undeserved, unsafe, and unwise.

"You'd be crazy!" concluded Mark Gerhardt as we sailed on *Rhapsody in Blue.*

"He's an asshole!" said my buddy Tony.

But I, and only I, had thought differently. *I* alone saw that there could have been unique contributing factors that accounted for Brian's questionable behavior, *I* who had felt an obligation as a sailor, *I* who had thought Brian deserved a second chance. Now I was accepting the rewards from that sympathetic, compassionate maturity with which I now credited myself.

"Oh, I'd *love* a cup of coffee," I said, thankful for the decisions I had made. How smart I was. How *mature!* "Toast, you say? Jam? Why sure, I'd love some. Hey, hand me that coffee pot!"

"We need to put up the spinnaker pole," Brian announced after a while.

"Sure! Let me just finish my coffee." I answered, still gleeful.

"Yes! Yes! Finish your coffee. There's no hurry; we have plenty of time."

Well, one cup of coffee turned into two, no surprise there, and I *did* indulge myself with a piece, well maybe two, of toast with jam. I was half-way through a bowl of Muesli when Claudia got up, an event which started another cheery round of "good morning," and "How did you sleep?" and "Would you like some coffee?" It was an hour or more later when the three of us—Brian, Claudia and I—went up on the foredeck with the purpose of putting up the spinnaker pole.

Now, for those who don't know, a spinnaker pole, when one is used, is mounted horizontally with one end affixed to the mast (about chin high) and with the pole extending out to one side or the other, several feet past the side of the boat. It's for holding one corner of the sail—be it a spinnaker or a genoa—far overboard, the preferred

288

trimming location when sailing downwind. It's a clumsy apparatus, a spinnaker pole, and several lines must be rigged to hold it in place: the topping-lift to hold it up, the fore-guy (also called the down-haul) to hold it down, the after-guy to pull it aft, and the sail with its sheet pulling forward.

The spinnaker pole on *Allegretta* was approximately 25-feet long and weighed well over 100 pounds. It was added to the boat at some point after manufacture, and the installer, in addition to choosing a pole that was too big, omitted the installation not only of some important controls (such as the topping-lift and the fore-guy) but also the winches, cleats, turning blocks and sheet-stoppers, all of which make for the smooth and safe operation of a spinnaker pole. Everything about the pole was "jury-rigged," which means that you used whatever you could to accomplish the task of the item missing. A little bit of instruction would have been handy as well, but with Brian's poor leadership skills, this was one more item missing on the foredeck that morning.

A north breeze had come along while we were finishing breakfast, and since we were now clear of the straits and around the horn of Morocco, this new and building wind was still behind us, coming over our starboard quarter. Normally, if the wind comes from one side you put the sails out to the other, and I was a bit surprised when Brian announced that we would pole the sail out to windward. (Actually, I thought he had misspoken and I started setting-up the pole on the port side when Brian corrected me.)

"Tie the spinnaker halyard to the pole," commanded Brian. I released the tension of the halyard from one end and asked Claudia to tie the other end to the pole. At this time I still credited Claudia with being an experienced sailor, accustomed to "working the pit" on sophisticated Mediterranean racers. She had a bit of trouble determining which line was the correct halyard, and though by this time she had been on board *Allegretta* for three weeks, I figured she was new to sailing the boat. Being unable to identify one line out of the twenty or so that came down from the mast was not surprising. When she tried to tie the line to the inboard end of the pole instead of the outboard one, however, I became rather suspicious. When her bowline resembled the knot a five-year-old might tie, I knew we had another Drew Dickerson aboard.

It was the first time we were to raise the spinnaker pole, and though in time we would learn to do it like seasoned salties, our first attempt more closely resembled an episode of The Three Stooges. We must have rigged the fore-guy four times, always on the wrong side of at least one life-line. The lazy sheets—those not used unless the sail is tacked or jibed—repeatedly gave us trouble because Brian insisted they always be cleated. Grinding in the "topping-lift," we got the spinnaker pole up, but with the rocking of the boat it swung dangerously back and forth, threatening to bat someone overboard. Finally, we had everything ready, and with me grinding in the jib sheet with the electric winch and Claudia assigned to the genoa furling line, the lazy sheet and the fore-guy, we unfurled the genoa into the pole, adjusting six different lines as the sail filled with the wind. Brian stood on the foredeck, watching the operation progress and ready to take action if anything were to go wrong.

"Okay, release it!" Brian said, still looking up into the sail and facing forward so that nobody could hear him.

"Can't hear you," I shouted out. "What'd you say?"

"Release it! Release it!" Brian shouted back at us, visibly panicked this time. Claudia and I looked at each other, both of us confused. The operation was going perfectly and all six lines were being loosened or tightened as required. Was something amiss that we couldn't see? What did Brian want released?

"The down-haul dammit! Release the goddamn down-haul!"

Carrying on in full rage, Brian was jumping up and down on the deck, his back stiff with electricity and his arms flapping up and down like the flippers of a penguin. Claudia and I, now panicked ourselves and thinking we had caused something to go seriously wrong, were trying in desperation to figure out which of the several lines was the down-haul.

"Release the down-haul, God dammit! Can't you even release the fucking down-haul?" Brian's absurd demeanor only increased our own panic, taking away all ability to think clearly. Claudia released a line—not the correct one—and the pole dropped to the deck, barely missing Brian's head.

"Not the up-haul, God dammit," Brian screeched, choking on his words now, spit foaming from his mouth and tears dripping from his eyes. "The down-haul! The fucking down-haul! Don't you know what the..."

Okay, you get the picture: Brian in full rage; Claudia, who never in her life had handled so many lines, trying her best; me doing my best as well, but frankly at a loss as far as what to do next. Eventually we *did* get the sail set, and though it was on the wrong side, at least in *my* opinion, the wind filled it and pulled the boat along at a respectable six knots. Brian's rage continued even after the sail was flying, though by this time Claudia and I were ignoring him and going about our business. I went about checking that the three or four critical lines were all secured, and it was a sudden silence a few minutes later that alerted me: Looking up from my work, I noticed that Brian had left the foredeck and gone below to hide himself in his cabin. Claudia, seemingly unaffected by Brian's temper tantrum, was also below and had joined Guillaume and Malina who were awakened with the commotion. I remained alone on deck, feeling stunned by Brian's behavior and wondering which was going to fail next: the unstable sail held out into the wind, or the temper of the equally unstable lunatic captain.

Of course, this wasn't the first time I had witnessed Brian's severe temper tantrums. Very fresh in my mind were the tirades of the previous year: the yelling he gave me when my method of tying a line around a cleat differed from his, the panic he displayed when I didn't understand his (unclear) command regarding the mainsail halyard, the several botched docking maneuvers where his temper continued to escalate as the others and I fended-off from other boats.

It occurred to me that the frustrations giving rise to Brian's tantrums, both this year and last, were generally caused by his own poor communication. Brian had a soft voice to begin with, and he often spoke commands while looking forward and upward into the sails making it impossible to hear him. Pair this up with Brian's overall poor leadership skills and the absence of any pre-instruction of the task to be performed, and you end up with a confused crew, one that Brian often found impossible to tolerate.

I also took notice of the predictable manner in which Brian's tantrums progressed. Each tirade would begin with the misunderstood instruction, followed quickly by Brian repeating his command, this time at a full scream and often repeated two or three times. Coinciding with the screaming tirade were the physical attributes: the unmistakable stiffening of his back, the flapping of his arms, the hateful stare as if you had killed his first-born. Brian's entire head would turn beet-red during these times, his face often contorting as if pulled to one side by a demon. Veins would protrude from his neck, severe enough to give concern of a medical emergency. The verbal insults would begin, always blaming somebody else for the problem. (Brian never accepted blame for anything.) The rage would continue, increasing to incredible levels. But then at its very peak, when I really *was* thinking that a heart attack was imminent, his face would take on a saddened appearance and his entire body would go limp with exhaustion. Where previously he had been spitting his words in violence, he now would choke on his own voice with saliva thickening into foam around his mouth. Sometimes tears would come, an effect of total exhaustion caused by an internal refusal to give up his anger. He wouldn't be long, I learned. Regardless of his desires, he would be totally spent and would have no choice but to stop. He would retire to his cabin, shutting the door and remaining there for an hour or two. After recharging he'd get up, subdued and quiet. He'd go about his navigational duties, sometimes making a cup of coffee, and neither he nor anyone else would say anything about what had occurred.

I should have spoken to Brian about his temper tantrums; at least that's what I keep telling myself. I never did. On the other-hand, when an episode began, this most recent one for example, perhaps I should have simply retired to the galley for another cup of coffee, agreeing to return when and if he behaved appropriately. Maybe I should have punched him! I don't know. What I do know is that "to get along for the duration of the voyage" I always kept my reaction in check, thinking that a non-reaction would provide the best chance of diffusing the situation. In fact, I always doubled my work efforts to satisfy Brian during his tirades, thus only reinforcing his unacceptable behavior. Nobody ever challenged Brian on this. Nobody ever talked to him later in a conciliatory manner, seeking to correct a problem that made for an unhappy environment at the very least, and at times threatened the safety of the voyage. I think it unlikely that any of us could have made a difference, but I chastise myself for not ever trying.

When Brian got up from his recharging nap, rather quiet but in good spirits, he suggested that we unfurl the staysail and fly it opposite the genoa on the port side. It was a simple job, and though I was still wary of Brian at the time, he and I alone put out the sail, calmly and easily, as the others gabbed in the galley and prepared dinner. It was the first time I had witnessed the rig of double headsails flown wing-on-wing. I was impressed by the stability of the rig, and that if the wind were to vary 30 degrees in either direction, the rig wouldn't require any adjustment. I could also see that one of the sails had to be poled out, and yes— oh, this is difficult to admit—it would have to be the one to windward.

We carried on "wing-on-wing" for the remainder of the afternoon. The sails required no attention whatsoever, and the right-hand auto-pilot—*Allegretta* had two very reliable auto-pilots—steered a straight course with no difficulty at all. I sat in the cockpit looking out at the sea, keeping a casual eye for boats and changing conditions. Brian sat at his navigation desk, typing out some e-mails. We had survived our first 24 hours at sea.

Guillaume, as it turned out, was a superb cook, possessing an exceptional command of spices. On this occasion, which was Monday, our second evening out, he cooked up some onions in oil and garlic—as he did to begin most of his creations—then added some frozen fish and a can of snails. He did his magic with a few spices then poured the mixture over pasta, adding afterward some fresh ground parmesan cheese and a bit of parsley for decoration.

We chose to dine outdoors at the table in the cockpit—much to everyone's delight—and the two women added their flair with some attractive place settings. We all ate together family style, thankful that the downwind sailing didn't heel the boat over too much. As we sat down, Malina sang a simple melody:

Thank you for the food, thank you for the food.

"Where did you get that song?" I asked, thoroughly impressed, both with its simplicity and its focus on gratitude. "That's beautiful!"

"Oh, you haven't heard it all," Malina said. "There's more." She began anew:

Thank you for the food, thank you for the food.
Thank you for the fo-oo-ood, thank you for the food.

It's healing. It's healing. It's he-ee-ling us.
It's healing. It's healing. It's he-ee-ling us.
Tears came to my eyes. I'm such a woos!

As the sun went down, the NW wind strengthened and swung around to the northeast as we had expected right along. "We're flying too much sail," Brian said, so he and I furled the staysail, leaving out only a half-furled genoa. This we flew to leeward, held securely in place by the spinnaker pole. (Ha!) *Allegretta* plowed on at nine knots, as stable and effortless as could be. We ran our watches. At two hours duration, they were the easiest I had ever experienced. The night passed without incident, as did the next two or three days. The wind was strong—30 knots—but it was behind us and caused us no concern. A gorgeous ocean with 12 or 15-foot seas built up around us, putting *Allegretta* and her crew, at least those of us who weren't queasy, in our glory.

A fifth of all sailors get sea-sick. A fifth never will. Another fifth feel varying degrees of nausea. The rest are liars. Those new to sailing will be more susceptible, so I always figured we would have a significant problem with sea-sickness on *Allegretta.*

I had several *Transderm-V* patches with me, and I welcomed everybody to use them. Claudia accepted one the first night out. Malina and Guillaume each felt a fair degree of nausea, but elected to fight it with their "natural" methods. They felt queasy for a full week, but then they were both okay. Brian never felt a thing. I felt a bit queasy myself and put on a patch, though I was able to remove it after a day or two. Claudia, even with the patch which I replaced every few days, felt queasy for the entire voyage and vomited two or three times. She was a real trooper, however: she never complained and rarely even mentioned her discomfort. All in all, I think we lucked out.

The Canaries were 700 miles from Gibraltar, but we made some excellent runs and after only four days we were approaching the vicinity of the wonderful Spanish islands. I was looking forward to our planned stop at the island of Tenerife: I knew that dozens of boats from the Atlantic Rally for Cruisers would be there, and I was hoping to hook up with Dan Bower on *Skyelark of London* or some of the other sailors I had met. The ocean is huge, we all know, but the stops along the way are small and innumerable: The odds of running into old friends at a place like Tenerife are pretty good. It was to be a terrific stop.

"Mike, do you have any real burning need to go to the Canaries?" Brian asked me a day or so before our planned landing.

"Well, no. I don't have any burning need," I said. "It would be a wonderful stop. I think the others are looking forward to it. What do you have in mind?"

"I'm thinking we should skip the Canaries. It would give us more time in the Verdes. We've both been to the Canaries, and it's likely we'll stop there every year. But neither of us has been to Cape Verde, and we might never get back that way. It should be a unique African environment and there are several islands to visit. What do you think?"

It seemed like a good enough idea, and though it was unfair to *not* involve the others in the decision, in the matter of a few seconds we scrapped the plan to go to the Canary Islands. I should have argued against the change: I really *did* want to go to Tenerife; it really *was* unfair to the others; and as it was to be, Cape Verde was not that special. I agreed to the change—not that it was mine to decide— because of an impatience that overcomes me anytime I'm on a sailboat: When I'm in port, I can't wait to leave; when I'm at sea, I can't wait to get in. I saw the cancellation as a way to get on with the voyage, my impatience blinding me from all of the good reasons to stop at the Canaries. It was a bad decision, unfair to the others and wrong on many levels. Nevertheless, the decision was made and Brian and I were soon discussing whether we should sail upwind or downwind of the Canaries. An hour later, as I was telling

Malina about the change of plans, I saw the disappointment in her face as she quietly accepted the news. I knew we had screwed up.

To be honest, I thought the Cape Verde islands were only a few hundred miles south of the Canaries. It surprised me when I found out that our extension amounted to almost a thousand extra miles—a full week of added sailing at least. The wind continued strong, giving us several daily runs in excess of 150 miles, but the extension made for a 1700-mile sail out of Gibraltar. It was a long passage, especially for those on board new to sailing.

I passed most hours of the day sitting in the cockpit, reading one of the several novels *Allegretta* had aboard in her library. The previous year I had begun reading Mark Twain's *The Adventures of Tom Sawyer,* and I was happy to find it still aboard this year. I enjoyed Tom's escapades, empathizing with his childhood romance with Becky Thatcher, and I also devoured *The Adventures of Huckaberry Finn* by the same author. I got through *For Whom the Bell Tolls,* and eventually read six or seven books throughout the voyage. It was on *C'est si Bon* that I learned the pleasure of reading on a sailboat at sea, a pleasure I continued with on all of my voyages including the present one on *Allegretta.* Others read frequently as well, especially Malina who devoured book after book in three different languages: Polish, French and English.

One such day while sitting alone and reading in the cockpit, Claudia came up from the main cabin and sat—slouched, really—on the seat across from me. With her chin in her hands, she exhibited a dejected and sad expression, staring longingly behind the boat out at the sea where we had already passed. Moving only my eyes, I stole a quick glance at her, but had returned to my reading when I heard her exhale with an audible sigh, one clearly meant to gather my attention.

"Mike, do you ever get bored when sailing?" she asked. The question spoke volumes: Claudia had lost the enthusiasm she once had for the voyage. The long days of inactivity were too long, too inactive. She was bored and her boredom couldn't be alleviated by reading: reading a book in her non-native English was difficult for her. In the first few days she had occupied much of the day preparing the evening meal, but Brian had told her that she was cooking up all our food, and that cooking dinner in the morning wasn't a good idea either. She had nothing to do. It was her "big sail," her first ocean crossing, an adventure like no other, but only a few days into it, she had had enough. The beauty of the ocean had lost its charm; the wind in her hair no longer held her interest. She was now beginning to comprehend the size of the ocean and how very long the voyage was to be. I could empathize fully.

I recalled my own first ocean experience on *C'est si Bon* 24 years prior: *It should have been the very best sailing passage of my life,* I wrote as I sailed south of Bermuda, *but all I wanted was for it to be over.* I recalled also the voyage on *Skyelark of London:* Tina abandoned her first ocean experience halfway through: "I think I bit off too much for me to chew," was what she had told Dan the captain. Even on the recent voyage on *Rhapsody in Blue,* the captain and first mate conversed: "Why do we do this? It's not fun; certainly not comfortable."

"I do it only for pay," Bert had said.

With Claudia's simple question—"Mike, do you ever get bored when sailing?"—I knew exactly what she was feeling. I had been there many times.

"Oh, sure I do," I said, putting down my book. "I get bored on every passage. It's unavoidable. I simply turn off my brain when I have such thoughts. I just think: We always arrive at the end; if we haven't arrived, it's not the end." She laughed at my joke. "Why?" I asked. "Are you feeling bored?"

"Oui. I cannot believe how long [big] is this ocean. We are here forever already, oui?, and we still have a very, very big [long] time yet, no?"

"Well, yeah, it *is* a very big ocean," I told her in a consoling tone. "But listen: It's very normal to start re-thinking the voyage half-way through. I have noticed this on every voyage I have done. I think it happens to everybody. It's called 'Channel Fever.' I used to fight it. I used to think 'I must never wish my adventure away, not even one day of it.' But I have learned that 'channel fever' is very natural and you can't avoid it. The ocean is very, *very* big. One can't help but be bored. But I think you need to simply step back from yourself and observe your feelings without giving them any importance. Give yourself permission to be bored but don't let it become *you.* If you simply watch and observe your boredom, you'll see it diminish and drift away."

Claudia didn't realize it at the time, but many different emotions often run amuck out at sea. Boredom is the most common, I would think, but anger and fear are big ones too. False pride—that pumped up ego giving rise to a feeling of superiority—is common among captains, especially those "unofficial captains" such as Bertie on *Rhapsody* and Julian on *That Darn Cat.* As for me, an anxiety stemming from impatience frequently overtakes my psyche, destroying my otherwise content mental disposition. Sometimes I'm overly concerned about the slow progress of the boat; at other times there might be legitimate issues with the boat or crew. Worrying about these things won't help, of course, and developing a real anxiety about them is about the worst one can do. Still, it happens. Tania Aebi, the first woman solo circumnavigator said it well: "My emotions were stretched to their limits, and I knew better than to risk the torture of negative thoughts, but it was no use and I began hating the very sea I used to love so much." Out at sea, it's important to *not* let emotions take control, but that is certainly easier said than done.

On this voyage, my goal was to quell any negative emotions that arose in my mind, focusing instead on the lovely ocean and enjoying what should be a terrific downwind sail in the trades. I came to realize that any discontent I felt was not caused by conditions or events but by a mind that refused to find peace. "Let it all go," I told myself daily. "Don't allow negative thoughts to occupy my mind." For the most part I succeeded. Brian, with his escapade the second day out—"excitement," he would call it later—altered my disposition for a while, but for most of the voyage I was able to sit in the cockpit and look out at the sea occasionally as I read, enjoying the tremendous beauty of the ocean and reminding myself how lucky I was to be sailing across it in such lovely fashion.

"Channel Fever...," Claudia said slowly. "Yes, I have Channel Fever very, very bad." Learning the term for what she was feeling, and knowing it was a common malady, seemed to help. Claudia still wrestled with her boredom, but she learned to combat it in her own way. The anxiety would bother her all the way to Cape Verde, but there it ended: As the next leg progressed—the Atlantic crossing— she had the opposite feeling: not wanting the voyage to end!

In an astonishing coincidence, two days later Guillaume asked me the same question: "Mike, do you ever get bored while sailing?" Guillaume didn't exhibit the same demeanor when he asked me the question: He didn't slouch in the cockpit; he didn't stare longingly out at the wake of the boat; he didn't let out an exaggerated sigh to get my attention. He was with Malina at the time, the two of them smiling and asking something of interest: "Mike, do you ever get bored while sailing?"

"Well, yes, sometimes," I said. "Not too often anymore," I lied. "On this trip I'm trying extra hard to simply enjoy the voyage for what it is, and *not* be bored. I'm trying to abandon all thoughts of how long we've been out and how long we've got to go. So far I'm doing pretty well at it, but we're still just getting started. We'll have to see how I make out down the road. Why? Are you feeling bored?"

"No, we are not bored at all," they both said at the same time. Their smiles spoke as much as Claudia's frown had a couple of days before.

"I'm enjoying it immensely," claimed Guillaume, and I believed him. "I see that we are one with nature," he said. "We are not in charge. We must do as the wind and sea dictate."

"Well, I think you're exactly right," I said. "Fortunately, the sea is on our side these days. It has been a rather easy voyage so far, and we might have it easy all the way to the Caribbean. By the way, how are your stomachs?"

"Not good, not bad," Malina admitted, her smile diminishing just a bit. "We're okay."

I was impressed by this couple. They interacted well with each other, and both of them possessed a very healthy attitude about life. Incredibly, at least in my mind, they each spoke three languages, and at least one of them—English— surprising well. They were both university educated— Guillaume an engineer, Malina with a master's degree in Polish literature—and they both relayed stories of worldly experiences I found captivating. Malina's life in Poland began under the rule of communism and I wondered how her childhood in an area of newly born capitalism differed from that of someone in, say, Iraq.

"Living in Poland now-a-days, and also in France, do you regard yourself as being able to live freely?" I asked. Claudia was now joining the group as we spoke.

"Yes, now," said Malina. "Before, no. Under communism we couldn't leave the country. Now, especially with the European Union, we can travel freely to any country we want. If we were still ruled by communism, I wouldn't have been allowed to study in France. I would never have met Guillaume."

"I just realized something," Claudia said with a puzzled expression. "In Tunisia, we are not free: Most Tunisians can't leave the country. Everybody must be a Muslim. You can't speak out against the government."

"We would have a big problem with that in the United States," I said. "We have basic freedoms—Freedom of Speech, Freedom of Religion, Freedom of the Press—that we take very seriously. Claudia, how was it that you were able to get out of Tunisia to study and live in France?" I asked. "Did you receive special privileges?" It was a slip: Brian had shared the secret with me previously that Claudia's family had some money.

"I cannot believe we are not free!" Claudia exclaimed, distracted by the realization and avoiding my question, at least at first. Then: "No, I was married to a Frenchman ten years. I am divorced just three months."

"I'm sorry," I said. "It must be a difficult time for you."

"No," she said casually. "It is not a difficult time at all. I am very happy to be divorced. It was not a very, very good marriage, and I rather to be free anyway. Free from government; free from my husband. Just free. It is better, no?"

A few days south of the Canaries, the beautifully strong northeast wind we had been enjoying almost since Gibraltar lost its punch. It was still behind us and blowing at *almost* 15 knots, which in most cases would be plenty. Going downwind, however, and with a desired boat speed of six knots, *almost* 15 knots left *less than* nine knots of apparent wind. "She comes alive at 20 knots," said the captain. "We might need a little help from the engine."

We tried everything we could: putting out the full genoa, jibing the rig, flying the mainsail. Nothing could give us more than four knots of boat speed. We turned on the engine—which corrected the problem immediately—and it remained on for 30 hours. The wind continued to diminish and with the calmer conditions we saw dolphins for the first time.

Neither Guillaume nor Malina had ever seen dolphins before, and the marine mammals made sure they put on a good show. At first, 10 or 20 began swimming back and forth in front of the bow, but then scores more caught on to what the first had discovered and they came over too. Several of them jumped vertically out of the water with

302

flippers a-flapping, exhibiting the excitement normally reserved for children and Christmas. I enjoyed those dolphins very much for my own viewing, of course, but even more so for the obvious pleasure Guillaume and Malina—two avid nature lovers—were having. As I had discovered on prior voyages, the dolphins will remain as long they're watched, and Malina watched them until they were exhausted and could hardly break the water surface to breathe. She finally let them go, but others replaced them in time, and we were able to see dolphins several days in a row.

We were still a few hundred miles from the islands of Cape Verde when we started to see a distinct sandy haze in the air. I had heard of this haze before: It blows over from the Sahara Desert but lingers in a vast area several hundred miles wide around the islands. We could smell the odor of burnt sand from the haze, and before long *Allegretta's* decks took on a brownish color. We then saw a few dragonflies; they too had come with the wind the 300 miles from Africa. Soon we saw thousands of them—beautiful white little creatures—though not one ever came aboard. Flying fish also made their first appearance on the voyage as we sailed through the haze approaching Cape Verde. "They're only found in tropical latitudes," Brian informed us. Claudia collected a few dead ones found on deck and Guillaume cooked them up, gutted but whole. Most of the crew tasted the product. I did not. Claudia wrapped up two uneaten samples and for several days they remained in the refrigerator, staring back at whichever poor sailor happened to open the door and looked inside. Finally, I threw them away. Disgusting bastards, they are.

After his temper blow-out the second day out of Gibraltar, Brian largely maintained an improved temperament, which made me believe it might be out of his system. *Allegretta* was a happy boat as long as Brian remained in a good mood, and for much of the passage to Cape Verde, life was good. I was Brian's best hand on

303

board—perhaps because of the inexperience of the others—and the two of us worked well as a team in the operation of the boat. Communication wasn't Brian's strong suit, so instructing the rest of the crew of important seagoing matters fell to me, a responsibility I didn't mind at all.

"You're a very good sailor," Brian told me one evening. "I'm glad to have you on board."

"You're a good sailor as well," I replied, "and a good captain. I was very happy when you chose to invite me with you this year," I continued. "You know, for me this voyage is all about finishing up business that was left undone a year ago. It was very important that I do this. I needed to see your good side. I left last year with a bad impression. I'm glad I came back."

We discussed the matter well into the night. I told him how unhappy I was to leave him under-staffed the year before and how I felt the obligation to make things right between us. I told him again how much I appreciated being brought back.

That is not to say we didn't have the odd tizzy between us: One night I found Brian asleep on watch with a ship bearing down on us. I altered our course before waking him, which set him off a bit. He also displayed a real surliness one day, shooting off F-bombs and swearing away like a trucker. It was a peaceful afternoon of inactivity and I couldn't imagine what might have frustrated him. I voiced a friendly, "Oh, settle down," which he didn't enjoy at all:

"Don't tell me to settle down!" he said. "Don't ever tell me to fucking settle down! You think I can't swear? I can fucking swear anytime I want. It's my boat. I can do anything..."

Oh brother! I was reminded of a similar occurrence in Gibraltar: Claudia had laughed at Brian when he tried to make a cup of coffee but had forgotten to add the coffee grounds. "Don't laugh at me!" Brian had yelled. "Don't ever laugh at me. I don't like that." I recalled also how Claudia had continued laughing even after Brian had scolded her. At the time her aloof reaction seemed disrespectful. As Brian's episodes became repeated, however, I began to think that Claudia's way of dealing with him was the best method possible.

On November 8, eleven days out of Gibraltar, Malina spotted land at eleven o'clock. We were still forty miles off and each of us spent the next several hours staring at the islands and planning what we might do once ashore. Dolphins visited us for a final showing, and the smell of burnt sand intensified as we approached the island of Sao Vicente, our destination in the eighteen island group of Cape Verde. The wind fell flat and we furled all sails and turned on the engine. Brian watched the charts and our progress from below. From there he could also alter the auto-pilot, which he did occasionally to parallel the shore of Sao Vicente a half a mile away. I stood on the aft deck, watching *Allegretta* glide along under power. We passed a navigational buoy or two, and as I called them out, Brian confirmed that we were passing them on the correct side. I saw the buoys of several fishing nets close by, but they were all sufficiently far off and we never had to alter course to avoid any of them.

Sticking his head up from the main cabin, Brian looked at me and called out, "I'm going down to the engine room."

"Okay," I replied. It was a mini-change-of-watch. No big deal. With Brian below, he wouldn't be able to watch our progress so he needed me to keep a look-out. Also, since he was in the engine room and with the engine running, he wouldn't be able to hear anything I might want to yell to him. Again, no big deal.

Brian was still below when the boat suddenly veered 90 degrees to the left, heading straight for the rocky shore of the island. I saw the mishap occur, and to prevent the boat from crashing into the rocks, I simply turned off the auto-pilot and hand-steered *Allegretta* to its proper course. A few

305

minutes later, Brian returned and I informed him of this maneuver.

"What??? Why didn't you tell me?" he lashed out. "I'm the captain of this boat. You should tell me when the boat goes off course and I will determine what to do. Why didn't you tell me? Why? Tell me why!"

I noted the stiffened back again, along with the reddened face, the protruding blood vessels in his neck, the hateful stare, the foaming mouth. I stood passively as another of his temper tantrums came into fruition.

"You said you were going into the engine room," I said calmly. I had thought this over and had made up my mind to under-react in this situation.

"I was *not* in the engine room," he shouted. "I was at the chart table."

"Well, that's what you said," I added matter-of-factly, looking off to the horizon. "Maybe you would prefer that I let the boat go up on the rocks..."

"Oh, you would do that? You don't care? Who do you think you are? I'll tell you who you are: You're just crew here like everybody else. Do you think you're the captain here? Well this is *my* boat here and *I* am the captain, and..."

On and on. There was no point in arguing back. It was a humbling experience for me—all of his escapades were—but I just looked off in the distance with apparent indifference. He continued for another few minutes, then announced, "*now* I'm going down the engine room," once again going below and leaving me in charge of the helm much as he had before.

I wish I could say that Brian's tirades had no effect on me, that I simply acted as a witness to the verbal lashings and disregarded them as the worthless, inaccurate products of immaturity that they were. The truth of the matter, however, is that his insults always hurt me. I saw too, that as his tirades were repeated, my own emotional reactions to them evolved:

The year before, when his initial tirades were directed at the trio of Lucille, Drew and me, often as we tried to fend-off because of Brian's docking mishaps, I took only small offense at the insults, my principal reaction being surprise or disbelief: *Why is he yelling at us when it is* he *that needs to control the boat?*

This year, Brian's first episode, the one just out of Gibraltar when we were first rigging the spinnaker pole, was extreme enough to leave me stunned and numb. Once again I wondered about the safety of the voyage and considered abandoning. I was asking myself if I knew all of the boat's systems sufficiently to operate it myself if, say, Brian were to have a heart attack during one of his tantrums, or fall overboard, or who knows what?

After the latest tirade, a totally unfair and humiliating verbal lashing given in front of the rest of the crew, an intense anger overcame me, stoked further by the injustice of me having no better choice but to simply accept it. And it was a lingering anger, one that continued to monopolize my mind two hours later when we reached the harbor for the city of Mindelo. I clung to my resentment, not wishing to release the anger I somehow decided was just. As the boat started to slow, however, I realized there was much work to do. I pushed my emotions aside and made ready to help set the anchor.

Mindelo Harbor on the Cape Verdean island of Sao Vicente is a large natural bay with the city of Mindelo tucked away in its deepest corner. Burnt brown mountains surround the bay—there is virtually no vegetation on Sao Vicente—and the trade winds funnel between these mountains, forming the very strong wind that forever blows out from the city and out of the bay toward the open ocean. Mindelo Marina, accompanied by a small but quaint restaurant, occupies the majority of the city's waterfront footage. Outside of its break-waters, commercial and recreational boats and ships are allowed to anchor without cost.

We motored into the bay at a slow speed and found a spot to anchor: half a mile out, but downwind from all of the other boats and in a large enough area of open water so that *Allegretta* could swing freely on her anchor. Brian handled the helm, bringing *Allegretta* to a stop, and Claudia worked the controls for the windlass, dropping the anchor at 6:00 ship's time, 11 days and one hour out of Gibraltar. With the setting of the anchor well-tested, we unlashed the dinghy and launched it over the gunwale using the spinnaker halyard. Customs was closed for the evening, so we showered up and made ourselves presentable to go to town. All cleaned up, we locked the boat thoroughly and dinghied in.

None of us, not even Brian, had been to Cape Verde before, but Brian had been told that Mindelo was a safe, friendly town, modern and with good facilities. "We need to find the Mindelo Yacht Club," he said. "Behind the yacht club is a coffee shop with free Wi-Fi." Brian's priority, like that of many of the others, was to catch up on internet and e-mail.

We tied up near some other dinghies already moored at the restaurant dock. The Mindelo Yacht Club was not to be found, nor any coffee shop near-by, nor free Wi-Fi. The waterfront bar was adequate and comfortable, however, serving all sorts of refreshments, snacks, and even light lunches. Several small tables surrounded the bar itself, each with a very necessary sun-umbrella. Wi-Fi was available, we were told, costing six euros for 100 GB.

We all went our separate ways, agreeing to meet back at the bar "an hour" later. (I was soon to learn that we were already on "Caribbean time," and the suffix "ish" had to be added to any mention of time.) My priority was to speak with Lisa, so right away I bought some internet time and Skyped a call to her. The connection wasn't good, and it took several tries before we connected, but it was a huge relief to finally hear her voice.

We had had offshore e-mail capability on *Allegretta* since the voyage began, and Lisa and I had used it, but the delicate yet crucial topics we needed to discuss didn't lend themselves well to e-mail. This changed when we were able to connect by phone.

I was able to tell Lisa that I loved her and that I valued our relationship, enough so that I didn't want to lose her. I told her I was still uncertain if I was capable of changing my life sufficiently to join her in the way she needed, but that I *thought* I could and I was willing to give it my best effort. It was all she needed to hear. We would still "meet at the door" when I finally got back home, but we were both on the same path, and both once again optimistic that we would plan a life of happiness together.

There are crossroads in life where a decision or an action is made, one that changes everything in life thereafter. The telephone conversation I had that day with Lisa was one of those crossroads. Had we not talked that day and made the decisions we made, Lisa and I would have each returned to our separate lives. It guaranteed nothing, our conversation, but it provided an opportunity that without it would never have existed.

Off the phone, I set about on a walk, anxious to explore the town of Mindelo. I wanted to see some local art, hear some African music, and check out the latest in African fashions. Leaving the marina property, I was approached immediately by a thin man in his forties wearing a NY Yankees baseball hat.

He was a good-looking black man with lighter, European complexion. He wore a stylish grey shirt and smart looking white pants, both neatly pressed. He didn't look poor. Though only 5'6" tall, he walked with purpose and enthusiasm, the latter evidenced by his easy smile, which unfortunately showed a full mouth of rotted teeth. He removed his sun glasses and greeted me in perfect English with no detectable accent.

"Hello sir," he said. "My name is Joe. I'm a tour guide for the island, and if there is anything you need, I'm the man who can show you how to get it."

I had come across people like Joe before. He really wasn't a tour guide at all; he was a family man who made his living not by giving tours but by telling you where you could find a tour guide. Likewise, he couldn't rent you a car, but he could tell you where the car rental agency was located. He could also locate a restaurant for you, or tell you where to get groceries, gas, laundry services or boat supplies. As he said, if I needed anything, he could tell me how to find it. I didn't really need him for anything at the moment, but I thought making his acquaintance might come in handy sometime later.

"What do you do, Joe?" I asked.

"Oh, I can do anything. I'm your man. What do you need? Are you familiar with the island?"

"Well, I *was* hoping at some point to take a car tour around the island. Do you have a car?"

"Yeah, I can get you a car," he said, not answering my question. "Look, you can go up the mountain," he said, showing me a map. "From there you can see the whole layout of the island. Hey, that's a nice shirt."

"I'm sorry, what did you say?"

"That's a nice shirt," Joe continued, referring to the yellowed *Skyelark of London* T-shirt I was wearing. "Sir, if you have any extra shirts like that, I'd love to have one."

"You want this shirt?" I asked incredulously.

"Oh, yes sir! Any shirt with a boat's logo on it."

I thought of the shirt I was wearing. Dan Bower had given it to me at the end of the *Skyelark* voyage. I treasured it then, but by this time it was almost three years old and pretty worn. "I'll give you this shirt, Joe. You can have it."

"Oh, great! Here take this one and we'll trade," he said offering to take off his own shirt.

"Well, no. Joe, I'll give it to you tomorrow. I'm going to town and I need the shirt right now." I started walking away, expecting him to leave, but he followed along with me. "Is there something else I can help you with, Joe?" I asked.

"Well, if you have any money, I could use some, sir. It's how I make my living, you know, and it's really been a slow day. I've got three kids at home and I don't have any groceries in the refrigerator. If you could *loan* me a bit of money so I could buy dinner for my kids..."

The nerve! First, he wants the shirt right off my back, and now money. "Not right now, Joe. Maybe later. I'm just off the boat and I've got to find dinner myself. You'll be fine, and tomorrow I'll bring you a shirt, but right now let me be so that I can enjoy the town."

"Okay sir," he said, following me as I crossed the street in an attempt to escape through the heavy traffic. "I'll let you be. Hey, do you need a restaurant? I know where all the restaurants are. I can find you a very good place to eat. What kind of food..."

He wouldn't quit. I waved him away as I crossed a side-street, then another, finally crossing through a marketplace quick enough so that he couldn't follow. I was finally free to roam on my own, but not for long: Every 30 seconds or so, another beggar would approach me, speaking as if he was my best friend, asking for money, and pestering me until I escaped. Traffic became my friend. I crossed a lot of streets that evening.

Most of the streets in Mindelo were small enough that we would call them alleys back home. The commercial buildings that lined the streets all butted up against one another, creating a wall of buildings on both sides of every street. A robust, well-secured doorway identified each separate business or residence, and often I saw a singular man, sometimes two or three, standing in these doorways, inactive except for watching the comings and goings of the street.

I recalled seeing the same practice in St. Thomas, and also back in the sixties in my hometown of Detroit. Remembering the dangers in these two places put me on

311

high alert as I walked the streets of Mindelo. Sometimes one of the doorway occupants would approach me and beg for money. Sometimes I was simply watched as I walked by. It seemed dangerous. In fact, *all* of Mindelo seemed dangerous. I felt as if I might get robbed at any time. I kept a brisk pace and walked down the center of the streets. It was a tactic I learned in Detroit, the safe way to walk in the "hood."

I wasn't long in my exploration, returning to the restaurant at the marina a little short of the agreed upon hour. Joe was on the cement walkway leading to the marina. This was the station where he did his work, where he spent most of his 12-hour work-day. He approached me again, his ever-present smile and enthusiasm apparent, and held out his hand to shake mine as if I were his best friend.

"Sir, how was your trip to town? It's a beautiful evening out, no? Say, did you find a nice place for dinner? You know, I know all the restaurants in the city. I can find you the best meal. What kind of food do you like, sir?"

Oh brother! I found Joe's enthusiasm refreshing, but he was also quite a nuisance. I had already guessed that he didn't offer anything of particular utility, but I figured I'd stay on his good side, not that I had any choice. He was "my man," the local expert that I could go to for anything, or so it appeared. To the other beggars, at least those in the area by the marina, I could say, "Joe's my man; anything I need, I go to Joe." It was a good tactic: Everybody knew Joe and with my phrase I would be left alone.

So, when Joe approached me this time, I stopped and shook his hand and asked him about *his* day, *his* home, and *his* family. I was surprised that Joe used to live in New York, though that explained his command of English, uncommon to the locals of Cape Verde. He had an ex-wife and an 18-year-old daughter still in New York, he told me, and also a brother and a sister who lived there.

"Why don't *you* still live in New York, Joe?" I asked him.

"I don't have papers, man," he said. "That's why I was booted out: I didn't have the proper papers."

"Can you get papers? I mean your daughter is there, your siblings are there. You speak English. Can't you get clearance to move there?"

"No! After 911? Man, nobody gets papers for the US anymore. And besides, now I got a wife and a couple kids here. I *gotta* stay, man."

"You *gotta* get a job, Joe. With a wife and kids, you can't be doing this. Aren't there any jobs here?"

"No, man. There ain't no jobs here. I do a bit of construction work," he said, showing me the callouses on his hands, "but there's not much work. I do whatever I can, and when I got nothing else, I come here. And as you see, I'm here all the time. Sir, could you give me a little something so I could get some dinner tonight? Anything would help, sir? Can you help me?"

I only had a few euros that I had brought from home. I gave him a 10-euro note, more generous than I intended. I figured I could spare it and, who knows, maybe it really would go to feed some kids.

"Oh, thank you, sir," he told me profusely. He should have left it at that: "Sir, don't forget: I would love to have that shirt. You know, it's hard to buy clothes on the money I make. And if you have any other shirts, or shorts. Or shoes, sir, I really need shoes. You've got an extra pair of shoes, don't you sir?"

He reminded me of a child reciting his Christmas list. I liked Joe. I liked his enthusiasm and his smile. I felt compassion for a man living in an impoverished economy that offered little support for its inhabitants. But his persistence was exhausting. Also, by this time I was running late and had to meet the others.

"Joe," I said, "first thing: My name is Mike, not sir."

"Okay, Mike," he said shaking my hand once again. "Yeah, I wanted to ask you your name. Okay, Mike!"

"Also, Joe, I'm going to do what I can to help you, but if you want my cooperation, you're going to have to give me some space. You know what I mean, don't you?"

He was a bit hurt but he got the message. He shook my hand, and with a wave and an "okay, man, I'll see you tomorrow," we went our separate ways. Good thing: There weren't any streets to cross in the marina area.

The rest of the gang was seated at the bar, each of them with their laptop or phone, heavily engaged in e-mail and social communication. It was dark by this time, and late enough that I was hungry for dinner.

"Anybody interested in dinner?" I asked. It didn't take long: Soon everybody was logging off and we were off for dinner. "Hey, we'd better be careful," I told the others. "This looks like a pretty rough town."

"Rough?" asked Malina.

"Dangerous," I said. "My first impression of the town is that it's pretty dangerous. You'll see."

We circled several blocks, trying to find a suitable restaurant. Joe caught up to us two or three times—he seemed to *always* be around—and though he was able to point out several possibilities, none of his suggestions seemed very good. Finally we found a suitable place run by a woman named Maria Anna. Neither large nor fancy, and with not a soul inside, the restaurant had outdoor seating and a promising menu with good prices. Maria Anna, a nice older woman and the owner of the restaurant, spoke very little English, but we finally all settled on a traditional dish of corn, beans and potatoes, with a single egg along with a small piece of poor quality fish (half the head?) placed on top. It was not the best meal I had ever had, nor the worst. It was filling, and at 25 euros for the five meals, the price was right.

On the way back, Guillaume and Malina suggested we all go to a bar they had heard about. "They have traditional music there," Malina pleaded.

314

"It's a bar, right?" I asked. "A place where you go and drink all night? Pay a cover charge? Dance? Get back at two o'clock?"

"You don't have to drink," Brian interjected. "You can just buy one drink and leave it in front of you all night. No one can make you drink it."

There was no way I was going to hang out at some bar in this dangerous town all night, nursing a drink and pissing off the establishment. "Hey, you guys go along if you want," I said. "It's way too dangerous for me, but you're on your own. Me, I'm going back to the boat."

They decided that, perhaps, I was right. (Gee, do you think?!!) We all returned to the boat, the others thinking they might go out the next night instead. I was in bed by 9:00 with the lights out, but the others stayed up drinking tea and playing cards. Claudia baked a loaf of bread, something she did most nights of the entire voyage.

Sometime during the night I heard some noise as if somebody were on deck. I got up and stuck my head through the deck hatch in my cabin. I looked around thoroughly, not seeing anything out of ordinary.

Malina heard something on deck during the night as well and sent Guillaume up to have a look. He, too, saw nothing.

Sometime in the early hours of the morning—still dark out—I heard a banging sound. I got up and noticed the door to my cabin was opened. I closed it and went back to sleep.

I woke up with the sun about seven o'clock, ate a bit of breakfast, and took a cup of coffee out to the cockpit. By this time Claudia was up, and we both sat in the cockpit as a sailboat motored by. I noticed it wasn't flying a flag. "That's strange," I said. "I thought it was the law that you flew a flag in a foreign country." That's when I noticed our own flag was missing.

"Where's our flag?" I asked in astonishment. I recalled we had mounted it the previous day but now it was gone. It was a new flag, one that I had brought from home and had given to Brian when I arrived in Gibraltar. It was a gift of good tidings, sort of a make-up gift. It was a wonderful high quality embroidered flag. "Where'd it go?" I asked again in disbelief. "The flag and the staff: they're both gone."

The others were up by this time. We all stared at the mounting bracket in the stern pulpit where the flag and its staff had once been. "Maybe the wind blew it away," I guessed.

"No, in all the years I've owned the boat, the flag has never been blown away by the wind," Brian said. "Somebody came aboard and stole it."

"My phone!" Claudia yelled. "My phone is gone. It was on the chart table, charging."

"You know, my cabin door was open this morning," I said trying to pull all the pieces together. "I *could* have left it open, but I wouldn't have thought so."

"Mine was open too!" said Claudia, her eyes now like saucers.

A thief had come aboard; there was no doubt. He had to have come by boat, since we were out at anchor. It was probably a fisherman, we figured. He entered the boat, opening both Claudia's door and mine to see each of us sleeping. He then slipped away, leaving both doors open, and taking with him whatever was easy to take and easy to sell. The phone was an obvious thing to take: it was in clear view on the chart table, easily picked up and put into a pocket, and it would readily sell in town. The flag puzzled me: Why would anybody from Cape Verde take an American flag? Was it a trophy? I couldn't imagine so.

"No, they're very much required in demonstrations where they burn the American flag," an Iraqi veteran friend told me later. "There's no place to get one in those far-away foreign ports. American flags are in big demand."

I recalled that a home of mine had once been burglarized about 30 years prior. Nothing major was stolen—a TV that didn't work, an old coat—but I had felt violated at the time. That same feeling of violation returned to me and the others aboard *Allegretta.*

Malina thought we should take up anchor immediately and sail for the Caribbean, a sharp contrast from her wish the previous night to stay out late at the bar. When Brian mentioned he wanted to do several repair jobs and that groceries and gas were needed, Malina stated that at the very least we should maintain watches day-and-night in case the thieves came back. It wasn't a bad idea, I thought, though I didn't cherish the idea of giving up uninterrupted nights of sleep. Claudia was more pragmatic: "I need to get my phone back," she cried. "My whole life is in that phone."

"You know, I'll bet that guy 'Joe' can get your phone," I said. "It's got to be on the black market by now. We might have to pay, but I'm thinking he'd be our best bet."

So, we finished up with breakfast and showers, and grabbed our laptops and whatever else we each wanted to take into town. I made sure I had the shirt I had promised Joe and also a nice Gortex hat I never wore. We latched all of the boat's hatches—and *not* because it might rain—then locked the boat thoroughly and dinghied in.

Upon reaching shore, Claudia and I made it our mission to go after the phone. We found Joe on duty at his work station. He saw me right away, smiled fully, and held out his hand.

"Good morning sir! How are you today? Did you have a good time out on the town last night? Did you..."

"Hello Joe! Yes, we're fine. Joe, this is Claudia, another crew member on the boat. Joe, we had a bit of trouble aboard last night. We need your help."

I told him about the theft. He said he had never heard of any trouble on boats before. He had no idea who would do it. "Nobody has access to a boat," he told us. "The marina is fully secured. Nobody can get in, and we're all too

317

poor to have a boat anyway. Maybe it was somebody off a yacht."

"No, it wouldn't be anybody from a yacht," I said. "A boat person would take a winch handle, or the GPS—something for a boat. No, this was a phone and a flag: things that could be sold ashore. I'm thinking it was a fisherman, Joe."

"Yeah, it could be a fisherman," he said, totally amazed with the realization. It struck me odd that the idea didn't occur to him immediately. He was either a liar or stupid, I thought. I gave him the benefit of the doubt and believed the latter.

"Joe, we need that phone and we need you to find it for us. You know the markets. Find it Joe. Find that phone. Look for the flag. If you find the flag, you'll find the phone. We need your help, Joe. Can you get it for us?"

"I'll *try*," he said, and my hopes of success plummeted. Thievery in Mindelo, the same as in other impoverished areas, would be a popular form of business. The thieves would be known by anybody familiar with the street, as would the avenues with which stolen goods were processed. I was hoping that Joe was astute and would know exactly where to look. We would just have to give him the assignment and wait and see...

"Joe, if you find that phone you'll get paid. We know the rules of the game and we don't mind playing. But we need that phone. You know the street, Joe. Do your thing."

"Well, like I say, I'll try but I don't know..."

Okay, we had given him the assignment. He would either succeed on not. We also wanted to go to the police station and file a report. We weren't thinking the police would find our phone, but Claudia needed a report for insurance reasons. When we mentioned this, Joe was right on cue: "Hey, I can take you to the police station. C'mon! It's right this way."

I wanted Joe to get started on checking his sources and finding the phone, but I realized we didn't know where the police station was, and we might need a translator as well. We accepted his assistance and the three of us began a half-mile walk to the station. We were continuing along toward the north end of town when Claudia pointed across the street and asked, "Isn't that the Police Station there?"

"Oh, yeah! That's it! That's the Police Station right there," Joe said with pride.

"Nice job, Joe," I said under my breath.

We walked into the Police Station, a shoddy and dusty, uncomfortably warm building. The woman at the reception desk didn't speak a word of English, nor did the investigating officer assigned to us, nor did a second woman, Amelia, the one who eventually wrote up our report. Joe acted as a translator. It was the first time Joe had been of any real help to us.

We were ushered to a small room with Amelia where she loaded a blank report form into a typewriter. (I hadn't seen a typewriter in years!) "What is your name?" was her first question.

It turned out to be a complicated question to answer. Claudia was born in Tunisia, and her name wasn't really *Claudia* but rather an Arabic version of it. Also, it was written using the Arabic alphabet and there were questions regarding its translation. It took the two women, with Joe as translator, fifteen minutes to get Claudia's first name recorded. The surname wasn't any easier: Claudia had failed to get her passport changed with her divorce, so now it differed from the driver's license she was using for ID.

I was getting a bit frustrated, sitting in the hot room. I could understand the difficulty Amelia was having, caused by the unique complications of the name, but when she also had trouble entering "white phone" to describe what was stolen, I was starting to doubt the utility of what we were doing. It was about an hour and a half later when Amelia said she needed a statement from Brian, the captain of our boat. She would also have to send an officer out to the boat to get some more specific information and take some photographs and, of course, he was busy at the time. "Would you be available at 3:00?" she asked us.

"Sure, 3:00 would be fine. Does the officer speak English?" asked Claudia.

"No, he doesn't," said Amelia. "But we'll send a translator with him."

"Can we get a copy of the report as it is right now?"

"No, it's not ready. You'll get a report when it is finished."

"You know, we only need it for insurance reasons. What you have now would be fine. Is there any way we could get what you have now?" Claudia pleaded.

"No."

So, we left the station no better off than we were before, walking three abreast and with Joe tagging along. I was expecting what was to follow and it wasn't long in coming:

"Can you guys please pay me for the help I gave you?" Joe asked.

"What do you mean 'help?'" asked Claudia. "We don't have a report, we don't have a phone. What help have you given us?"

Joe's request was reasonable; Claudia's answer was *not*. We very much had required Joe's facilitation and translation, and we had occupied two hours of his time. For these things you pay. Claudia should have understood this as well as anybody; I couldn't believe she was putting up an argument. The two dickered back and forth, with Claudia finally handing Joe some English pound money—three one-pound coins and several others of smaller denomination.

Now, Cape Verde has its own currency, called "escudos." Banks and most places of business will accept escudos, euros, or US dollars, but nobody on Cape Verde—not even the banks—will accept coins of British currency. The amount of money Claudia gave Joe was insufficient as well as in a useless currency.

He turned to me and pleaded his case: "Mike, I *gotta* get paid," he begged. "I got kids. You guys took two hours of my time. I can't do this for free. You gotta help me."

"You should get it from Claudia," I told him, clearly within her earshot. "Tell her what you need." It was a waste of energy: Claudia told him she didn't have any other money, which brought him back to me.

"How much do you need, Joe?" I asked.

"I don't know," he said. "How much you got? Two hours, Mike! That's a big part of my day..."

"Give me a figure, Joe. What would make you happy?"

"Mike, I got kids! This British money is no good to me. I need to buy food..."

I finally got him to settle on 10 euros, a lot of money for him, but really only enough for two gallons of gas or two of the inexpensive dinners we had enjoyed at Maria Anna's. I gave him the money, making him agree that it was adequate, then also the shirt and hat I had brought for him. His smile returned and he thanked me, but he never said a word to Claudia or even looked her way when he left us. Claudia and I continued to town without him, never mentioning Joe, the money, the report, or the follow-up visit by the investigating officer.

It occurred to me that Amelia had never asked, and Claudia had never identified, the name of our boat or that it was not at the marina but out at anchor at the far end of the harbor. There was no way any officer could meet us later, and we were never going to get a police report. And with the way Claudia had snubbed Joe, there was no way he would try to find the phone for us. *"Let it go,"* I told myself. *"This one is clearly not my problem."*

Guillaume and Malina had found a small French market in town, one surrounded by several pastry and coffee shops, and which happened to be a door or two down from an internet café. The shops enclosed a small courtyard with several small and inviting tables, and with the free Wi-

Fi and French-speaking proprietors, it was a perfect setting for Guillaume and Malina. We never had to look far to find them; they spent all of their time at this French market.

There was also a shop that had a telephone service, and for one euro you could call and talk for one minute to most places in the world. Poor Claudia, without a phone but still with serious needs to "connect," she spent a lot of time in this area as well, talking on the phone, doing e-mails, or socializing on *Facebook*.

Claudia led a busy life, much more complicated than mine or that of anyone else I knew. The business of her divorce hadn't been completely finished at the time of the voyage, and she was still heavily into negotiations with her ex-husband. She had also been terminated from her job as an architect in St. Tropez, and her ex-employer was suing her in court for misrepresentation. (She hadn't received a salary in eight months, she told us.) Additionally, she was frantically trying to sell an apartment she owned in St Tropez—*frantically* because she was flat broke and didn't even have enough cash (or credit) to buy a plane ticket out of the Caribbean. Claudia spent hours on the computer in communication with her ex and her lawyer, trying to prevent a meltdown of her unstable world. She also had a few boyfriends on hand—one in Tunisia, another in New York, and a third in Puerto Rico—and she was e-mailing and calling these fellows, trying to get any one of them to buy her a plane ticket and/or give her a place to stay.

Brian also spent several hours each day doing e-mail—he at a table near the marina, and probably for the more essential reason of conducting business. I was the only one who wasn't tied to a computer. I had my e-book with internet and e-mail capability, and I sent Lisa a note most days, but I left all other incoming e-mails unanswered, spending only five or ten minutes each day doing the e-socializing that the others found so necessary.

So on this day, with everybody else's nose in a computer, I set about to take my big tour of the town. I must have walked every street in Mindelo by the time I was done, checking out the town and its people, the three market places, and the two art museums—one Portuguese, the other African. I saw a woman cutting up a hundred-pound tuna in the fish market and another one carrying over a thousand eggs in cartons all balanced on her head. I watch several groups of men playing cards at an outdoor courtyard, and several athletic men and women doing some very rigorous exercises in a park. The town didn't look so dangerous to me anymore. Persistent beggars were still numerous, but I didn't find them bothersome. I saw that the architecture was Portuguese (Cape Verde was a former Portuguese colony) but that the people were clearly African. They spoke "creole," Joe had told me, a created language of their own.

My tour covered the entire town, occupying a couple of hours of my time. Seeing a new town such as Mindelo doesn't normally take me long: I check out everything once and then I'm done. I was in no hurry on this particular day. I walked slowly and took a few pictures, but I didn't talk to anybody at all. I would have loved to meet and mix with a few locals, but everybody approaching me was looking for a hand-out. I don't blame the people: they are poor and without opportunity. I was rich, by comparison, and a bountiful source of dinner money. I gave away a few dollars, but each time I did, a flock of others would gather around asking for their share. I carried only a few small notes—US dollars, euros, Cape Verdean escudos—knowing in advance the extent of my loss either to beggars or to thieves. With my tour finished, I returned to the marina bar and asked Brian to dinghy me back to the boat. I had had enough of Mindelo, at least for the time being. We still had a couple of days and a few things to do before we left Cape Verde—we needed provisions, fuel and water—but I planned to spend the majority of my time on the boat, reading and relaxing. Like I say, it doesn't take me long to check out a new place. Never has.

Back at the boat that afternoon, with the others all ashore with their computers, I sat in the cockpit, enjoying my solitude with a cup of coffee and a new book: *Life of Pi*. Every so often another boat would pass close by: sometimes a fisherman in one of the small skiffs they popularized, sometimes a cruising sailboat coming in off the ocean and looking for a suitable anchorage. Often the fishermen in skiffs would approach me on *Allegretta*, holding up a huge lobster and asking in words I couldn't understand if I wanted to buy it. I enjoyed their encounters but chased them away. We had plenty of food and their lobsters were always way too big. If I had bought one, I wouldn't have known how to cook it.

In my lazy inactivity, I was standing on the teak aft deck when I looked down and saw the unbleached outlines of where two ice coolers were once stored. They were a couple of large white ice chests, not for our use on the voyage, but needed by Brian for charters later. The straps he had used to secure the coolers were still in place. The coolers, however, were gone.

Could we have had another theft? Truly, I had seen many boats come by, several of them with fishermen. Was it one of them? Coming aboard in broad daylight would be a bold move, but no bolder than the actions of the beggars I had encountered. I looked through the boat, hoping to find that the coolers had been stored inside. No luck. I couldn't believe it: We had been robbed a second time!

Another skiff of fishermen approached, they too wanting to sell me a lobster. "Did you take our phone and coolers?" I asked them, not so kindly. They might not have understood my words, but their hasty retreat told me they understood my emotion. My nasty stare kept all others away as well.

We carried walkie-talkie radios to aid communication between those of us ashore and those aboard, and Brian called me a couple of hours later, asking me if I wanted to join him and the others for dinner.

Knowing a thief might return at any time, I declined the dinner invitation, happy to eat aboard anyway. I mentioned nothing on the radio; I didn't want to ruin everybody's joyful night out. The group returned at 11:00—which concerned me: it was several hours after I expected them—and it was then I told them about the second theft.

We discussed a rotation of night watches, but I reasoned that one of us alone would offer little resistance to a thief in the middle of the night, one that might well be armed. Brian mentioned that we should leave as soon as possible, and though I liked the idea, it wouldn't help us much that night. Eventually, we decided to remove everything possible from the deck and lock ourselves in the boat as we slept. I even locked my cabin door that night.

We awoke in the morning and were discussing the thefts when Malina recalled she had taken a photograph of the stern the previous morning. She retrieved her camera and reviewed her most recent pictures. Indeed one was of the stern. The flag was missing and so were the coolers. We had *not* had a second theft; the coolers were taken during the first, along with the phone and flag.

The discovery that we had suffered only one theft relieved some worries, but all of us still favored getting away as soon as possible. We spent the morning completing some repairs to the spreader lights that Brian deemed necessary, and later we went to the grocery store and stocked up with provisions. We were hoping to leave that very evening, but couldn't get through Customs, it being Sunday, and Assad, the one person who could clear yachts, didn't work Sundays. Resigned to wait until the next day, we returned to the boat and spent an uneventful night out in the bay, swinging away on the hook. As we had the night before, we locked ourselves into the boat, but we never heard any noise on deck that night, and no robbers came by either.

In the morning, Brian and I launched the dinghy and powered over to the customs office. The office was open—

Assad was in, thank God—and 20 minutes later we were all set to go. Returning to the boat, we secured the dinghy to the deck, raised the anchor, and motored over to the fuel dock. We topped off the tanks, purchasing 100 gallons of fuel; Guillaume paid, thus settling his bill with Brian. We motored through the harbor with *Allegretta's* hardworking crew storing dock-lines, fenders, and shoes—all "land gear" that would henceforth only get in our way. We headed west out of the bay, paralleling Sao Antao, another island of Cape Verde, but smaller and much greener than Sao Vicente. We were off for our Atlantic crossing—the tenth for Brian, my third, and a first attempt for the other three. We were bound for St. Martin, 2160 miles away.

The stop at St. Martin wasn't in the original plan for the voyage. None of our French crew had obtained a US visa, however, so we had no choice but to stop on French St. Martin and let them off. St. Martin was on the route to St. Thomas and the stop shouldn't have taken any time at all, but Brian said he wanted to pick up a few items at a marine store. Later he would say that he also wanted to visit some friends while at St. Martin. "It won't take long," he promised. We were there for three days. Caribbean time: you gotta love it!

Brian often bragged that *Allegretta* always made 150-mile days, an exaggeration it seemed to me, but even at 150 miles/day, our passage to St. Martin would take more than two weeks. We would be at sea a long time, not the longest passage I had done—that would be the 18-day crossing on *That Darn Cat*—but still a long passage.

I wanted to avoid some of the mental pitfalls I had experienced on previous passages. I especially wanted to *not* wish away even a single moment of the passage. My goal for the entire voyage had always been to "live in the moment," passing days at sea in total contentment, unconcerned with however much time was required to complete it. Now on the final leg, with all worries and apprehensions either resolved or worn away with time, I vowed that this would be the passage where I would finally attain that goal. *One day I will be wishing to have just one more experience, any experience at all,* I reminded myself. *Don't wish away what should be one of the very best experiences of them all.*

It was with this objective in mind that I sat aboard *Allegretta,* gazing out at the sea as we motored away from the islands of Cape Verde. Downwind of the islands the wind fell flat and it wasn't until mid-afternoon, with us well out of the sight of land, when a stable breeze finally materialized and we started thinking about setting up a downwind rig of sails.

It was a southeast wind, not northeast as it had been before. We would still fly a double headsail rig, but this time the pole would be off to the port side and this proved to be quite problematic. On the port side, we had to use a spare staysail halyard as a topping-lift, and since that halyard fouled with the radar supports near the masthead, the pole would also require a roping mechanism called a "bridle" which would redirect the lead of the halyard. Brian, Claudia and I began working as a threesome to make a bridle and rig the pole, a frustrating task made worse by an exceedingly hot mid-day sun and the pesky rocking motion of the boat created by the "moderate" sea. As a team, we weren't working well, and it wasn't long before the situation and elements proved too much for Brian's patience.

I was in the cockpit handling the winches when I noticed Brian's irritation as he and Claudia worked on the foredeck. Guillaume and Malina sat near the companionway, uninvolved but eager to help if asked. Brian was calling instructions back to me to pull in one line or let out another. His words were often inaudible and I had to ask him for repeats several times. At first he simply looked back at me in irritation and shouted his repeated instruction, but as his frustration increased, he glared at me angrily, screaming the order multiple times, soon getting himself into a full fury. The emotional energy only added to the sun's heat, and soon sweat was dripping abundantly from his face and neck. I knew his tolerance limit wasn't far off. An error on my part of pulling in the wrong jib sheet sent him over the edge. I watched as his lips pulled back, exposing teeth clinched so tightly they made his head shake. Tears dripped from his eyes and he struggled to choke out the repeated words of his instruction. "Pull in the sheet! Pull in the sheet! Pull in the sheet!" he said.

I saw again the stiffened back, the protruding veins, and all the other physical and verbal features of another emotional episode. In his fury, he let go of the staysail halyard and the outboard end of the pole bounced off the deck and dragged in the water. I started to come forward to help retrieve it when he held out his palm and stood erect, giving me the fiercest glare he could muster.

"Stay!" he commanded. "Do you hear me? Just fucking stay! Don't come up here. Just stay!"

Now, the command "Stay!" is something you might give a dog, a slur that made me so indignant I wanted to *attack* him like a dog. It was an insult that exceeded all others. He was disabling me. Disempowering me. It was as if he was telling me, "You're a useless ass and we're better off without your help. Do us a favor: Stay the fuck away!" I felt insulted, angry and hateful all at the same time. I wanted to grab his throat and didn't dare go forward, knowing surely I would have punched him had he been within my reach.

"Just fucking stay!" he went on. "Do you hear me? We don't need you. I said stay! Just fucking stay!"

"I *am* fucking staying!" I yelled, and I realized I was losing my own temper and needed to keep my anger in check.

"And stop fucking watching me. You're making me nervous," he added.

Well, I *had* to watch him: the damn fool could have fallen overboard the way he stood on the rocking foredeck, arms flapping like a penguin and screaming away in a full rage. I maintained my watch, a stare meant to antagonize I'll admit.

Brian's verbal ranting continued, even as Claudia caught the run-away staysail halyard and the two of them used it to haul the pole out of the water. Overheating in the sun, they remained on deck for another hour, rigging the pole and sail. I stood on the aft deck in the shade of the awning, watching the activity and grinding in the odd line as needed. Every now and then Brian would look back and yell another "Stay!" or "Quit watching me." These I ignored, realizing by then the irritating effect of my stare. I fully loathed the man by this time. My stare was the one method I had for revenge.

I had never reacted to Brian's tirades—not to this one, not to any of the others. I had always figured that any reaction would only worsen the situation and that it was best to remain quiet and take my lumps. (I learned a lot about humility with Brian.) But after the umpteenth demeaning command to "Stay," a moment of indiscretion overcame me, and I hurled a verbal assault of my own:

"Oh, fuck off!" I yelled.

Fuck off. I had heard the two words for the first time as a teenager in Canada. I can recall thinking of it as a senseless phrase, but at the same time realizing its unquestionable volatility. It was the ultimate verbal stone. *Fuck off* meant that you were worthless scum. *Fuck off* said that I was banishing you from my world. And *fuck off* was permanent: Fuck off meant *always* fuck off. Fuck off forever. Fuck off and die! It was a phrase I didn't use often, but after working in a factory for 30 years, I had learned to deploy this special weapon with lethal precision.

Well, my weapon hit its mark. Brian's back immediately arched and he began circling the deck in baby steps up on his toes as if he were about to pee in his pants. He glanced back at me with a look of betrayal and disbelief. He was stunned. His only capable crew on board had taken up arms against him. He had never seen my anger and he didn't know how much more of it I had within me. But I was bigger than he was, and stronger. He must have realized that if I chose to attack, he'd have a difficult time defending himself.

He wants a fight, well now he's got one.
But he ain't seen me crazy yet!
                    Miranda Lambert

Brian's temper tantrum didn't quite end with my F-bomb. He and Claudia were nearly finished anyway, so after a moment or two of recuperation he came to the cockpit and began complaining about several apparent deficiencies in my handling of matters back there—none valid, I might add. He was more like a crabby old maid than a sea captain, and I grinned at him mockingly, still angry but not about to do anything harmful. Finished at last, he retired to his cabin as he did after all of his escapades. We were all very glad when he did.

Guillaume and Malina were each horrified at my outburst, realizing that both capable sailors on board were out of control with their tempers. I didn't know it until much later, but they had always been terrified of Brian and his temperament, and grateful that I had not reacted to him thus far. They regarded me as the one person on board who could hold things together and save the voyage from catastrophe. With Brian gone to his cabin they could express their concern:

"Mike, what happened? What went so wrong?" they both asked and I could see their worry. I put my finger to my lips and pointed at my feet. Brian's cabin was directly below us, and through an opened window he could hear every word we said.

"It's going to be all right," I said. "I'm sorry I lost my temper. Everything's fine now." My words seemed to soothe them. Everything *was* okay. We couldn't control

330

Brian's temper, we all knew, but I had to control mine for the voyage to succeed. "I'm fine. Don't worry," I said again.

Dinner was a somber occasion that night. Guillaume cooked up some chicken and potatoes, and since we had lots of fresh fruits and vegetables, the women were able to make a big salad. Four of us ate at the cockpit table, enjoying one another's company. Brian, after a two hour "re-charging" nap, ate at his navigation desk. He remained there for the rest of the evening, not saying a word and keeping to himself.

He and I hadn't spoken since the afternoon. I remained angry well into the night—angry at how I was treated and angry that Brian took no ownership in the problem or its resolution. I knew that somehow we would have to get back to a talking relationship, however, and I knew that it would be me, not him, who would have to initiate the effort. It wasn't fair, that's for sure, but it had to be done.

Recall that I had done this before: with Julian on *That Darn Cat* and with Bertrand on *Rhapsody in Blue*. It's a humbling experience, making amends, and I'll be damned if it doesn't always seem to fall in my court. On *That Darn Cat,* I was legitimately at fault, at least in part, so I can see why it fell to me to reestablish good relations. I recall that my efforts worked quite well that time—thank you very much. With Bertie, I don't believe the issue between us was my fault—and my efforts to re-establish cohesion weren't nearly as successful either—but I still credit myself for taking the initiative. It *did* repair the rift between Bertie and me, to a large degree anyway, and generally speaking that is what happens when amends are made.

On Allegretta, the captain should have apologized: It was *his* behavior that was repeatedly absurd and abusive, and only *his*. It was *his* boat, *his* charge and *he* was the most senior among us. Most folks of would own up to these facts and apologize right away, but Brian's ego and immaturity didn't allow him to do this.

So, it fell to *me,* and it was *me* that walked over to Brian at his navigation desk later that evening. As I said, we hadn't spoken a word, and it took a few seconds before he realized I was standing over him, right next to where he sat. I looked him in the eye for several seconds then held out my hand. He shook it and I gave him a slight nod, a totally silent gesture that might have said, "It's over. We can be friends now. All is forgiven." He said nothing as well, but nodded back in agreement and I walked away and went to my cabin. The amends were complete. We never spoke of the matter again. The next morning I met him on the foredeck, and with a manly grunt and perhaps a word or two we acknowledged that the wind had changed. We took down the spinnaker pole, the one that had caused so much commotion the day before, and set the main and genoa. We work well together. It was almost as if nothing had ever occurred.

That is not to say that Brian and I were going to be good chums ever again, in spite of how we treated one another. To be honest, I didn't really like him anymore and figured I probably never would. For my part, however, I settled into my now familiar routine of reading in the cockpit and gazing out at the sea, reminding myself to live in the moment and enjoy every minute of the passage.

Speaking of the captain: For the rest of the voyage he was often in a foul mood, complaining about this and that, and bitching away like an old maid. By this time we were all familiar with his ways, however, and each of us had our own methods of dealing with him.

Only Claudia was oblivious to Brian's destructive nature, but Claudia was oblivious to many things. I recall one time when Brian was playing some Pavarotti pieces on the stereo, normally something to enjoy, but played at full volume because he wanted to drown out a conversation Malina and I were having, one that he didn't enjoy. (Both of these were common: Brian not enjoying our conversations, and Pavarotti played at full volume.) The loud music was an

332

obvious assault, a childish one indeed, but it certainly did work to quell the conversation. Not recognizing the assault, Claudia sat in cockpit with her eyes half-closed and her opened hand suspended in mid-air, totally enamored with one of the tenor's favorite arias.

For the most part I was able to pass my days happily, but I'd be lying if I told you Brian's repeated humiliations didn't have a significant effect on me. His foul moods, and the fact that I never knew if one would develop into another meltdown, affected me more and more as the crossing progressed. Even the overly-loud music—what I came to think of as "The Pavarotti Chinese Torture"—wore away at me. Beginning about halfway across the ocean, and increasing until its end, I felt some old childhood fears start to surface, fears that I had forgotten long ago.

My father had quite a temper when I was young, and he would often come home from a stressful day at work in an angry mood. I didn't realize it at the time, but my mother told me years later that he used to take his anger out on his children, and since I was the oldest boy, I normally received the largest share. I developed an intense fear of my father, always wondering if I was going to receive a verbal or physical lashing when he came home. That fear was with me throughout my entire childhood, and by the time I was in high school, I was so shy I would cross the street if someone, especially a girl, were to walk toward me on the same sidewalk. In time the fears left me—or so I thought—and eventually I forgot about them altogether.

That same ever-present fear I had felt as a child revisited me on *Allegretta* halfway across the ocean. Though I had no reason to fear Brian—hell, he was a skinny old man—I always wondered if he was going to go into another of his tantrums and I would be humiliated in front of the others once again. Brian's repeated foul moods were like the smaller pre-eruptions of a geyser, and the Pavarotti Torture constantly reminded me that the "boss man" was always near-by. The reverberating fear in my core grew to surprising proportions. By the end of voyage, I felt like that same shy teenager, cowardly crossing the street, afraid of his own shadow.

Guillaume and Malina had by this time become my favorite comrades on the voyage. (Mind you, the competition was limited.) Like me, they also enjoyed sitting in the cockpit, and we spent many a day enjoying the sea together. They often sat with one's head in the other's lap, content to spend their time in a romantic closeness that seemed to come to them very naturally. Guillaume had brought a ukulele and he would play it while Malina lay with her head in his lap reading a book. One time, with positions reversed, Guillaume slept in Malina's lap as she lovingly stroked his beard. Guillaume was asleep—at least it seemed so—but he was in obvious ecstasy with a grin that went from ear to ear. By nature, both Guillaume and Malina were happy, content people, pleased with themselves and the world around them. Malina often sang songs throughout the day—Polish and French folk songs—and it occurred to me that a person who sings while going about life's inconsequential affairs must be very happy indeed.

As for the sailing, after the first day with the eventful spinnaker pole rigging, the wind clocked to the north and we struck the pole and flew the main and genoa, a very fast rig on *Allegretta*. We raced along at nine and ten knots, but the propeller shaft spun excessively fast, resulting in a bad vibration. (There was previously a brake that would stop the shaft from spinning, but it had broken and been removed some time before the voyage.) Brian thought this might cause a dangerous water leak where the shaft ran through the hull, so we reefed all sails to slow the boat down. (Pooh!) The north wind blew for only a few days, and was eventually replaced with the NE trade wind, which unfortunately, never gathered the strength we would have liked. For most of the crossing we had light but sufficient wind of 15 knots. For four full days we had almost no wind, however, and we had to run the engine for all of this time.

(We siphoned the fuel from the barrels on deck, never actually using this fuel, but we would have been bone-dry without it.)

The wind, when it blew, came from behind us, sometimes over the port quarter, sometimes starboard. Brian and I would meet on the foredeck each morning after breakfast and set the rig. The topping-lift and fore-guy issue became nothing more than a minor inconvenience, and we even started "poling out" the genoa to leeward by putting a swivel block on the end of the mainsail boom and running the genoa-sheet through it. We worked well enough together, Brian and I, and I tried my best not to harbor any resentments toward him. In the last third of the crossing, the trade wind filled in rather nicely. *Allegretta* sailed toward the windward islands of the Caribbean *with a bone in her teeth,* finally showing her metal and recording several days of 150 miles or better.

Other than the issues with personnel, or more correctly: with the captain, we experienced almost no problems during the voyage on *Allegretta.* We had plenty of water and fuel, no sickness aboard (other than a very little sea-sickness), and *Allegretta* sailed a true course, reaching all of her planned ports in good timing. Also, the fuel barrels on deck didn't give us any trouble, the inexperienced crew proved to be sufficiently helpful, and although Brian's temper proved to be an issue much as it had the year before, I never noticed a single nautical decision or sailing maneuver that was compromised by his temper. In fact, none of the apprehensions I had before the voyage—other than Brian's temper—came to fruition. We had a couple of breakages aboard—a module for the generator blew, as did a high pressure hose on the water-maker—but Brian had sufficient spare parts aboard and these were repaired underway. We also had very good weather for the entire voyage, and while some may claim that the constant 100 degree temperature we endured was a bit stuffy, we had no squalls or storms and only a cupful of rain.

One might conclude that *Allegretta* proved to be a capable and seaworthy ocean cruiser, but the truth is she was never fully tested on this voyage. "It was my easiest crossing ever," Brian would say several times. I still shudder when I think about those fuel barrels on deck, and indeed, the inexperienced crew *would* have been problematic had a significant storm occurred. Some of the safety equipment, especially the MOB gear, was inadequate as well—certainly not "seaworthy." We did well—and I'm thankful for that—but we were very fortunate on this voyage, and that cannot be denied.

Speaking of *Allegretta:* by the end of the voyage she was a pigsty! Other than washing up the dishes, not one moment had been invested in cleaning her since the voyage began. Samples of our collective 500 meals were trampled into the floor matting, enough to create a slipping hazard. Food stains and dropped pieces of bread, cereal, cake, and other foodstuffs covered the table cloth and seat covers. An unfamiliar observer would think we had eaten without silverware or plates. The refrigerator was a horrid mess and the dozen or so incredibly soiled dish rags and towels that littered the galley stunk like hell. Outside, the deck had so much dirt and filth, one could barely see its ugly grey color. Dried blood from several scraped knuckles added a very special flair, as did the snot, spit, and occasional drippage of other bodily fluids. We should have cleaned the boat, that is certain, but no one ever made the effort. Not even once.

The crossing would eventually be completed in 16 days, 4 hrs. Brian was glad to be in: "I had forgotten these things take so long," he said. Guillaume and Malina were still terrified of Brian and very happy to get to St. Martin and leave the whole episode behind them. Claudia said she had hoped the voyage would last a few more days. Claudia always marched to a different drummer.

We anchored in the *Baie du Marigot*, the same bay in which we anchored after our crossing on *That Darn Cat* two years prior. We launched the dinghy and motored to shore, once again finding a closed customs office. We walked the lovely French town of Marigot and I was able to convince the crew to eat dinner at *Oplangeur Bistro*, the same restaurant the crew of *That Darn Cat* and I had dined at and enjoyed.

Brian had promised me that our stop at St. Martin "would only take 15 minutes," but Claudia, Guillaume and Malina were all flying off the island—Claudia to New York, the others to Dominica—and all of their flights were a day and a half hence. We spent the time enjoying town, such a better place than Mindelo. It was just after noon on Thursday, November 28—American Thanksgiving—when Brian took the three French citizens ashore in the dinghy so that they could catch their flights. As they motored away, I stood on *Allegretta's* foredeck, fondly waving the others goodbye.

They were about half way to shore when I noticed that the dinghy had stopped, and I guessed it had finally run out of gas. I knew they had no paddles. I was wondering what they would do. I heard Brian and a man from a boat at anchor yelling back and forth. I figured Brian was asking for help.

Suddenly I saw the unmistakable stiffening of Brian's back, coupled with a set of arms that flapped like the flippers on a penguin. I was a distance away but I could clearly hear the two men arguing in combat. I shook my head in disbelief: How could *anyone* possibly get in a fight while motoring a dinghy by a boat at anchor? I laughed until my gut ached.

I didn't know what to expect when Brian returned to the boat, being that we would be alone—our first time ever. While we were still underway I had considered jumping ship once we reached St. Martin, but in the two days since we had landed, he had been treating me like a brother. With this much improved environment—plus the fact that he really did need my help—I decided I would see him through, all the way to St. Thomas. I did this for me, however, not him: *I* wanted to finish up unfinished business; *I* wanted to fulfill my obligation as crew; *I* wanted to make amends; *I* wanted to end this voyage at St. Thomas, a very special place to *me*. Nevertheless, Brian was being extremely pleasant—and would remain so until I bid him farewell.

"I have some friends on the island and they have invited both of us to their home for a Caribbean Thanksgiving dinner," Brian told me. "I think you would enjoy their company. Would you like to go?"

"Absolutely!" I said. "That sounds like wonderful fun!"

And so, toward evening we took the dinghy into town and went to the home of Alicia Conner, a 95 year old native of St. Martin, meeting her there and her daughter Maria, a banking vice-president who lived and worked on St. Thomas.

We walked in a few circles to find Alicia's house, but with the boisterous peeping frogs in the field next door—"a real nuisance," Maria said—I don't think I would have trouble finding it again. Maria greeted us with a welcoming smile, the bright red lipstick she wore matching the flower print on her Caribbean dress. She pulled open the robust steel gate that secured the yard, and welcomed us to her mother's home as the frogs next door screamed in our ears.

Inside we met Alicia, a gentle and proud black woman who had lived through poverty and repression, but who had retained faith in God and in goodness and had found a way to raise five children, one of whom had died of heart disease. "Heart disease runs in my genes," she told me. "It killed my son, and it's killing me too, but I ain't dead yet, so let's cel-e-brate!"

We sat in Alicia's modest living room and talked. She had a million stories, and I wanted to hear a million more. I was captivated by the accounts she told me about growing up on a sugar plantation. They lived in company-owned

338

employee housing—old slave quarters—and everything was supplied either by "the company" or their own ingenuity.

"On the mainland, the depression was going on," Alicia told me. "But we didn't know nothing about that. We had our chickens. We had our cow. All the fresh vegetables we want. Milk. Butter. Eggs. And the company give us money and clothes. What more you want?

"And prohibition? Lord, we made our own rum in the kitchen, and it was *good* rum too! Of course we didn't drink no how, 'cause of the Lord. Just a little. Well, maybe some more. But we didn't need no prohibition. Sheeit! Whatcha going to need that for?"

On and on. Alicia sure could tell stories. I was good and hungry—and the smells from the kitchen only increased my appetite—but I listened to Alicia with great interest, knowing I might never again have the opportunity to hear Caribbean folklore *first-hand*. As Maria finished the cooking in the kitchen, Brian helped her and put dishes on the table. He was so charming, Brian. No one would have ever believed the behavior of his I witnessed only a few days prior. He had a second side, a wonderful side. Life with Brian would be so different if he could simply learn to control his temper.

We had turkey for Thanksgiving dinner, turkey wings: "We just eat the double-bone part of the wing," Alicia said. "The double-bone part is the best part."

It was true! We ate only turkey wings, and Alicia had the butcher give her only the portion that had the double bone. They were tender and juicy, and served with a spicy Caribbean gravy. I don't think I've ever tasted such delicious turkey, but I admit the company and the atmosphere biased my opinion. Along with the turkey we also feasted on potatoes, green beans and fried plantains, and after indulging in some home-made cake and ice-cream, the two sailors were stuffed and tired. We bid the ladies good-night and walked through the darkened streets of Marigot, glad to find our dinghy still locked to the wharf.

339

We stepped aboard and freed the lock, but before he started the engine, Brian did something totally unexpected:

"Mike I want to apologize for the *excitement* I caused during the voyage," he said. "Really, I'm sorry for all the trouble I caused you. You showed a tremendous ability to accept my angry behavior without reacting to it. That ability must be very helpful to you in life."

I thought about his words. It was big of him to apologize. A little too late, but still, it was big.

"You know, if Lucille were here, it never would have happened," he added.

"Oh, how's that?" I asked.

"When I get that way and Lucille's around, she knows to say 'Brian stop!' and then I stop. It's just that those other guys were so useless and..."

Okay, not a perfect apology, but considering whom we're working with: good enough!

"Well, I appreciate the apology, Brian," I said. "Thank you." And without another word, Brian pulled the rope to start the engine and we motored back to *Allegretta*.

Back aboard, I was in bed quickly and I lay awake overcome by a sense of gratitude like never before. I was thankful to meet my new friends, Alicia and Maria Conner. They welcomed me so thoroughly into their home. The meal was delicious, yes, but I will never forget the stories Alicia told me of growing up on a Caribbean island during the depression. Brian's apology was special too, and for this I was also thankful. It took away a lot of pain. It made the voyage worthwhile. What a wonderful Thanksgiving indeed!

It wouldn't be until late afternoon when we left the next day. Brian wanted to do some repairs to the windlass, and between going back and forth to the marine store to buy parts and waiting for the shipment of two coolers to replace the ones stolen in Mindelo, the day was used up quite thoroughly. It was a long day of waiting for me, the boredom briefly interrupted when we made a required stop

340

at Alicia's house to pick up some items of Maria's that Brian was taking to St. Thomas.

The screaming frogs directed us to their home and Maria greeted us once again with her gorgeous smile as she pulled open the big steel gate securing the yard. She wore another colorful print dress and full make-up, again with bright red lipstick that, in the Caribbean sunshine, highlighted her thick lips and perfect white teeth. I handed her some flowers I had brought and she kissed me, purposely, I think, leaving a substantial mark of proof on my neck.

"Good afternoon fellows," she said to both of us but not taking her eyes off mine. "Thank you for the flowers, Mike," she said, cradling them like a child. She invited us into the house where we chatted like children and she loaded us up with the cargo we were to deliver: two large suitcases and a 50-pound burlap bag of rice. All the while, Maria dipped her chin and looked at me with make-believe innocent eyes, flirting with me non-stop. I was flattered, that's for sure, but her efforts were all for naught: I was already taken.

Lisa and I had been talking and e-mailing the entire voyage and by this time we had a workable plan for our future. The e-mails were important, no doubt, but two telephone conversations—the one I made from Mindelo and another one I was able to make the previous night while at anchor—evolved our plans more than anything else. Yes, I was a sailor and long-time bachelor and had always wanted my space and freedom, but by this time at Marigot, I was finally ready to offer Lisa what she required and deserved: a permanent, committed, cohabitating relationship. It was my intention that was important to her, she had told me. If my intention was to simply date her without commitment, this she wouldn't accept. If, on the other-hand, my intention was to pursue the type of relationship she desired, then she would do anything in her power to help me with that intention.

341

It took me years to come around to Lisa's way of thinking. I had to first live my life as an adventurous single man, discovering along the way all that a bachelor's way of life has and does *not* have to offer. I also had to date a million women—okay, maybe not a *whole* million—and find the very one that suited me best. Once I found that woman—and we're talking about Lisa—I had to date her for four years and fall totally in love with her. And then I had to lose her and unequivocally recognize the void that loss created.

And I had to sail several *Ocean Passages*, finally sailing across the ocean with a crazy lunatic captain on a boat and voyage with enough issues and problems to keep me awake at night before the voyage began, worries significant enough that my principal concern was that this woman I love, the one that suits me better than all others, might not ever know just how much I loved her.

And when I had done all this I was finally ready, ready to start a new voyage, a voyage more important, more rewarding, and more challenging than any *Ocean Passage* could ever be. It has always been my nature to be lucky, and it was just my luck that when I was finally ready to begin this voyage with Lisa, she was ready to begin it with me.

So, we picked up our cargo, Brian and I, and we set sail for St. Thomas with a strong north wind that came at us from the starboard beam. Squalls were all about, no surprise in the Caribbean, so we put a couple of reefs in the mainsail and left the genoa half-furled as well. We set four-hour watches and sailed all night, working together as well as any team could. Shortly before noon the next day we laid anchor in a small anchorage just west of Charlotte Amalie harbor on the south side of St. Thomas. It was where I had arrived on *C'est si Bon* 24 years earlier, chasing the sun and living the Sailor's Dream. Had I come full circle? Surely I had.

The voyage was over, a grand voyage indeed. All of my other voyages had had one objective, and that was to sail

342

from start to finish. This voyage—"the easiest crossing I have ever done," said Brian—had involved more difficult and elusive objectives, those of closure, obligation, and forgiveness. It had not been easy—and I had taken my lumps—but it had been successful. I could leave with a clear conscience. I had made my amends. I had fulfilled my obligation. I was ready to take on a new and different adventure, one that would require all of the wisdom I accumulated on this and all of my prior *Ocean Passages*.

Made in the USA
Las Vegas, NV
18 January 2024

84516366R00204